WRITING
RESEARCH PAPERS

Second Edition

W · W · NORTON & COMPANY also publishes

THE NORTON ANTHOLOGY OF AMERICAN LITERATURE
edited by Ronald Gottesman et al.

THE NORTON ANTHOLOGY OF ENGLISH LITERATURE
edited by M. H. Abrams et al.

THE NORTON ANTHOLOGY OF MODERN POETRY
edited by Richard Ellmann and Robert O'Clair

THE NORTON ANTHOLOGY OF POETRY
edited by Arthur M. Eastman et al.

THE NORTON ANTHOLOGY OF SHORT FICTION
edited by R. V. Cassill

THE NORTON ANTHOLOGY OF WORLD MASTERPIECES
edited by Maynard Mack et al.

THE NORTON FACSIMILE OF THE FIRST FOLIO OF SHAKESPEARE
prepared by Charlton Hinman

THE NORTON INTRODUCTION TO LITERATURE
edited by Carl E. Bain, Jerome Beaty, and J. Paul Hunter

THE NORTON READER
edited by Arthur M. Eastman et al.

THE NORTON SAMPLER
edited by Thomas Cooley

and the NORTON CRITICAL EDITIONS

WRITING RESEARCH PAPERS

A Norton Guide

Second Edition

MELISSA WALKER
MERCER UNIVERSITY ATLANTA

W • W • NORTON & COMPANY • NEW YORK • LONDON

Library of Congress Cataloging-in-Publication Data
Walker, Melissa.
  Writing research papers.
  Bibliography: p.
  Includes index.
  1. Report writing.   2. Research.   I. Title.
LB2369.W25 1987   808'.02   86-7118

W · W · Norton & Company, Inc.
500 Fifth Avenue, New York, N.Y. 10110

W · W · Norton & Company Ltd.
37 Great Russell Street, London WC1B 3NU

ISBN 0-393-95574-5

1 2 3 4 5 6 7 8 9 0

CONTENTS

PREFACE TO THE SECOND EDITION

Writing Research Papers: A Norton Guide provides all the necessary guidance and information for students to do research and produce satisfactory research papers, but it goes beyond that. To counter the notion some students bring with them to college that research is a senseless exercise having to do with footnotes and index cards, this book tries to teach the spirit and value of independent learning. It helps students appreciate that learning to do research on their own can be an exciting part of their college experience and that the skills acquired can serve them in other academic endeavors and throughout their lives.

This text contains instruction in basic research skills: narrowing a topic, using library sources, recording information, and organizing material. It provides guidance in the process of writing and documenting a research paper: writing rough drafts, revising, preparing a bibliography, integrating sources, and producing a final accurate copy. In addition to general instruction appropriate to research in all disciplines, there are clear examples for reporting and documenting according to three styles commonly used in undergraduate assignments: the styles of the Modern Language Association (1984), the American Psychological Association (1983), and the scientific number system used in many technical and scientific papers.

The second edition of *Writing Research Papers* expands certain sections of the text, updates others, and refines and clarifies particular details of the process of doing research. The chapter on organizing material has itself been reorganized and clarified. In addition to discussing the forming of a topic sentence and outlining (the presentation of evidence), it also defines expository and persuasive papers and illustrates with detailed outlines ways of organizing each. The discussion of paraphrasing, incorporating quotations, and integrating sources is enriched by the addition of many more specific examples, providing students with a wide range of models.

In the first edition, the chapter on the new MLA style of parenthetical documentation with a list of sources, prepared in consultation with the director of MLA publications, reflected what at that time was the most current version of the new 1984 MLA style. Since then, the MLA has fine-tuned some details, and this edition reflects those clarifications. I have expanded the number of sample documentary citations to include less traditional sources, such as material retrieved from databases. I have also added detailed instructions and some fifteen examples to illustrate various ways to cite sources in the paper itself. The section on documenting with the new APA style now includes a comprehensive list of sample citations.

For the convenience of teachers who want to use endnotes or footnotes, I have brought together in one place, Appendix A, the instructions for citing sources with notes, an expanded list of sample citations, and a sample paper documented with endnotes followed by a list of sources.

A new sample paper—"The Need for Education to Combat the Psychological Effects of the Nuclear Threat on Children"—illustrates the development of a strong persuasive argument. Each of the three main sample papers, illustrating student research in the major divisions of the college curriculum—the humanities, the social sciences, and the natural and applied sciences—is now preceded by a discussion of the nature of research in those divisions and in the various disciplines within them.

A vast amount of material is newly available through computer databases, and the possibilities of the computer search have therefore been greatly expanded. This edition includes a selected list of databases illustrating the kinds of material available through the use of computers. The annotated bibliography in the appendix, which has itself been expanded and updated, now indicates those traditional sources (such as PMLA) available on-line. To explain how to do a computer search, this edition describes the procedure in general terms, breaks it down into specific steps, and illustrates it with a particular student's computer search.

This text is appropriate for students doing research based on library sources alone, but it also can be adapted to broader projects. As a comprehensive guide to research across the curriculum, it expands the concept of research to include activities beyond the library.

I have found that students learn best by example, so I have illustrated the hows and whys of research by periodically following the process of four student research projects from the selection of a topic through gathering material, organizing, writing a first draft, revising, and producing a final paper. Students thus learn how to do their own research and to write research papers by learning general principles and studying examples of actual research in progress. For example, the discussion of the general principles of revision is followed by excerpts from revised rough drafts of the student papers. The completed student papers are reprinted at the end of the text.

The paper in chapter 11 is documented by a bibliography with references cited in parentheses in the text, the preferred style of the Modern Language Association. The one in Appendix A, a documented essay on a literary topic, uses the more traditional form—also endorsed by the MLA—of documentary notes and a bibliography. The sample in chapter 12 illustrates the American Psychological Association (APA) style of documentation as well as the use of an abstract; and that in chapter 13 is documented with the simple number system widely used in science and technology and recommended by the American Chemical Society.

Not only different students but also the same student at different times will face varied research tasks; this text can help with different kinds of research assignments. In addition to the four featured student papers—ranging in length from 1,500 to 3,000 words—a short paper of only 800 words on Eleanor Roosevelt's work for women serves as a model for short assignments used either as preparation for a longer project or for courses that require a series of short papers rather than a single long one.

The annotated list of selected reference works in the appendix introduces some of the most valuable works in the library. With the help of experts in various disciplines, I have chosen works that are likely to be useful, as well as those thought to be indispensable. I have tried to include only works that are usable by undergraduate students, however, and to describe in a concise note the main features of each. There are, of course, many other useful reference works in all fields, but this list should serve as a beginning, leading students to the shelves of the reference room where they will find other works appropriate to specific projects.

While this book is specifically designed as a textbook for that part of the freshman composition sequence that includes instruction in the methods and tools of research, it is also intended to act as an easy-to-use guide that students will consult whenever they undertake a research project. Students who keep this text on their desks will have easy access to authoritative, up-to-date information about planning and carrying through a research project. Since learning to do research is a central activity in learning to learn, *Writing Research Papers: A Norton Guide*, kept as a ready reference, may prove useful throughout the college years and beyond.

ACKNOWLEDGMENTS

I would like to thank the many people who contributed to the preparation of the first edition of this book and who have continued to offer support and encouragement while I prepared the second edition: my husband, children, parents, and friends, who have given positive suggestions and patiently stood by; my colleagues at Mercer University, who have used the book with their students and have helped make it better; my teachers, who taught me that learning how to learn is only a first step; my students, who used early versions of the book and led me to understand what they really need to know; and those students who have used the first edition and have proved its usefulness by completing exciting research projects of their own.

Others made it possible for me to have the time and quiet needed to write. I am grateful to Mercer University for giving me leave for a term to begin the work and Eleanor West of the Ossabaw Island Foundation for providing a retreat from other responsibilities. I am particularly grateful to Dean James Yerkes, who helped me make the time to finish this revision.

For their many suggestions and constant encouragement I thank Jerome Beaty, Richard Bondi, Roberta Chesnut, Jay Knopf, David Goldsmith (all of Emory University); Elizabeth Penfield and Ann Torcson (University of New Orleans); Blanche Gelfant (Dartmouth College); Michael Lund (Longwood College); Nancy Kearns, Paul Douglas, Missy Williams, and Mat Mancini (Mercer University). I am grateful to those who read the manuscript at various stages and offered helpful advice: Edra Bogle (North Texas State University); Rosa B. Calvet (Broward Community College); Peter Dusenbery (Bradley University); Constance Gefvert (Virginia Polytechnic Institute and State University); Richard E. Meyer (Western Oregon College); and David Yerkes (Columbia University). I am grateful as well to my colleagues around the country who used the first edition of this book and who have taken the time to write words of encouragement and to provide guidance for this revision. For their evaluations and suggestions, I would like to thank Dennis Eddings (Western Oregon State University), Peter Peterson (Shasta College), Norma Rudinsky (Oregon State University), and Laura Zlogar (University of Wisconsin).

I am particularly grateful to Walter Achtert, the director of Book Publications and Research Programs of the Modern Language Association, for his very careful attention to the chapters that illustrate or use the style of the 1984 *MLA Handbook,* and for keeping me up-to-date about corrections and changes since then. His patience and good humor in several late-afternoon telephone calls helped immeasurably in clarifying details of the MLA revision.

During the writing of the first edition, the American Psychological Association also revised its style manual. I would like to thank Leslie Cameron of the APA for helping ensure that the format and citations of the psychology paper conform to the current authorized style.

Many librarians have helped me along the way. I wish to express special thanks to Virginia Tiefel, head of the undergraduate libraries at Ohio State University, who read the chapters on library sources and offered valuable suggestions; I am also indebted to her 1982 article, "Libraries and Librarians as Depicted in Freshman English Texts" in *College English.* I would like to thank the reference staff at the Woodruff Library at Emory University— particularly Nancy Books, Alan Clark, Luella Davis, Francine Henderson, Irene Malleson, Eric and Marie Nitschke, Tarina Stephens, and Mary Ellen Templeton—for answering my endless questions. Finally, I would like to thank Judith Brook and Deb Robinson, librarians at Mercer University, for their guidance in updating the annotated bibliography, expanding the lists of bibliographic citations, and patiently teaching me about databases and computer searching.

All these people have contributed their knowledge to this book but are not, of course, responsible for any errors that may have found their way into the text.

Barry Wade, my editor at W. W. Norton, was involved in every aspect of the creation of the first edition, and has shown the same care and thoroughness throughout this revision. I am extremely grateful for all he has taught me and for the countless ways he has helped. I would also like to thank others at Norton: John Benedict for his encouragement, which has helped more than he knows; Victoria Thys and Heather Warren for their concern and hard work in planning and carrying through this revision; Marian Johnson and Patricia Peltekos for their splendid copyediting, which saved me from many errors and ensured consistency; and Roy Tedoff and Diane O'Connor for their patient help in turning my manuscript into a book.

WRITING
RESEARCH PAPERS

Second Edition

1

UNDERSTANDING WHAT RESEARCH IS

An Introduction to Research

You may think of research as something you do in laboratories and libraries, usually as a requirement for a college course. But think for a minute. When you or your parents or friends are in the market for a new car, what do you do? You probably read consumer guides, visit car dealers, and talk to other people about their cars. When you look for a job, you may study the want ads, check bulletin boards, and ask around among your friends. Choosing a college or academic major or graduate school, deciding on a career, settling on a place to live, buying a house—all these activities require research.

While the word *research* has come to mean a serious, systematic activity, one requiring hard work, dedication, and perseverance, it once referred to a man's effort to win a woman in love or marriage, rarely a systematic business. The common element, however, in a lover's suit and a scholarly inquiry is found in the first two letters of the word. The prefix *re-* has the general sense of "back" or "again" and suggests repetition. The struggle to obtain what is personally desirable, socially good, or intellectually true is usually a matter of searching again and again.

To try again and again to understand other people, the natural world, and social and political structures is a significant step toward living consciously and deliberately. Researching has probably already played an important part in determining what you think and what you do. The skill with which you conduct research in the future can have a significant impact on the quality of your life, influencing how you perceive the world and what choices you make.

1

EXPLORING

Before setting out to investigate a subject systematically, it is helpful to recall that you are a natural investigator. You have been conducting informal research all your life. As an infant you conducted research primarily through your hands and mouth, often grasping, dropping, and grasping the same object again and again, until one day you were able to hold it and make it your own. As a two-year-old you probably discovered the nature of a dog by feeling it; perhaps you learned an unforgettable lesson about canine behavior by examining its teeth or pulling its tail.

As soon as you could talk, you discovered that there are shortcuts to knowledge, and so you began to ask questions: Does that dog bite? Is the stove hot? What is that thing? You probably never stopped asking questions, although the nature of those questions may have changed: What is inflation? How does a camera work? What did Martin Luther King accomplish? What are genes?

By the time you have enrolled in college, your success as a student depends on how much responsibility you take for your own learning, particularly on how you try to answer questions. Following through on questions can help develop habits that will make learning a part of your daily life, not just as a student, but in the years to come. Questions have a way of leading both to answers and to other questions, and the search for answers can help you keep alive—or recapture—the curiosity that comes so naturally to a child.

As an adult—particularly as a student and researcher—it is important that you learn to discriminate, to choose which questions seem the most important. It is not a good idea to look up every word you do not recognize in a difficult text, to ask professors to clarify every statement that you do not understand in a long lecture, or to go to the library for information on every subject about which you would like to know more. Rather, it is more productive to look up those definitions that you need to understand an author's main ideas, to ask a professor for clarification when independent study of the text still leaves you baffled, and to select topics of particular interest to explore in the library.

The issue is not *whether* you will need to conduct research, but *how well* you want to do it. The success you will have in finding information is dependent on both your attitude and your skills.

The first step in good research is gathering the available facts. Whether you are trying to discover the best way to go from one place to another on public transportation or a politician's stand on particular issues, you want to begin with the facts. If you consult a published bus schedule or a campaign brochure, you may only have just begun. To verify the reliability of the bus schedule and the campaign brochure, you may need to talk with people who actually ride a particular bus route in the first case and to consult the senator's voting record in the second. Does the bus actually run on time? Are the candidate's campaign promises reflected in his or her voting record?

Getting at the truth of what has actually happened is perhaps one of the most challenging of human efforts, and often the more we know about a subject the more we are aware of the difficulty of achieving absolute knowledge. Consider the physician who is asked to bring relief to a patient suffering from the most common of human ailments: a headache. To really help, the doctor must consider the possible causes of pain: Is there stress in the patient's life or some chemical imbalance in the patient's body? Has the patient had too much to drink or eaten food containing monosodium glutamate or other substances that cause headaches? There is no way to be certain what has happened in the body to cause pain, but a careful physician will consider the evidence for each of the possibilities and make a judgment about the best treatment and the best way to prevent future headaches. In daily life, people frequently have to gather evidence, reach conclusions, and take action without having reached absolute certainty; but conclusions are more likely to be valid if they are based on evidence that has been carefully collected.

Once the evidence has been gathered, the researcher must learn to understand and evaluate it. The first step in this process is learning when to trust and when to doubt the validity of sources. A book on the wonders of marine life by a skin-diving instructor probably does not contain the most reliable information about sharks; a study of cholesterol funded by the egg industry would not have the same authority as one conducted by objective researchers. A general biologist who personally opposes the development of procedures for creating test tube babies may overemphasize the dangers, while another who has a grant to do genetic research may understate the risks of such procedures. But the unreliability of sources, or at least the fact that they present material from a particular perspective alone, is not always obvious, and you may sometimes need to investigate the author to make that judgment. Learning to identify a person's special interests and prejudices can help you determine if that person is likely to slant a presentation of facts to lead to a particular interpretation. Of course you will not always be able to judge the authority of a text or a person's oral statements, but you can ask yourself what assumptions are behind what you read or hear. It is a good idea to suspend judgment and to get a balanced view of any subject before you reach conclusions, before you take a stand on controversial ethical issues, assume a political position, adopt a theory of human personality, or accept a set of standards for judging a work of art or literature.

There may be issues in these areas about which you keep an open mind all of your life and about which you never feel that you have reached final conclusions. There will be many times, however, both in school and in everyday life, when you will ask questions that have definite answers, when it will be reasonably clear what processes are at work and what events produce certain results. You will be able to study and determine how the heart functions to pump blood through the body, how the sun is used to heat water, what diseases have been linked to cigarette smoking, how a computer stores information, and how certain tax laws favor the rich. And, of course, you can study many events, the circumstances of which you will be reasonably certain about, while the causes remain a mystery. That about 400,000 people attended the Woodstock Festival is not questioned, but the social forces that contributed to that phenomenon are more difficult to discover. That a spy plane known as the U-2, piloted by Francis Gary Powers, was shot down over Russia on May 1, 1960, is certain, but what motivated scheduling the flight just before a planned summit conference between Eisenhower and Khrushchev is still a matter for speculation.

As a student researcher, you will mainly be concerned with discovering for yourself what other people have already studied more exhaustively than you will be able to do, and one of your tasks will be to distinguish between what is known and what is still open to further research. At times you may want to conduct original research to test the conclusions of others (as in interviews, polls, and surveys), and occasionally you may wish to design an original research project (such as correlating the eating and exercise habits of a group of students with their academic achievements). Though most of the time you will be researching what is known, your research report will still be original: You will be the one to make sense of the facts and to arrive at your own conclusions.

REPORTING

When you do research, you ask questions and look for answers; you find some answers and identify questions that you cannot answer; and usually, even when you are doing informal research, you make some kind of record of what you find. You record an address, write down a memorable quote, jot down figures, or take notes from what you read. When you conduct a systematic and sustained research project, you may not be sure of what you have learned until you organize and try to make sense of what you have found. Writing a formal research paper is a way of making connections and reaching conclusions. By outlining your findings, writing a first draft, revising, documenting your sources, and producing a polished final paper, you will not only try to make sense of your research, but you will also try to communicate what you have found as clearly as possible to others.

The requirements for writing research papers depend on the purpose of a given assignment. The kind of topic (assigned or selected), the time allotted for researching it, the number and kinds of sources consulted, the methods used to record information—these may vary from one research project to another. The purpose of a particular assignment will dictate the organization, the length, and the style of documentation of a final paper.

In all cases, however, you want to report your research in a paper that is organized, clear, readable, and interesting. The real value of a research report depends on what you as a researcher have discovered and how well you tell others about it. The outline, title, list of sources, and notes are details that can help you record and communicate the conclusions of your research so that how you arrived at those conclusions will be perfectly clear to your reader. A good research paper will reflect your best effort to make what you have discovered understandable to others.

An Introduction to Resources

An unusually large number of resources for satisfying your curiosity is available to you in college. You probably have more sources of information and more experiences than you have time to use. Even in a small college community there are more people with experiences different from yours than you will be able to talk to, and there are more books even in a small college library than you can read in a lifetime. Learning to find and tap the resources around you is an important skill both in formal education and in everyday life.

The research resource that most people think of first is the library, and it is the place on a college campus where you will find the largest concentration of sources. But there may be other academic resources for you to explore, such as the bookstore, the computer center, or a museum. Beyond every college is a town or city with public establishments, businesses, and even shops and restaurants that may serve as resources for learning. Finally, the people you already know—family members, classmates, teachers, friends, and acquaintances—as well as those you can arrange to meet—other professors, experts from the community, specialists in one field or another—will prove to be living sources of information and opinion.

THE LIBRARY

A college library is an inexhaustible and ever-changing storehouse of information. New books, periodicals, and other sources of information are constantly being added to the collection. An academic library benefits from the knowledge of many people on the college campus, since faculty members from all disciplines keep up with the latest books, magazines, journals, and other information sources so that they can select the best ones for the library.

Of course not all college libraries are the same; each reflects the institution it is part of—the courses in the curriculum and the interests of the faculty and students. A school of technology will certainly have much more information on technological and scientific subjects than will a general liberal arts college, while a university with a business school will provide a full range of books and periodicals on economics and the various aspects of business.

You will discover the valuable resources of your own library only by spending time there, so take a few minutes to explore: find the periodicals, the reference books, the stacks, the circulation desk. You can easily find your favorite magazines, but if you look further you may discover many other journals and newspapers that you will enjoy reading. You can probably find books by your favorite authors that you have never read, as well as books containing information that is new to you on a subject you know well.

OTHER ACADEMIC RESOURCES

The main college library is the most obvious research resource on the college campus. But there are many others. Some institutions have more than one library, and most have other resources for independent learning. To find them you might begin by asking the following questions: Is the library collection all in one place, or is it spread out in several locations? How many libraries are there? Is there a museum? an art gallery? Does your institution publish a newspaper? a magazine? an academic journal? Is there a computer center? a theater? a lecture series? Some of these questions can be answered by studying your catalog or by talking with other students. Others may require some investigation.

For example, what does your college bookstore have to offer? To answer this you may want to go there and spend some time. Browsing among the shelves and skimming texts can help you choose your courses more carefully and learn something about the many courses you will not be able to take; and, when you are trying to decide on a major, you will want to survey carefully the texts used in the discipline that interests you. Finally, when you choose a research topic, you may want to find out if your topic is being studied in a course on your campus; you may want to examine the assigned books and in some cases consult the course instructor.

THE COMMUNITY

Your college is part of a larger community—whether a small town, a huge metropolis, or something in between. Often there is an exchange arrangement between the services of a college and those of the greater community. You may be able to use the public library, borrow materials from public organizations, or attend meetings or lectures at other institutions. Each community has its own individuality: its traditions, civic organizations, political climate, cultural and social identity, businesses, and public services. It is a good idea for you to know something about the greater community in which your college is located and to find out which of its institutions are available for your use. Again you will want to ask questions: Is there a theater? a museum? an art gallery? (In large cities, you will want to ask how many such places there are and whether there are specialized ones.) What cultural events are there? What is the ethnic makeup of the population? Are there many people from other countries? Are there consulates to serve them? What about public libraries, other academic institutions, social services, historical associations, religious organizations, institutes, and foundations? What is the economic base of the community—its trade, manufacturing, and management organizations? What kinds of shops and restaurants are there?

If there are commercial bookstores in your community, you may want to begin there. When you visit such a store, you will usually find books that reflect the interests of a town or a particular neighborhood. It is a good idea to learn how the books are classified before you begin to explore the shelves. If you plan to spend any time browsing in a bookstore, you will probably be able to discover for yourself how the books are organized. If not, people who work in bookstores usually will help, and they typically like to talk about the books they sell. Remember also to look for used-book stores and those that specialize in certain types of books, since these stores can often help you find hard-to-get or unusual materials for your research.

PEOPLE

Learning what people have to teach us may be more difficult than learning the content of a book or the holdings of a library. People we meet do not provide us with a table of contents, an index, or a card catalog, nor can we punch a button to receive a printout of their interests. Rather, we have to ask questions: What kind of work do you do? What are your hobbies? Have you traveled very much? Where have you lived? Simply by chatting with your classmates, you may discover that some are citizens of other countries, some have intriguing hobbies, and others have special skills. Making such discoveries often requires that you listen carefully to what other people have to say and that you resist talking too much about yourself.

Some people are very reluctant to talk about themselves, and you may have to work hard to learn what they have to teach you; others welcome the opportunity to talk about their interests and will usually do so without much prodding. You may be surprised to discover that it is still possible to talk to people who came of age during World War I, and probably many of them would like to tell their stories of that time. Most of the people you know who are over sixty-five could tell you detailed stories about the Great Depression, Prohibition, or the rise of the labor movement; about Babe Ruth and Greta Garbo; or about the first airplane they saw. Some people you know may have special interests that have led them to become experts on subjects such as gardening, nutrition, or handicrafts; jazz, vintage cars, or baseball; photography, carpentry, or solar energy; genealogy, early movie history, or science fiction.

The rich and varied experiences of the people you meet in your daily life and those you seek out for a special purpose can be a valuable source of learning. Tapping these resources may not be so difficult if you realize that you are using the same sorts of skills involved in exploring libraries, other academic resources, and your community—skills that will lead you to ask questions again and again.

2

CHOOSING A TOPIC

Doing independent research is a valuable way to enrich your study of the courses you take in college. What you learn in class or from assigned textbooks will probably be more enjoyable and meaningful if you also explore aspects of the subject on your own. Once you learn research techniques, you will be able to go to the library or to appropriate experts to learn more about the topics in your courses that particularly interest you. Some courses include assignments specifically designed to teach you how to do research and to write a paper based on what you have found. The first step in that process is to find a topic—a specific aspect of a general subject—or to adapt an assigned topic to the resources available to you.

The choice of a research topic, like the choice of a friend, is not usually made after a systematic investigation; rather, it is the consequence of circumstances and actions involving both conscious effort and luck. The professional writer deciding on a subject for a new book, the graduate student choosing a thesis, and the college student selecting a topic for a limited research project all have the same general set of resources: where they live and where they have been; the people they know and those they have known; what books they have read and what they have done. The particular details of people's lives determine their existing interests as well as what new subjects they are able to learn about.

Five Important Activities

Whether your instructor assigns a topic or asks you to select your own, there is a process you need to go through to adapt a topic to your own interests and abilities. The early stages of any research project should include the following five activities:

1. Budgeting time

2. Following and developing interests
3. Letting ideas brew
4. Asking the right questions
5. Making a commitment

BUDGETING TIME

Throughout your project, you will need to budget your time. While this is not always easy, since you may not know how long particular activities will take, it is important that you plan from the beginning how to use the time you have. Begin by making lists. If you have four weeks set aside for a research project, then decide what you hope to accomplish each week. Your first decision will be to decide how many hours or days you can allot for choosing a topic. Remember that if you exceed your budget at one stage, you will have less time for other tasks; and you may need to revise your budget every few days. It is also a good idea to coordinate your research project with your other responsibilities. For example, do not schedule the final writing of your paper the day before you have a major test for another course.

FOLLOWING INTERESTS

Once you stop and think, you will probably find that there are many subjects you would like to explore. One way to begin to choose a subject for research is to recall what interests you already have, to think about what you already know, and to consider how to build on what you know.

Perhaps you already have one or more strong interests. You have played the guitar, the piano, or the drums for years; you have read science fiction, mysteries, or contemporary novels; you have raced bicycles, participated in swim meets, played soccer or football; you are an expert on cars, movies, rock and roll, or batting averages; you have operated computers, worked in a business, or cared for small children; you have worked in a community organization, for a political group, or for a newspaper; you have spent time in the wilderness, traveled, or lived in another country. You may be able to use what you already know as a context for new knowledge. For example, the student who has raced bicycles for years will already have some of the background necessary to study the most famous bicycle race, the Tour de France; a student who is interested in computers and in music would be prepared to study the development of electronic synthesizers; and another who has lived in Nicaragua may want to study recent political upheavals in that country.

In choosing a subject for research, you will want first to think about what you already know and what you have to build on. The next step is to consider those subjects that you think you want to learn about. Perhaps you would like to take up painting, photography, or organic gardening; you would like to learn more about alcoholism, drug rehabilitation, or weight reduction programs; you are considering studying psychology and would like to know something about Sigmund Freud, Carl Jung, or Karen Horney; you want to be more physically fit and to learn about aerobic exercise, nutrition, and yoga. When you select your courses and when you decide on a major, you will consider what you want to know; you should also consider that question when you choose a subject for independent research.

You may also want to consider what you think you ought to know. A research project can provide you with an opportunity to build a foundation that you need for future learning or to enhance some subject that you are currently studying. Perhaps you are planning to take a course next term in existentialism and you have been told that you should know something about Kierkegaard; or you decide to research the Spanish Civil War, which your Spanish teacher mentions frequently; or you want to learn about Maria Montessori's ideas about how children learn since you have a part-time job in a day-care center.

You may already know of several subjects that you have an interest in and would like to research. There may also be subjects suggested in your classes, by your instructor, or in this book about which you are curious enough to want to learn more. Before you commit yourself, it is wise to take time to consider the possibilities. You may want to make three lists:

1. A list of subjects that you already know something about
2. A list of new subjects that you would like to explore
3. A list of those items on the first two lists that are appropriate for your assignment

LETTING IDEAS BREW

By now you probably have many ideas, and it will be good if you can take the time to think about each of them. Discuss your ideas—even seemingly trivial or fleeting ones—with as many people as possible: friends, family, faculty, or others who may know something about the subject that interests you. Other people—your teachers or the reference librarian—may discourage you from pursuing some ideas because of the difficulty of finding materials or simply because a subject is not compatible with the goals of a given class. Once you have arrived at a subject that is acceptable to your instructor, give yourself time to determine whether it is one you want to pursue for three weeks, a month, six weeks, or in some cases more. Live with your ideas for a while; let them brew.

ASKING QUESTIONS

Next you will want to explore possibilities by asking questions. You may ask your classmates, your instructors, or other people what they can tell you about the possibilities you are considering. You may want to look up several items on your list in encyclopedias or other general reference books. If you decide in advance how much time you can give to exploring possibilities, you will find it easier to draw the line at the appropriate point and say, "I must decide now."

Often the final decision about a topic can be made simply by jotting down questions to which you would like to know the answers. This technique is particularly helpful if you have identified a general subject area and broken it into a number of particular topics. The best topic sometimes emerges when you study the questions and think about how they might be answered.

It will be easy to choose your topic if there is one thing in particular you want to know more about. Look at the list of questions you have made about possible topics and see if there is one that you would most like to be able to answer. When several questions interest you, ask yourself which is the most important, the most relevant to your studies, the most challenging, or the most suited to your resources.

MAKING A COMMITMENT

After you have selected a subject, done a little background reading, and talked to your instructor and others about it, you will probably be ready to make a commitment. Remember that you will live with a research topic for several weeks, and so you should stop and ask yourself if you have a sincere interest in the subject. If the answer is yes, then proceed with the conviction that you will not change your mind. You are now ready to begin your research by focusing on a limited, manageable topic.

Exploring a Broad Subject

Many students begin a research project by studying a particular person—Mary Wollstonecraft, Thomas Jefferson, Emma Goldman, Ralph Nader, Albert Schweitzer, Martin Luther King, Jr., Clare Boothe Luce, John Lennon—but a study that simply summarizes the events and accomplishments of a person's life is not very meaningful. Such summaries are usually available in general encyclopedias and other reference works. While students with a strong interest in an individual person will first want to read general sources to learn the outline of his or her life, they will then want to focus on some particular aspect of that life. Imagine, for example, that you are interested in Eleanor Roosevelt. You begin your study by consulting the *Ency-*

clopedia Americana index, which leads you to a single article about Eleanor Roosevelt. Although the article is only one page long, you identify the following aspects of her life as possible topics for research:

1. Activities during World War I
2. Work in women's organizations in the 1920s
3. Career as an educator: The Todhunter School
4. Radio program
5. The furniture factory at Hyde Park
6. Syndicated newspaper column, "My Day"
7. War work: World War II
8. Role in the formation of the United Nations
9. The United Nations Declaration of Human Rights
10. Fighting for the underprivileged and racial minorities
11. Contribution to Adlai Stevenson's campaign

Each of these topics, suggested by a general encyclopedia article, is appropriate for student research. There are other aspects of Eleanor Roosevelt's life—her childhood, her struggles with her mother-in-law, and her personal suffering—that may be interesting, but that you will not be able to research as thoroughly as her role in public life. It is, after all, people's accomplishments and their roles in society that are reported in newspapers; studied by scholars; witnessed by observers; and, finally, recorded and analyzed in periodicals, books, and films.The events of private lives are often obscure, rarely recorded accurately, and seldom accessible to researchers. A short paper based on one student's discoveries about Eleanor Roosevelt is found on pages 125–129.

Focusing a Subject: Two Examples

Once you have committed yourself to a subject, you will want to take some time to explore possible ways to focus your study: talking to people about it, doing some background reading, and thinking about what aspects of the subject most appeal to you. Again, decide on how much time you can afford to spend before you begin concentrated research.

It can be helpful to see how other students break down large subjects and finally focus on a particular topic. Consider the progress of two students who start with general subjects and arrive at manageable, limited topics.

Michael Gold enjoys going to the movies and watching old movies on television. Studying his college catalog, he is surprised to discover that academic courses are offered in film history, film appreciation, and film theory. When Michael is asked to choose a topic for a research project as part of his freshman English course, he immediately thinks that he would like to learn more about the history of film. Michael first goes to the library and consults the *Encyclopedia Americana*. He looks up "film" and "movies" and finally finds an article entitled "Motion Picture." (It would have been quicker to use the index, but Michael enjoys browsing in encyclopedias.) After reading the article, he concludes that one way to approach the subject is to break it down into different types of movies. Michael then visits his college bookstore and examines the textbooks that are used for film courses. Skimming through one book, David Cook's *History of Narrative Film*, he soon discovers that there is much more to learn about film than he had thought. At lunch one day, he talks with a student who is taking a film course. He asks her a few questions about the course and discovers that she is studying films that have influenced film making. By asking more specific questions, Michael learns the titles of important films he has never seen and of those that have attracted a cult following of fans who see them over and over again.

Based on what he already knew about movies and what he has learned from a little preliminary research, Michael begins to jot down ideas. The subject is so broad that he finds it helpful to divide it into rough categories. In a few minutes, he has produced this:

TYPES OF FILM

Comedy	Fantasy	Spy
Western	Gangster	History
Spectacle	Horror	Musical
Social Realism	Thriller	War
Political Propaganda	Detective	

TYPES BY NATIONALITY

American	German	Swedish	Soviet
French	Italian	Japanese	

OTHER TYPES

Feature films	Documentaries	Animated films
Shorts	Blockbusters	

LANDMARK FILMS

The Great Train Robbery (1903)	Citizen Kane (1941)
Birth of a Nation (1915)	Rebel without a Cause (1956)
The Battleship Potemkin (1925)	2001: A Space Odyssey (1968)
The Jazz Singer (1927)	

TECHNIQUES AND SKILLS OF FILM MAKING

Editing	Dubbing
Processing	Special effects
Adapting music	Scriptwriting
Sound	Adapting scripts from other media

OTHER APPROACHES

Great actors	Equipment
Great directors	Industry vs. art
The star system	The economics of film production

FILM AND SOCIETY

Censorship	Political propaganda
Cult films	Social values on film
Violence and film	

Michael looks at the lists he has made, somewhat amazed at the possible approaches to a subject that he thought he knew something about. He considers researching a particular film genre, such as the Western or the musical, but after some background reading in Cook's *History of Narrative Film*, he realizes that the Western has really spanned almost the entire history of film and the musical began with the first talking movies. Not quite sure how to limit such broad subjects, Michael considers other possibilities. In doing so, he checks the topics that interest him and consolidates them in another list:

```
American films
Social realism
Social values
Great actors
Feature films
Cult films
Rebel without a Cause
```

A little baffled about how to limit his topic, Michael puts his list aside and decides to come back to it later. The next day, he considers the list again and begins to see that all of the topics that he has checked are related. *Rebel without a Cause* is a landmark American feature-length film; it is a film of social realism that is an indictment of certain social values. Its star, James Dean, is considered by some to be one of the most charismatic actors of the twentieth century, and, what is more, he became a cult figure. Michael takes a clean sheet of paper and writes the following questions: How does a film like *Rebel* come to be made? How can we account for its success? What influence did it have? Was James Dean's charisma responsible for its impact?

Carol Garcia came to college with the intention of becoming either a mechanical engineer or an architect, interests that grew from personal experience. She remembers very well the time when her family's life began to change because of the rising cost of energy. Her parents discovered one hot summer day that they could no longer afford to use air conditioning; the following winter they installed a small wood stove to heat the family room. The year before Carol left for college, her father put up storm windows throughout the house to cut down on heat loss. In spite of these changes, the house was still not very comfortable on cold days, and it was particularly stuffy on hot, humid days.

Carol is taking courses in both physics and English; and when her English teacher assigns a research project, she decides that she would like to research a topic relevant to her study of physics, perhaps some aspect of applied physics. After making a list of possible subjects, she decides to study ways to heat and cool homes with small amounts of energy. She considers "wood stoves" as a possible subject, but she soon discards it as too simple. Visiting the school of architecture, Carol sees an announcement for a lecture by a solar architect, which she attends the next day. His topic is the economics of active solar heating systems. Carol goes to the library, consults the card catalog under solar energy, and checks out a book entitled *Rays of Hope*, by Dennis Hays. After reading the chapter about energy and shelter, she jots down these possible topics:

```
Active solar heating systems
Active solar cooling systems
Solar hot water heaters
Solar collectors
Passive solar heating design
Solar electric cells
Indirect solar energy: wind power
```

Carol studies her list and eliminates wind power and solar electric cells, which she discovers are rarely used to generate electricity for heating and cooling. When she reads about active solar systems that cool and heat rooms by collecting the sun's heat outside and then pumping it inside mechanically, she learns that they are expensive. She then eliminates active solar systems as a topic, since what she really wants to know is how to build a house so that it can be heated cheaply. Carol has found her topic by identifying the question she wants to answer: How can a house be designed—or an old one remodeled—so that it can be heated cheaply? The answer: by using design features that capture the sun's heat without the use of expensive mechanical devices. Carol's research begins to take shape as she asks other questions: What are these features? How do they work? What are their advantages and disadvantages? Carol jots down these questions, and at the top of the page she writes a tentative title: "Design for the Future: Passive Solar Homes."

Carol's topic is already more focused than that of Michael Gold. She has very specific questions that will yield definite answers. Michael, on the other hand, has decided simply to find out what he can about a particular film. His actual research will lead him to unexpected discoveries.

Adapting the Assigned Topic

College teachers frequently ask their students to research some aspect of a general subject. A psychology teacher, for example, may assign a term paper on some aspect of developmental psychology, an economics teacher on deficit spending, a physics teacher on applied technology, and an English teacher on twentieth-century fiction. Students who are assigned such general topics face the challenge of narrowing the broad subject area to a manageable topic. Such was the experience of David Harris, whose instructor required all students to research some aspect of child psychology and to write a paper based on the research. David studied the table of contents and the index to his textbook and considered various possibilities, but a visit home one weekend focused his thoughts. His eight-year-old younger brother, whom David was fond of but whom he didn't normally give much thought to, woke up screaming from a nightmare. Shaken, David learned from his mother that John had been suffering on and off from nightmares for months; they all involved a nuclear explosion and the end of the world. David returned to college determined to learn more about the effects on children of growing up in a nuclear age.

Other assigned papers are much more specific. Sara Maxfield's instructor assigned different twentieth-century writers to each student. Sara was specifically asked to learn what she could about Toni Morrison and to write a documented essay based on her research. In an essay on women's literature in the *Harvard Guide to Contemporary American Writing,* Sara read both about Toni Morrison and also about Alice Walker, another black writer whose novels have been published roughly over the same time as those of Morrison. With the approval of her instructor, Sara decided to read a novel by each writer, to do some research about the careers of each, and to write an essay based on what she learned. Although such a specific assignment eliminates the need to break down a broad subject, Sara still had the job of adapting the topic to her own response to the material.

EXERCISES

A. The items in the following list include a general subject area on the left and a specific topic on the right. Identify other topics related to each subject.

1. From "All-Time Best Sellers" to "Public Response to *Gone with the Wind.*"
2. From "Racism in America" to "The Internment of Japanese-American Citizens during World War II."
3. From "Third-Party Presidential Candidates" to "Henry Wallace for President: 1948."
4. From "Photography as an Art" to "The Photographic Achievement of Diane Arbus."
5. From "The Early Space Race" to "Sputnik: The Aftermath in American Education."
6. From "The Growth of Professional Football" to "Vince Lombardi and the Green Bay Packers."
7. From "Student Activism in the Sixties" to "The Early Days of Students for a Democratic Society."
8. From "The Rock Festival Phenomenon" to "Woodstock."
9. From "The Civil Rights Movement" to "Mississippi Summer: 1964."
10. From "Ethical Problems in Medicine" to "Do We Have a Right to Health Care?"
11. From "Computer Science" to "Computers and Unemployment: The Solution or the Problem?"
12. From "The Pros and Cons of Various Investment Options" to "Investing in Rental Real Estate."

B. Study the list of reference works in the appendix of this book. Then go to the library and find one of the specialized encyclopedias or dictionaries such as the *Encyclopedia of American History,* the *McGraw-Hill Encyclopedia of Science and Technology, Grzimek's Animal Life Encyclopedia,* or the *International Encyclopedia of Social Sciences.* Browse through it looking for material that interests you. Then make a list of general subject areas and another of specific topics that would be appropriate for student research.

C. Make a list of your interests, including sports, fashions, music, books, people, places, hobbies, occupations, and ideas.

D. Make a list of topics you would like to know more about.

E. Select a book from your own collection—perhaps a textbook—or one from the library on a subject that interests you. Study the index, and make a list of the topics that would be appropriate for student research.

3

IDENTIFYING LIBRARY SOURCES

An academic library has many resources for informal learning as well as for formal research. A knowledge of the material and services available in your own college library is essential to your success as a student. When you can easily use your library, you will be able to supplement required reading, pass an hour of leisure browsing among books and periodicals, or pursue independent research. This chapter will introduce you to the main resources of an academic library, and it will indicate the kinds of material available in different sections of the library. There are more resources described in this chapter than you will use for a given research project, but you should know that there is library material to help you answer most research questions. The next chapter gives instructions for using the various library resources, including specific information about collecting and recording references for a research project. You may want to read these chapters in your academic library so that you can find the parts of the library as you read about them.

Libraries and Librarians

Some large universities may have several libraries: one library for general use, plus more specialized ones for the schools of law, medicine, or agriculture, for example, or a central library with several branches. But most universities have one main library for the general collection. Although most of your library work will take place in the main library, you will probably be allowed to use other campus libraries as well.

The number of books in academic libraries varies, from under 100,000 volumes for small colleges to several million for a few large universities;

and the sizes of the library buildings also vary, from one-room structures to buildings with several stories. But regardless of the size of the building or the number of volumes in a collection, all academic libraries will have the following: a reference department for books that are used in the library and that cannot be checked out; a collection of periodicals (newspapers, magazines, and professional journals); a card catalog or a computer catalog (or both), which lists all the material in the library; a circulation desk, which often serves as an information center; a section for circulating books (often referred to as the "stacks"); space for microforms, non-print material, reserve books, and special collections.

Libraries may have sections of rooms, individual rooms, or even separate floors designated for material on specific subjects and for different kinds of material. If you are not familiar with the layout of your library, you may want to take an informal tour to locate and become familiar with each department. (See the exercises at the end of this chapter.) Some libraries will provide you with a map or a formal tour. In any case, you will probably be more at ease in a library after you explore it on your own.

The people who work in libraries have various kinds of skills. Some are part-time student workers who only check out or reshelve books. Others are highly trained, sometimes specialized, librarians whose responsibilities may include selecting and ordering new books, cataloging books, or managing the circulation department. Librarians who are mainly responsible for providing personal services to the patrons of the library are usually called reference librarians. It is important that you learn to identify the different members of the library staff. The person who checks out your books is probably a student worker; someone in an office behind the circulation desk may manage the circulation of books as well as the reserve room; a reference librarian will have a desk or office near the reference section.

The Reference Section

Any member of the library staff can answer general questions—where the card catalog is or where the recent issues of newspapers are stored—but when you have questions about a specific research topic, you should ask a reference librarian. Some reference librarians are specialists in reference materials on particular subjects—science, social science, or literature, for example—and in a large library, there will probably be several reference librarians, along with other staff people whose job is to help you find what you need. Once you have located someone who is willing to help you, you should be as specific and clear as possible about what you want to know. Perhaps you are looking for some recent articles on word processors. You find a reference librarian and ask where the *Readers' Guide to Periodical Literature* is located, thinking that you will find some magazine articles. The librarian points to the appropriate shelf, and you eventually locate a few superficial articles in news magazines that may not have been what you were really interested in. If, however, you had explained from the beginning that you wanted to find information on the technology of word processors, the librarian could have led you to *Applied Science and Technology Index,* which cites articles in specialized journals of technology rather than in popular magazines. You should always tell a reference librarian exactly what you are looking for rather than ask for reference works that you think may have the information.

Remember that reference librarians can help you do your work, but they do not do it for you. Think of them as consultants, people with whom you can discuss your research and who will then make suggestions. It is usually best to have a short conversation with a librarian to explain your research project, what you have already found, and what you hope to find. Michael Gold, for example, went to the reference desk, noted the librarian's name on a sign at the front of the desk and explained that he was doing a research project on the movie *Rebel without a Cause,* and that he had found information in a few books and several magazines, but that he needed help finding articles in film journals. The librarian suggested that Michael consult the *International Index to Film Periodicals* and that he look under the name of the director as well as the title of the film. Within a few minutes of doing so, Michael had made a long list of articles, some of which he found in his library and two of which were extremely useful for his project.

Before you ask a reference librarian for help, make sure that you have done what you can to find material. Read this chapter carefully, study the annotated list of references at the end of this book, and find out if there is a guide to your library. Once you have done these things, feel free to ask questions. When you find someone who is willing to help you, it is a good idea to come back to the same person for any further questions. Since librarians usually work shifts, you may want to ask when a particular person will be available.

The reference area of the library contains books that cannot be checked out, books such as dictionaries, bibliographies (lists of books and articles), encyclopedias, indexes, and other catalogs of information. Many reference books are intended to provide small pieces of information as quickly as possible—the spelling of a word, the publication date of a book, the birthplace of a famous person. Others, such as encyclopedias, give an overview of large topics; and still others, such as indexes and bibliographies, help you find information in periodicals and other books. For a description of specific reference works, see the appendix of this book.

GENERAL ENCYCLOPEDIAS

Encyclopedias are familiar to most students, but you may need to be reminded that the three major encyclopedias in English differ from one another in significant ways. *Collier's Encyclopedia* has an accessible style and balanced coverage emphasizing the kinds of things taught in American colleges. It is factually reliable and up-to-date. A general, comprehensive index makes it easy for you to find what you are looking for, and an annotated bibliography suggests further reading. Both index and bibliography are in the final volume.

The *Encyclopedia Americana,* aimed at a similar readership (age fifteen and up), is approximately 30 percent longer and features twice as many articles. The *Americana* is particularly strong in the history, culture, and geography of the United States and Canada; 40 percent of its entries are biographies, and it includes brief articles on particular works of literature, music, and art. It is generally up-to-date on urgent topics such as political upheavals, but because the revision is spread out over a period of years, some articles are not current. An effective general index is easy to use, and bibliographies of recommended reading are included at the end of all major articles and many shorter ones.

The *New Encyclopaedia Britannica* is the least accessible of the three both because of its sophisticated style and because of its elaborate three part structure: the Propaedia, which outlines the world of knowledge; the Micropaedia, which provides short articles on many subjects and serves both as a ready reference and an index; and the Macropaedia, which contains in-depth, signed articles. The *Britannica* emphasizes international subjects and historical data. Leisure and previous knowledge of a subject are sometimes necessary to appreciate the abstract discussion, and it is often difficult to find all the material on a given subject because of a complicated and sometimes inadequate system of cross-references. But at times the effort required to use the *Brittanica* is worthwhile. Its depth and complexity make it more informative and authoritative in the long run.

The *New Columbia Encyclopedia* is an excellent single-volume reference work that provides reliable information on a wide range of subjects in condensed form. It is particularly useful for quick reference—getting an overview of a person's life or work, discovering the exact location and size of a state or country (there are maps), learning the average size of a particular breed of dog. The articles are cross-referenced, and many of them include lists of books for additional reading.

These are all good encyclopedias. The best one for you will depend on what you want to find out, how much time you are willing to spend, and how much you already know about a subject.

ENCYCLOPEDIA INDEXES AND BIBLIOGRAPHIES

The general index of a standard encyclopedia may refer you to a number of articles that treat your subject, but you will find that consulting the encyclopedia index will be more productive for some topics than for others. For example, the *Encyclopedia Americana* lists seven subheadings under "Conscientious Objector," while "Woodstock Festival" is included only under "Rock Music." At the end of some encyclopedia articles, you will also find a list of books used or recommended by the author of the article. One encyclopedia may provide a useful bibliography on a subject for which no references are cited in another standard encyclopedia. A case in point is the *New Columbia Encyclopedia*, which lists five books on the subject of conscientious objection, while the *Encyclopedia Americana* lists none. You may therefore want to consult all the standard encyclopedias before going to more specialized reference works. Note the following excerpt from a general encyclopedia index:

*Motion, Newton's laws of: *see* Newton's laws of motion
Motion, Perpetual: *see* Perpetual Motion
MOTION PICTURE 19–505 ——————————————— main entry: volume 19, page 505
   Academy Award 1–71a
   Acting 1–123
   Argentina 2–268; 17–30
   art and technique 19–506
   Audiovisual Education 2–671 fol.   list of other articles with infor-
   Australia 2–751   mation about motion pictures
   Brazil 17–31
   California 5–205
   Camera 5–272
   Canada 5–443
   Cartoon, Animated 5–740
   Censorship 6–161, 163, 165, 167; 7–429
   China 6–589
   Cinemascope 6–728
   Cinerama 6–729
   Civil Rights 6–771 ————————————— volume
   Comics 7–374
   Communication 7–427 ———————————— page
   Copyright 7–772
   Czechoslovakia 8–411
   De Mille, Cecil B. 8–683
   Disney, W. 9–180
   documentary 19–537
   Education 9–729
   Electronic Video Recording 10–176
   exposure meter 17–458
   France 11–832
   Friese-Greene, W. 12–95
   Gaumont, L. 12–348
   Germany 12–650
   Great Britain 13–296
   Griffith, D. W. 13–492
   history 19–516
   Hollywood 14–298; 17–754
   India 14–928
   Journalism 16–219

—— **suggestions for further information**

SPECIALIZED REFERENCE WORKS

General encyclopedias are the most widely known of the books in the reference section, but their usefulness will be very limited for serious student researchers looking for material on a particular subject. There are many other reference works that you should know about—indexes and bibliographies; yearbooks and almanacs; and numerous specialized reference works, including directories, dictionaries, histories, and specialized encyclopedias. These specialized works will usually offer a more thorough treatment of a subject than that given by a general encyclopedia. For example, you are more likely to find an in-depth treatment of behavioral psychologist B. F. Skinner in the *International Encyclopedia of the Social Sciences* than in the most recent edition of *Collier's*.

The annotated list of reference works in the appendix of this text will help you identify specialized reference works appropriate to particular research projects.

The Periodical Section

The most relaxed spot in a library is usually the current periodical section, where students can be found sitting in comfortable chairs, reading magazines, or consulting movie schedules. In this area there are two kinds of periodicals: popular magazines and newspapers—such as those you can buy on newsstands—and scholarly or professional journals, which contain articles for specialists and most of which are available only by subscription. Back issues of periodicals are stored in bound volumes or on microform—sometimes in the periodical room and sometimes in the stacks.

PERIODICAL INDEXES

Indexes to periodicals are usually shelved in the reference section of the library. To locate material in magazines, newspapers, and journals, you will have to use a variety of indexes. For popular magazines, you can consult one of the following:

The *Readers' Guide to Periodical Literature* (New York: H. W. Wilson, 1900 to date) is useful for finding articles (by subject or author) in 150 popular magazines. Supplements are published every two weeks, so it can be used for very recent publications. Bound volumes consolidate all the entries with a single alphabetical listing. The following is an excerpt from *Readers' Guide:*

∗ MOVING of machinery
    Huge generator moves on planks. il Pop Mech
      103:109 Mr '55
MOVING of structures, etc.
    Cash-and-carry houses. D. X. Manners. il Read Digest 68:145-7 Ap '56
    Hotel takes a ride. il Pop Mech 103:139 Je '55
    Houses that move around. D. Isaak. Am Mercury
      82:89-91 Mr '56
MOVING of trees. See Tree planting
MOVING picture acting
    Strange doings of actress at practice. il Life
      42:96-8 + Ja 28 '57
    That wonderful, deep silence; difference between stage and screen. S. Winters. il Theatre
      Arts 40:30-1 + Je '56
    When you take a screen test. M. Arnow. Good H
      142:38 + Ja '56
MOVING picture actors and actresses
    American women pick: our favorite stars. P. T.
      Hartung. pors Womans Home C 82:12 Je '55
    Amour and the man. pors Sat R 39:29 O 13 '56;
      Reply. D. Beams. 39:23 N 10 '56
    Bells are ringing. L. Lerman. il Mile 44:81-5 + N
      '56
    Bogart on Hollywood. il Look 20:96-8 + Ag 21 '56
    Bright young stars in fashions for off-stage
      hours. W. Cushman. il Ladies Home J 72:68-9
      My '55
    By any other name. Mr Harper. Harper 210:80-1
      Mr '55

∗ Material from *Readers' Guide to Periodical Literature* is reproduced by permission of The H. W. Wilson Company.

Discovery: British women are beautiful. il Look
    20:26-30 + Ag 21 '56
Fans choose; Photoplay magazine winners. News-
    week 45:90 F 14 '55
Film pioneers' roll of their living immortals. il
    pors Life 40:116-23 Ja 23 '56
Foreign accent in starlets. M. Nichols. pors Coro-
    net 40:44-55 Ag '56
Glamor gallery; Italian screen stars; photo-
    graphs. Theatre Arts 39:72-3 My '55
Greatest stars; Timeless stars; Glamour in our
    time; Star system in 1956; Newcomers. il Cos-
    mop 141:28-37 O '56
Hollywood actors win $80 day for now. Bsns W p
    170 Mr 24 '56   — date of periodical
Hollywood and its people. R. Gehman. il Cosmop
    141:46-51 O '56
Hollywood fathers. il Look 19:38-41 Jl 12 '55   — pages
Hollywood hobbies. il pors McCalls 83:16 + O '55
Hollywood revisited. L. Rosten. il pors Look   — author
    20:17-28 Ja 10 '56
Hollywood tragedies. E. Honor. il Cosmop
    141:38-9 O '56   — title of article
Hollywood, unhitching post. I. C. Kuhn. Am Mer-
    cury 80:7-11 Ja '55   — name of periodical
Hollywood's search for new faces. S. Peck. il pors
    N Y Times Mag p28-9 O 7 '56
Hollywood's search for stars. T. M. Pryor. il pors — illustrated
    N Y Times Mag p 14-15 + Je 12 '55
I make up Hollywood; ed. by P. Martin. W. West-
    more. il Sat Eve Post 229:17-19 + Ag 4; 30 +
    Ag 11 '56   — volume
Idols of Italy. il Look 19:100 + N 15 '55
Look annual movie awards. il Look 17:26-31 Mr
    10 '53; 18:122-4 + Mr 23 '54; 19:100-4 + Mr 23
    '55

Magazine Index, now used by many libraries, is currently available in
both microform and on-line computer readings. It lists articles from twice
as many magazines as *Readers' Guide*, but it is useful only for recent articles
since a current reel indexes only the last five years. There are printed volumes of the deleted material, but none go back earlier than 1976. Articles
are arranged by both subject and author, and the subject headings are often
much more specific than those in *Readers' Guide*. For example, film reviews
are listed by title of the film, books reviews by the title of the book, and
consumer goods under brand names.

INDEXES TO NEWSPAPERS

The *New York Times Index* lists all major articles that have appeared in that
paper from 1913 to the present. It is kept up-to-date with supplements
published every two weeks. There is also an index for selected articles for
the years 1851-1912. Articles are listed by subject. Entries in recent volumes give the exact location of each article, an indication of length, and
usually a brief summary of content. Note the following excerpt from the
New York Times Index:

*MOTION Picture Arts and Sciences, Academy of. See also
Head, Edith, D 7. Motion Pictures—Awards, F 18,19,24,
Mr 12,23,29,31, Ap 1,2,3,12, O 22, D 26
MOTION Picture Assn of America (MPAA). See also
Motion Pictures, Ja 16. Motion Pictures—US, My 24,
O 8. Television—Cable TV, My 15   — main heading
MOTION Picture Daily. See also Television—Programs,
Catch a Falling Star (TV Program), My 10
MOTION Pictures. Note: US and gen material are under —— explanation of how articles are
subject subheads. Foreign material is under geog subheads.   organized
Specific films are under subhead Revs
   See also Pornography (for inclusion). Theater and —— other suggested headings
performer names
   Vincent Canby movie quiz; illustrations, Ja 4,II,15:1
   Edwin Bigley, asst to Jack Valenti, pres of Motion Picture
Assn of Amer, reports that Pres Carter viewed some 500
films during his tenure in office, more than double that of any
previous Pres (S), Ja 16,III,6:6
   Kirk Honeycutt article on Lillian Michelson Research —— (S) indicates a short article
Library, which provides meticulous background information
for writers, designers, dirs, and art dirs to recreate authentic
stories, sets, props and costumes (L), Mr 1,II,18:1; comment
on Acme-Dunn optical printer, used to enhance certain —— (L) indicates a long article
special effects in films; noted developers of printer, Linwood
G Dunn, Cecil D Love and Edward Furer, were recognized
with Oscar for technical merit; illustration (M), Ap 3,IV,5:1
   Comment on problem of old movie film that fades; Henry
Kaska, spokesman for Eastman Kodak, Larry Carr of Amer —— (M) indicates an article of
Film Inst and filmmaker Martin Scorsese note preservation   medium length
steps that are being taken to improve situation (M), Ap 5,
III,19:1
   Natl Center for Jewish Film is established by Jewish —— brief summary of
Historical Soc; will be located on campus of Brandeis Univ   article
(S), My 3,70:6
   Gregory Peck comments on acting opposite Sophia Loren —— author of article
(S), Jl 20,II,8:3
   Bob Harelson, head of Berry Auction Co which specializes
in movie memorabilia, comments on trends (S), Ag 7,III,8:5 —— date
   Universal, Paramount, M-G-M, and United Artists have
joined together to form Lorgn, United Internatl Pictures, to
distribute films abroad (S), O 6,IV,28:6 —— section
   Vincent Canby article on effect that society's repression
has on filmmakers' styles; notes works of Frank Ripploh,
Andrzej Wajda, Dusan Makavejev and George Cukor (M), —— page
N 15,II,23:1
   Russell Baker humorous article on how old movies would
change if they were to be produced today; drawing (M), D —— column
20,VI,p17

There are subject indexes for other newspapers. *National Newspaper Index,*
available on-line and on microform, lists articles from the *Christian Science
Monitor,* the *New York Times,* and the *Wall Street Journal.* Although some
libraries do not carry microform files for all of these newspapers, they can
usually be obtained through inter-library loan. The *Times* [of London] *Official Index* is often helpful for international and especially British topics. The
Wall Street Journal Index is helpful for locating up-to-date information on
business and economics.

GENERAL INDEXES TO SCHOLARLY ARTICLES

The following indexes—actually one work with several title changes over the years—covers scholarly articles in the humanities and social sciences from 1907 to the present:

Readers' Guide Supplement and International Index covers articles from 1907 to 1919.

International Index to Periodicals, 1920 to 1965.

Social Sciences and Humanities Index, 1965 to 1974.

Since 1974, this index has been published in the following two parts:

Humanities Index lists articles published from 1974 to date.

Social Sciences Index lists by subject (anthropology, economics, psychology, etc.) articles published from 1974 to date.

INDEXES TO SPECIFIC DISCIPLINES

There are many indexes to specific disciplines, some highly specialized. Some are limited to periodicals, such as the *Art Index;* others combine an index to periodicals with lists of books on particular subjects, such as the *MLA International Bibliography.* A list of specialized indexes appears in the appendix of this book, along with an explanation of how each might be useful. You may want to explore the shelves of the reference room of your own academic library to discover what specialized indexes your library carries.

CATALOG OF A LIBRARY'S PERIODICALS

After you have located articles you want to consult in periodicals, you need to find out if they are in your library. Libraries catalog periodicals in several ways: in a separate serial catalog, in the main card catalog, on computer printouts, or on microform catalogs. You can easily find out which system a library uses by consulting a reference librarian or a printed guide to the library's resources. All systems, however, will give you the same basic information: which issues the library has; their location in the library, indicated by a call number; and whether they are bound, unbound, or on microform.

If articles that seem particularly important to your research are not in your library, you may want to try to get them from another library. To identify libraries that have a particular periodical, use the *Union List of Serials,* which catalogs periodicals in the United States and Canada through 1965. For articles after that date, consult *New Serial Titles,* which is kept up-to-date by periodic publication. Most academic libraries have a service for obtaining from other libraries copies of articles from periodicals that they do not have. Usually students pay a small fee to cover the cost of copying and mailing the article.

The Card Catalog

The card catalog is usually located in a conspicuous place in the library, sometimes near the entrance, sometimes near the circulation desk. The card catalog consists of individual three-by-five-inch cards stored in small drawers in a series of cabinets. For most books in the collection there will be at least three cards: an author card, a title card, and a subject card. Individual poems, short stories, and longer works of imaginative literature—fiction, poetry, and drama—usually will not have a subject card, though any type of work may be cited on additional cards for editors, illustrators, or translators. Each item in the catalog is assigned a unique identifying number called the call number, which is in the upper left corner of each card. Whether your library uses the Dewey decimal system or the Library of Congress system for classifying books, you will need to record the complete call number before you try to find a book in the stacks or before someone can retrieve it for you.

CLASSIFICATION SYSTEMS FOR BOOKS

To locate a specific book, you need to understand the classification system used by your library. Most libraries use either the Dewey decimal or the Library of Congress system of classification. Although it is not necessary to memorize the classification systems, you will find it easier to use a library if you know which system it uses and what kinds of books are in the general categories.

The *Dewey decimal system* uses a number system to classify books into these ten major categories:

000–099   General Works
100–199   Philosophy
200–299   Religion
300–399   Social Sciences
400–499   Language
500–599   Pure Science
600–699   Technology (Applied Science)
700–799   The Arts
800–899   Literature and Rhetoric
900–999   General Geography and History

These major divisions are then subdivided by tens. For example, the numbers 810 to 819 designate American literature, with 813 indicating American fiction. Additional numbers indicate the content of a book.

Under the Dewey decimal number is an author number made up of the first initial of the author's last name, a code number assigned to the author's name, and the first letter or letters of the book's title. The combination of the Dewey decimal number and the author number is unique. It applies to one book only. In a library where you have access to the stacks, you can locate a book easily with a complete call number. Note this example for Cleanth Brooks's *William Faulkner: The Yoknapatawpha Country:*

American fiction ⟶ 813.52 ⟵ period (1900-1945)

Subject (Faulkner) ⟶ F263B ⟵ author (Brooks)

The *Library of Congress system* uses twenty-one major divisions, each indicated by a letter of the alphabet:

A   General Works
B   Philosophy, Psychology, and Religion
C   History and Auxiliary Sciences
D   History: General and Old World
E–F History: North and South America
G   Geography, Anthropology, and Recreation
H   Social Science
J   Political Science
K   Law
L   Education
M   Music
N   Fine Arts
P   Language and Literature
Q   Science
R   Medicine
S   Agriculture
T   Technology
U   Military Science
V   Naval Science
Z   Bibliography and Library Science

Additional letters and numbers indicate more specific categories, and, as with the Dewey decimal system, an author number designates a particular book within a category. The following call number is for Erik Erikson's *Identity: Youth and Crisis:*

Psychology ⟶ BF697 ⟵ subject (personality)

author's initial ⟶ E7 ⟵ identifying number

Although it is not necessary to memorize categories and subcategories in the Library of Congress system, you will find it easier to use an open-stack library if you know in a general way where the books in different categories are found.

AUTHOR, SUBJECT, AND TITLE CARDS

The difference between author, subject, and title cards is simple. An author card contains all the information of the other two, but the first item is the last name of the author. And the subject card is identical to the author card, except that the subject heading is typed at the top. Cards on different books vary according to the content of the individual book. Consider the following examples:

AUTHOR CARD

E **Lash, Joseph P**   1909– 807.1   Eleanor and Franklin; the story of their relationship, based on R572   Eleanor Roosevelt's private papers [by] Joseph P. Lash. Foreword by Arthur M. Schlesinger, Jr. Introd. by Franklin D. Roosevelt, Jr. New York, Norton [1971] xviii, 765 p. illus., geneal. table (on lining papers), ports. 24 cm. $15.00 Includes bibliographical references. 1. Roosevelt, Eleanor (Roosevelt) 1884–1962.   2. Roosevelt, Franklin Delano, Pres. U.S., 1882–1945.   I. Title. E807.1.R572   72–152667   973.917'0924 [B] ISBN 0–393–07459–5   MARC Library of Congress   71 [7]

TITLE CARD

Eleanor and Franklin E **Lash, Joseph P**   1909– 807.1   Eleanor and Franklin; the story of their relationship, based on R572   Eleanor Roosevelt's private papers [by] Joseph P. Lash. Foreword by Arthur M. Schlesinger, Jr. Introd. by Franklin D. Roosevelt, Jr. New York, Norton [1971] xviii, 765 p. illus., geneal. table (on lining papers), ports. 24 cm. $15.00 Includes bibliographical references. 1. Roosevelt, Eleanor (Roosevelt) 1884–1962.   2. Roosevelt, Franklin Delano, Pres. U.S., 1882–1945.   I. Title. E807.1.R572   72–152667   973.917'0924 [B] ISBN 0–393–07459–5   MARC Library of Congress   71 [7]

SUBJECT CARD

ROOSEVELT, ELEANOR (ROOSEVELT) 1884–1962

E   **Lash, Joseph P**   1909–
807.1   Eleanor and Franklin; the story of their relationship, based on
R572   Eleanor Roosevelt's private papers [by] Joseph P. Lash. Foreword
           by Arthur M. Schlesinger, Jr. Introd. by Franklin D. Roosevelt, Jr.
           New York, Norton [1971]

              xviii, 765 p. illus., geneal. table (on lining papers), ports. 24 cm. $15.00

              Includes bibliographical references.

                 1. Roosevelt, Eleanor (Roosevelt) 1884–1962.   2. Roosevelt, Franklin Delano,
              Pres. U.S., 1882–1945.   I. Title.

           E807.1.R572   72–152667
                              973.917'0924 [B]
           ISBN 0–393–07459–5   MARC
           Library of Congress   71 [7]

    If you know both the author and the title of a book—as you would if you located it in a bibliography—then look for it under the author. That way you may find other books on your subject by the same author. When you are ready to look for sources under subject cards, you will want to try to identify all the appropriate headings.

    You will also find heading cards in the card catalog, which will list other subjects that may lead you to related material. For example, you may find a card with the heading SOLAR POWER that directs you to "see SOLAR ENERGY" or another headed SOUL MUSIC that directs you to "see MUSIC, POPULAR."

Comcats and On-Line Computer Catalogs

Many libraries now use cataloging systems that depend on computers to help organize and update the library holdings. Some use what is called a COMCAT—Computer Output Microfilm Catalog. The COMCAT consists of microforms (see p. 36) and microform readers or screens (usually placed conveniently around the library) that display the information traditionally stored in the card catalog. The COMCAT is used instead of a card catalog, though some libraries that use this system may also have a small card file for cataloging materials that have not yet been added to a microform. Most libraries that use a COMCAT system update the records every three months. If you are using a COMCAT and cannot find what you are looking for, check to see if there is a supplementary file for recent acquisitions.

    Each listing in the COMCAT will give all the information— and sometimes more—that is found in a traditional card catalog. The information, however, may not be in the same order: For example, some catalogs will give the call number at the end of an entry, others at the beginning. In any case, individual libraries will provide explanations—usually posted near a catalog microform reader—for how the information is organized as well as instructions for using the COMCAT.

On-line computer catalogs provide up-to-date information directly from a computer. With this system you request information by typing key words (such as author, title, subject) into a terminal; you then read the answer directly from a screen. All the information about the library's collection is stored as electronic signals rather than as photographs on microforms. Some libraries now use on-line catalogs for regional library holdings, such as those of selected libraries in a city, a state university system, or a section of the country.

Both the COMCAT and the on-line computer catalog are used instead of traditional card catalogs. If any of the libraries you use have either of these systems, you should become familiar with how they work before you have the pressure of a deadline. You will probably find that if you study the instructions carefully and practice using the systems, you can easily and quickly find which books are available to you.

Other Book Catalogs

You may want to compile a list of all the books on your topic that you think you would like to consult, even if they are not in your library. Some of them may be available from interlibrary loan, or you may be able to borrow directly from other libraries or friends. There are bibliographies—lists of sources—on many subjects. Many of them are complete books themselves. To find out if there is a published bibliography on your topic or the general subject you are studying, you may consult the *Bibliographic Index*, which is published in cumulative volumes every year; it lists both single volume bibliographies and those incorporated into books and journals, many of which will not be available in small libraries (see p. 257). Easier to use than the *Bibliographic Index* is Eugene P. Sheehy's *Guide to Reference Books*, which includes an annotated appendix indicating which reference works have bibliographies.

Books in Print is a multivolume work that lists all books in English currently available for purchase by bookstores and libraries. There are volumes that list books alphabetically by author and others that alphabetize by title. Both volumes include complete publication information for each listing. In addition, the *Subject Guide to Books in Print* classifies books by subject and the *Paperbound Books in Print* lists those books published only in paper, as well as those in both paper and hardcover. Any of the volumes of *Books in Print* may be helpful for identifying very recent books that may be ordered but not yet cataloged in your library.

Computer Databases

Computer databases are now available in almost all fields, and new ones are added periodically. Information retrieval services called vendors provide access to bibliographies, indexes, and other reference works. Two vendors frequently used in academic libraries are Dialog and BRS/Search. The following selected list incudes some of the more commonly used databases in various fields appropriate for student researchers:

GENERAL REFERENCE WORKS

Academic American Encyclopedia
An up-to-date general encyclopedia; the on-line version is updated quarterly. See page 259.

Biography and Genealogy Master Index
Serves as an index to more than 600 biographical dictionaries, directories, and handbooks of authors, providing access to information about historical and contemporary figures in all fields. See page 261.

Book Review Index
Cites the sources of book reviews appearing in more than 380 journals. See page 261.

Books in Print
Provides instant access to the most recent editions of this multivolume work and its supplements. See page 33.

Facts on File
Provides weekly news summaries of contemporary events ranging from politics to sports. See page 262.

Magazine Index
Offers broad coverage of general-interest magazines on a wide range of topics. See page 261.

Marquis Who's Who
Updated quarterly, this on-line database contains detailed biographies on nearly 90,000 individuals. Corresponds to the printed publications *Who's Who in America* (see page 258) and *Who's Who in Frontier Science and Technology*.

ON-LINE INFORMATION SERVICES IN THE HUMANITIES

America: History and Life
A comprehensive guide to finding information on historical topics. See page 264.

Historical Abstracts
Provides citations and abstracts of periodical literature in history. See page 264.

MLA Bibliography
Indexes books and journal articles published on the modern languages, literature, and linguistics. See page 266.

The Philosopher's Index
A comprehensive index to books and periodicals in philosophy. See page 268.

Religion Index
Provides indexing and abstracts to articles on various aspects of religion. See page 268.

ON-LINE INFORMATION SERVICES IN THE SOCIAL SCIENCES

ERIC
The complete database on educational materials from the Educational Resources Information Center. Contains *Resources in Education* and *Current Index to Journals in Education*. See page 272.

Moody's Corporate Profiles
For information on U.S. business. See *Moody's Manuals,* page 271.

PAIS International
Contains information from the *PAIS* bulletin as well as a foreign language index. Covers all fields of social science. See page 269.

PsycINFO
Covers the world's literature in psychology. Corresponds to *Psychological Abstracts*. See page 270.

Standard and Poor's News
Provides general news and financial information on more than 10,000 U.S. companies. See page 271.

ON-LINE INFORMATION SERVICES IN THE NATURAL AND APPLIED SCIENCES

American Men and Women in Science
Provides biographical information on scientists actively working in all scientific fields. See page 274.

Compendex
The on-line version of *Engineering Index*. See page 277.

Medline
> One of the major sources for biomedical literature. Corresponds to three printed indexes: *Index Medicus, Index to Dental Literature,* and *International Nursing Index.* See page 275.

SCISEARCH
> Contains all the records published in *Science Citation Index.* See page 275.

The Circulation Desk

The circulation desk is not only the place where you check out books; it is also the place where records are kept on all books that are not on the shelves: those that are checked out, on reserve, or being repaired. Staff people behind the circulation desk can usually tell you where books are and when you can expect to use them. If you have reason to think that a book has been stolen or misplaced, you should report it to the circulation desk.

The Stacks

Libraries shelve books that can be checked out in an area usually referred to as the stacks. In some libraries, the stacks are open, which means that you have free access to the circulating books. You can browse among the shelves, take a book down to skim it, carry it to a library carrel, or check it out. In open stacks, it is easy to find books on a particular topic and to select individual books directly from the shelves. In a library with closed stacks, you must make your selections from the card catalog, fill out a request form, and wait to have a book brought to the circulation desk.

The Microform and Non-print Collection

Microform is the general term for all information stored as very small images called microimages, which are actually reproductions of printed material—books, newspapers, periodicals, and documents. To use microforms, you must have a machine called a reader, which enlarges the print to a readable size. The most common microforms are microfilm, microfiche, and microprint. Since most libraries have some material on more than one type of microform, you should use the general term when inquiring about these materials. Non-print material is the term used to refer to audio tapes, videotapes, records, and films. Some libraries store these materials in a separate room near the equipment necessary to use them. You may want to learn to use the machinery before you need to use it under the pressure of an assignment.

The Reserve Book Section

Academic libraries have a section for books that have been set aside for use by students in a particular class. You will, however, usually be allowed to use reserve books in the library, and in some cases, you may be able to check them out overnight. When a book that you want is not on the shelf, you should ask at the circulation desk whether the book is on reserve. In some libraries, reserve books are kept behind the circulation desk; in others, they are in a separate section or even a special reserve reading room.

Special Collections

Library materials that require unusual care are kept in a separate room, often behind locked doors, or in a separate building. Old or particularly valuable books, fragile materials, letters, manuscripts, and all rare publications are usually kept together in the special collections room. There may be times when you will consult material in the special collections or when you will design a research project based on the collections of letters, manuscripts, or other rare or unique materials to which you have access. Once you have discovered what particularly valuable material your library has, you should ask whether it is available to students and what procedures you should follow to use it.

Library Services

ASSISTANCE IN FINDING INFORMATION

The circulation department will provide you with information about the whereabouts and availability of circulating books. The reference department will help you answer more specific questions on a wide range of topics. Even after you have studied the annotated list of reference works in the appendix of this book, you will probably need some guidance about the best reference work to consult for a particular question. For example, David Harris wants to find out something about Robert Coles, the author of one of the books he is using for his research. He goes to the reference room and looks for information in several encyclopedias. When he does not find what he wants, he asks the reference librarian, who suggests that he consult *Biography and Genealogy Master Index*. There he finds Coles listed in several reference works, including *American Men and Women of Science, 1979*, where he finds the information he needs.

INSTRUCTION IN LIBRARY USE

Many libraries provide pamphlets, maps, and other materials that explain how to use a particular library's services and resources. Some provide tours, workshops, or formal classes in library skills. It is a good idea to look for notices about these services or to inquire at the circulation or reference desk. Your college catalog may explain which of these services are available to you.

ASSISTANCE WITH COMPUTER DATABASES AND NETWORKS

Many libraries offer a service that uses a computer to search databases, providing lists of sources on subjects in a wide variety of fields, including business, medicine, law, science and technology, education, the humanities, the social services, and numerous narrow disciplines within these large categories. In most libraries, you will need to ask a librarian to assist you in your search (see p. 46).

Another service commonly provided by libraries is access to a national bibliographic network, which uses computers to link libraries all over the United States and Canada (see p. 50).

STUDY AREAS AND STORAGE SPACE

Certain sections of a library are designated for quiet study, and some libraries have carrels that can be reserved for use by individual students. Most libraries have space set aside for typing. Many also provide lockers where students can leave their books and papers overnight. You will need to take the initiative to find out if any of these services are available.

COPYING SERVICES

Using a library's copying service can save you time. Most libraries have coin-operated machines that students can use to copy single pages, whole articles, or even chapters in books. Some have staff people who will make copies for you, usually for a small fee. At all times, of course, you will want to respect the copyright laws that make it illegal for you to copy large portions of a book rather than purchasing the book. The law allows you to copy for educational purposes up to a chapter in a book, three articles in an annual volume of a periodical, and a story or a poem from an anthology.

INTERLIBRARY SERVICES

Libraries exchange various services, ranging from reference assistance to copying services. If your library does not receive certain periodicals, you may be able to get copies of articles from them from another library. This service is usually arranged through the reference section, where you will need to fill out request forms and pay a small fee for copying.

You may be able to borrow books from other libraries through a loan system arranged by your college library. To do this you will usually need to consult with the reference librarian, fill out a form, and sometimes pay a small fee. In some cases, you will be able to obtain a book very quickly; in others, there may be a considerable wait. In any case, ask how long it will take to get the book and respect what restrictions, if any, the lending library places on its use and on the length of time it is lent. Many libraries limit the interlibrary loan service to graduate students and faculty; others provide the service in a limited way to undergraduates. Before you try to find books in other libraries, find out if it is possible for you to borrow them.

EXERCISES

A. On your own take an informal tour of your college library. If a map or other guide is available, use it. Otherwise, you may need to ask a few questions of the library staff before you locate everything. The following activities should lead you to all the sections of the library:

1. Visit the section where the current periodicals are shelved. Select a popular magazine that attracts your attention and skim it, stopping to read articles that interest you.
2. Locate the bound periodicals and skim through a single volume, such as a few months of *Look* or *Life*.
3. Find the reference section of the library, identify the reference desk, and find out which staff people are the reference librarians.
4. Find out how the books in the library are cataloged. Are they on traditional cards or on microform?
5. If the stacks are open, browse among the circulating books and note whether the library uses the Dewey decimal system or the Library of Congress system.
6. Select a book that interests you, or, if the stacks are closed, select one from the card catalog and fill out a request form for that book. Take the book to the circulation desk and follow the procedure for checking it out.

B. Go to the periodical room of the library and select a number of magazines that attract your attention but that you have not seen before; then look at the scholarly journals and find one that interests you. Skim through the periodicals you have selected, reading carefully any articles that seem particularly valuable.

C. Go to the section of the library where encyclopedias are shelved.

1. Select a noncontroversial topic in which most people have some interest, such as "Dogs." Look the topic up in the three major encyclopedias. What differences and what similarities do you note? Are there cross-references within the article? If you wanted to buy a dog, which article would provide you with the most practical information for choosing the right breed?

2. Choose a subject you feel you know rather well—classic cars, nuclear energy, Nigeria, the Civil War, football, piano composers —and see how much you can learn from reading articles in two encyclopedias. Read carefully to see if you can spot any errors, out-of-date material, or opinions stated as fact.

3. Choose a controversial topic such as abortion or arms control and look it up in three encyclopedias, using the index to find all the articles that treat the topic. Note the varied treatments and whether the material in each encyclopedia is current; then make a list of the suggested further reading on the topic in each encyclopedia and compare the sources, noting particularly the dates of each. Do some sources appear in more than one encyclopedia? in all three? Which article gives you the most thorough, up-to-date treatment of the topic?

D. Visit the reference room again.

1. Look up B. F. Skinner in the following reference works: the *American Heritage Dictionary*, the *New Columbia Encyclopedia*, *Collier's Encyclopedia*, and the *International Encyclopedia of the Social Sciences*. You will find that each is more detailed than the last; as you proceed through each of the last three sources, jot down three facts not found in the previous source or sources. Jot down publication dates of Skinner's major books. Look to see if his work is discussed in more than one entry in the last source, and look up the titles of his works *Walden Two* and *Beyond Freedom and Dignity* to see if they are treated separately. Notice that the *International Encyclopedia of the Social Sciences* also has a *Biographical Supplement* that is indexed separately. You may find so much material in the final source that you will only have time to skim it.

2. Locate the *Readers' Guide to Periodic Literature* and select a volume for a year in which Skinner published a major book (1961 for *Walden Two* and 1971 for *Beyond Freedom and Dignity*). Look up Skinner and note how frequently articles were published about him in periodicals for those years.

3. Find the *Book Review Digest* and skim the reviews of one of these books. Would you be interested in reading the book?

E. Writing exercises.

1. Go to the library at a busy time and observe the activities of the people there. Write a paragraph or more describing how people are actually using the library.
2. Evaluate your own library. Make a list of the library materials and services mentioned in this chapter, and then find out which are available in your library. Write a paper in which you describe the resources in your library.

For students who are ready to begin a research project

3. Write a paragraph or more about the library resources that you expect to use for your topic.

4

USING LIBRARY SOURCES

When you go to the library to research a topic that truly interests you, you may find that your greatest difficulty is limiting the amount of time you spend finding and reading articles and books. It is a good idea to plan the steps of your research and to estimate in advance how much time you can spend looking for library sources. You will probably be more efficient if you allow several hours for each session in the library.

Preparing to Work in the Library

Before you begin collecting library material for a particular project, you will want to do the following:

1. Become familiar with your college library: locate the circulation desk, the reference desk, reference books, the stacks, the periodicals, and the card catalog (or COMCAT).
2. Obtain writing materials such as cards, paper slips, writing pads, etc.
3. Study suggestions for making source cards (see pp. 51–53).
4. Examine examples of note cards in chapter 6 (see pp. 80–90).
5. Decide which style is best for documenting your paper (see pp. 131–132).

SELECTING WRITING MATERIALS

You will save time if you always have enough writing material with you: three-by-five-inch cards for recording sources; five-by-eight-inch cards for note taking; a legal pad for your first draft; pens and pencils; and a large manila envelope, folder, or some other container that you use strictly for your research. To some extent, the kinds of materials you use will be a matter of personal preference. Some students enjoy using different-colored cards so that they can coordinate colors with types of notes or use one color for direct quotations and white cards for all other notes. (This also would help you avoid accidental plagiarism.) You may prefer more flexible slips of quality paper to the stiff index cards. Regardless of color or size, individual note cards have the advantage of being easy to organize when you are ready to write your first draft and individual source cards can be quickly put in order to form your list of sources. Whether you use long or short writing pads or small or large note cards should be determined by the scale of your handwriting and the directions of your instructor.

USING THE APPROPRIATE DOCUMENTATION STYLE

Decide which documentation style you will use for the final bibliography and notes of your paper before you make your source cards. Chapter 9 and the sample paper in chapter 11 use the style recommended by the Modern Language Association. The sample paper in Appendix A is documented with endnotes and a bibliography, a form that is also endorsed by the Modern Language Association. The third sample paper (chapter 12) uses that of the American Psychological Association, and the last sample paper (chapter 13) follows the guidelines of the American Chemical Society. (Your instructor may advise you about which style you are to use.) To save time later, record bibliographic information as it will appear in your list of sources.

REVIEWING AVAILABLE SOURCES

The order in which you collect your sources will vary from one research project to another. Since most researchers continue to narrow their topics as they explore sources, it is best to begin with general sources and move to more specific ones. You will probably consult library sources in approximately this order:

1. General reference works such as encyclopedias, bibliographies, dictionaries, and handbooks
2. The card catalog, COMCAT, or computer catalog
3. Other book catalogs and specialized bibliographies
4. General periodical indexes
5. Specialized periodical indexes

COLLECTING SOURCES: A CHECKLIST

Finding the sources that you expect to use involves a number of activities that have already been suggested in this book, but it is helpful to review these activities before you begin to take extensive notes. Although you have been advised to move from general to specific sources, you will probably backtrack, and even after you have found most of your material, you may go back to the card catalog or consult an index under a different heading. Always keep a record of your progress, noting specific volumes of indexes as you consult them. Before you conclude this stage of your research, you will want to do the following:

1. Locate and read articles in general encyclopedias and specialized reference works.
2. Make source cards for books and articles on your topic suggested in these sources.
3. Consult the list of subjects in *Library of Congress Subject Headings.*
4. Consult the card catalog and record titles and call numbers of promising books.
5. Check out appropriate books.
6. Consult other book catalogs and bibliographies.
7. Study general periodical indexes for magazines and newspapers.
8. Explore specialized periodical indexes for scholarly journals.
9. Discover which periodicals are in your library and locate the ones you want.
10. Photocopy articles that you want in full.
11. Discuss with a librarian the possibility of doing a computer search.
12. Fill out interlibrary loan forms for books available from other libraries.
13. Request copies of articles in periodicals from other libraries.
14. Locate non-print material—records, tapes, microform—on your topic.
15. Make a card for each source using appropriate bibliographic style.

Some of these steps will not be appropriate for all topics. For example, your library may not provide a service for borrowing books from other libraries; there may not be any non-print material available on your topic; and abstracts (brief summaries) may not be available for journals in the particular discipline you are researching.

DEFINING AND EXPLAINING WHAT YOU WANT TO KNOW

Before you plan your search strategy—the steps you expect to follow in locating material—try to define what you want to know. If you can condense your research questions to a single sentence, you will be able to explain quickly what you want to find out to the reference librarians and others who may guide you to appropriate material. A simple statement of what you want to know can also serve as a guide to keep you on the subject

and to help you decide quickly which sources should be profitable and which, though interesting, are in fact irrelevant to *your* project. You might write a summary statement similar to one below.
I want to know:

1. how a house can be designed to be heated and cooled economically
2. how the nuclear threat affects children and adolescents
3. about the people who created the film *Rebel without a Cause*
4. the similarities and differences between Toni Morrison's *Sula* and Alice Walker's *Meridian*
5. about Eleanor Roosevelt's work to help women

Librarians and others can be much more helpful if you explain as precisely as possible what you want to know rather than ask general questions. If you want to learn about Eleanor Roosevelt's public activities in the 1920s, say so instead of asking for general information about her life.

Planning the Steps of Your Search: The Search Strategy

Try to identify the steps on the checklist above that will be helpful for your topic. Some topics will not be treated in general encyclopedias. For example, a subject like the psychological effects of the nuclear threat does not even appear in the *Encyclopedia Americana*. When David Harris failed to find books on his subject, he decided to do a computer search, which yielded a number of valuable sources. For help in devising a search strategy—a plan for locating material—consult the annotated list of reference works in the appendix of this book and make a list of those that you think will be helpful.

Before he made a plan, Michael Gold made a list of the steps that led him to his topic:

1. Studied the article on "Motion Pictures" in the Encyclopedia Americana.
2. Read the chapter on movies in the 1950s in David Cook's History of Narrative Film.
3. Watched a video tape of Rebel without a Cause.

He then devised the following plan:

1. Consult the World Encyclopedia of Film and the Biographical Dictionary of Film.
2. Check the card catalog under Rebel without a Cause, James Dean, and Nicholas Ray.
3. Check out books that look promising.

4. Consult the <u>Readers' Guide to Periodical Literature</u> for 1955 and 1956 for reviews of <u>Rebel</u> and articles about James Dean.
5. Ask the reference librarian for guidance.

After Michael completed these steps, he identified other areas that he wanted to explore and expanded his plan to include the following:

6. Consult the <u>International Index to Film Periodicals</u>.
7. Read Robert Lindner's 1944 book, <u>Rebel without a Cause</u>.
8. Consult <u>Book Review Digest</u> for reviews of Lindner's book.
9. Check <u>Readers' Guide to Periodical Literature</u> for more recent articles about Dean, Ray, or <u>Rebel</u>.
10. Check <u>Essay and General Literature Index</u> for chapters in books.
11. Locate and photocopy promising articles.
12. Begin reading.

DOING A COMPUTER SEARCH

A computer search of an appropriate topic using carefully chosen subject headings, or descriptors, and a database that covers the topic can yield many useful sources in a very short time. A skilled searcher can combine more than one descriptor at a time and in this way find narrowly focused sources that would take hours to find in more traditional indexes. Topics such as business, medicine, or chemistry are best searched with a computer since databases in these fields are up-to-date. For example, the update for *Standard and Poor's News* is daily, for *Chemsearch* biweekly, and for *Medline* monthly. Some databases provide abstracts—short summaries—of the articles as well as all the information you need to locate them.

A computer search, however, can be expensive, so inquire about cost before you begin. Not all topics are suited for a computer search since some databases cover only a limited time period. Databases are constantly being updated and extended back in time, so inquire about the time period covered by each database you plan to search.

In order to help the searcher find material for you, you must explain your topic in some detail and answer any questions that arise. For this reason, you should not begin a computer search until you have limited your topic adequately. Once this is accomplished, a searcher can combine terms in several different ways, using one of three connectors: *and, or,* and *not.* For example, when Carol Garcia was looking for material on solar energy, she might have instructed the computer to locate sources that contain the words solar *and* energy. Someone researching energy sources other than nuclear energy might ask for energy *not* nuclear. (The *not* connector must be used with caution since it would exclude articles that discuss nuclear energy along with other forms of energy.)

Some topics are particularly suited for a computer search. David Harris found that searching the card catalog and the indices in book form was very tedious and nonproductive. "Nuclear war" in the *Library of Congress Subject Headings* eventually led him to "atomic warfare—psychological aspects," but he found nothing in his library's card catalog. Next he turned to *Psychological Abstracts*, but searching one subject at a time proved to be so tedious that David felt overwhelmed and gave up. He then consulted a reference librarian, who explained that with the help of a computer, he could search several subject headings at once. He made an appointment with the librarian who specializes in computer searches and together they planned the search.

Considering the material covered in the various available databases, the librarian recommended a search in ERIC and PsycINFO. After listening to David explain his topic and consulting the Thesaurus of ERIC Descriptors, beginning with nuclear warfare, the librarian then identified four other descriptors she could use to limit the topic: young children, childhood attitudes, children, and adolescents. Using the *and* as well as the *or* connector, she instructed the computer to look for sources that contain nuclear war *and* childhood attitudes *or* children, *or* young children, *or* adolescents. She then searched for articles on the subject of nuclear warfare and found 347 items. When she checked for material on any of the other four, she found there were 33,803. By directing the computer to identify those sources about nuclear warfare that contain information about children, childhood attitudes, children or adolescents, she found a manageable 25 articles. Following a similar procedure, she searched PsycINFO and found 50 sources, some of which overlapped with those from the ERIC database. Since David had plenty of time to do his research, he requested an off-line printout, which came in the mail within five days. Pages 48–49 show a small portion of the printout of the sources David located in his computer search.

The computer search was very helpful for David. Not all of the sources he found were appropriate or available, but he very easily located several sources on the list, which led him to still others. In a short time, David felt he had more information than he actually needed.

To do a computer search in most libraries you will need to follow these steps:

1. Fill out a form for a search request.
2. Make an appointment and meet with a computer librarian (a professional searcher).
3. With the librarian's assistance, choose the databases to search, determine the cost of the search, and decide whether you want the infor-

PRINT-OUT OF SOURCES LOCATED THROUGH A COMPUTER SEARCH

HARRIS — NUCLEAR WAR

DIALOG File 11: PSYCINFO - 67-85/NOV (Copr. Am. Psych. Assn.)

72-23763
   A decisionmaking approach to nuclear education. Special
Issue: Education and the threat of nuclear war.
   Snow, Roberta; Goodman, Lisa
   Harvard Medical School, Boston
   Harvard Educational Review, 1984 Aug Vol 54(3) 321-328
CODEN: HVERAP   ISSN: 00178055
   Journal Announcement: 7209
   Language: ENGLISH Document Type: JOURNAL ARTICLE
   Describes a US senior high school curriculum that addresses
4   areas: personal values as a basis for political views,
technological aspects of the nuclear arms race, the history of
the   nuclear   arms   race, and action for social change. The
program's   content, focus, and structure are detailed, and its
effects   on   student   attitudes   are   discussed. Excerpts from
student   essays   are   presented,   and   examples of appropriate
class projects are suggested.
   Descriptors: NUCLEAR   WAR   .(34567); STUDENT ATTITUDES
.(50300); EDUCATION .(16000); CURRICULUM .(12810); HIGH SCHOOL
STUDENTS .(22930); ADOLESCENCE .(00920)
   Identifiers: high school curriculum, decisionmaking approach
to nuclear education, high school students
   Section Headings: 3530 .(CURRICULUM PROGRAMS & TEACHING
METHODS)

72-23746
   Resistances to knowing in the nuclear age. Special Issue:
Education and the threat of nuclear war.
   Mack, John E.
   Harvard Medical School, Boston
   Harvard Educational Review, 1984 Aug Vol 54(3) 260-270
CODEN: HVERAP   ISSN: 00178055
   Journal Announcement: 7209
   Language: ENGLISH Document Type: JOURNAL ARTICLE
   Explores psychological reasons why educators and parents
resist   dealing with the nuclear issue, arguing that the
controversy   surrounding   nuclear   education reflects the
conflicts of society as a whole with regard to nuclear weapons
and   nuclear arms policy. Individual resistance, the avoidance
of   the   emotional   pain associated with nuclear war, and
collective   resistance, the result of a nation's political and
economic   assumptions   to   which citizens feel committed and
which they support through corporate structures, are examined.
The   psychological   attachment and personal emotional security
associated with alignment with these structures are described.
A   collectively   based   fear   among   those involved in this
hierarchy   of imparting a balanced view of Soviet ideology and
intentions   to adolescents also hinders efforts to provide
nuclear   education.   It is concluded that, if these collective
assumptions   are   not   questioned,   advocacy   for nuclear
education,   no   matter   how well-intended or impassioned, will
not succeed. (22 ref)

Descriptors: NUCLEAR WAR .(34567); EDUCATION .(16000); PARENTS .(36680); TEACHERS .(51690); ADULTHOOD .(01150)

Identifiers: psychological reasons for resistance to dealing with nuclear issue, educators & parents

Section Headings: 3530 .(CURRICULUM PROGRAMS & TEACHING METHODS); 2900 .(SOCIAL PROCESSES AND SOCIAL ISSUES)

72-23687

The role of education in preventing nuclear war. Special Issue: Education and the threat of nuclear war.

Markusen, Eric; Harris, John B.

Southwest State U

Harvard Educational Review, 1984 Aug Vol 54(3) 282-303 CODEN: HVERAP ISSN: 00178055

Journal Announcement: 7209

Language: ENGLISH Document Type: JOURNAL ARTICLE

Argues that education should play a crucial role in reducing the threat of nuclear war and examines the role of education in formulating and implementing policies and attitudes that caused the Holocaust of World War II Nazi Germany. A parallel is drawn to the role of American education in maintaining the nuclear arms race between the US and USSR. Aspects of US nuclear weapons policymaking and factors of psychological resistance (e.g., psychic numbing, apathy, ignorance, parochialism, distractions of daily life) that have limited citizen participation in nuclear decision making are examined. The propagation of nuclearism, in which organizations and individuals develop incentives to maintain the status quo of searching for nuclear superiority and of the readiness to wage nuclear war, as an institutional phenomenon is described. The concentration of power in these policymaking structures has eroded the democratic process as it relates to nuclear planning and policy. The potential of education to help prevent nuclear war and ways that educators are attempting to accomplish this task are discussed.

Descriptors: NUCLEAR WAR .(34567); EDUCATION .(16000); PREVENTION .(40290)

Identifiers: role of education in preventing of nuclear war

Section Headings: 3500 .(EDUCATIONAL PSYCHOLOGY)

72-22365

Between feeling and fact: Listening to children. Special Issue: Education and the threat of nuclear war.

Engel, Brenda S.

Lesley Coll, Program Evaluation & Research Group

Harvard Educational Review, 1984 Aug Vol 54(3) 304-314 CODEN: HVERAP ISSN: 00178055

Journal Announcement: 7209

Language: ENGLISH Document Type: JOURNAL ARTICLE

Contends that parents and teachers can learn a great deal about young children's attitudes and fears about nuclear weapons by closely attending to their behavior. A discussion that took place in a class of kindergarten through 2nd-grade children, who responded to a theme depicting them as ""bosses of the world,'' was analyzed. Ss' conversation revealed their attitudes toward war toys and war play and their inner distinctions between play and reality. Ways in which mation in an on-line printout available immediately or in an off-line printout that you will receive normally within five days.

4. Consult a thesaurus if available to find the appropriate descriptors (subject headings) to use for the search.
5. Devise a search strategy that will combine descriptors in the most effective way.
6. Begin the search, adjusting descriptors as needed. You may have to make another appointment to meet with the librarian to actually conduct the search.

USING A LIBRARY NETWORK

There are three major national bibliographic networks: OCLC (Online Computer Library Center), RLIN (Research Libraries Information Network), and WLN (Washington Library Network). These systems link libraries by providing computerized lists of books in the collections of libraries throughout the United States and Canada. A network is useful for a variety of purposes. You may, for example, use it to locate a book that is not available in your library or to verify publication information about a book that you do not have in hand.

IDENTIFYING SUBJECT HEADINGS

Certain indexes have their own guides to subject headings (sometimes called a thesaurus). Some include the guide in each cumulative volume; and some—the ERIC publications and *Psychological Abstracts*—provide a separate volume for subject headings. Still other indexes use the Library of Congress headings. Before you use an index, study the introductory material to find out how subjects are classified. When you are looking for books on a particular subject or articles listed in indexes that use the Library of Congress system, you should consult the *Library of Congress Subject Headings*. This and other guides may suggest headings that you would otherwise not think to consult.

FINDING THE RIGHT DATE

If you are studying the public response to a movie or a book, you will consult indexes to periodicals published at the same time or shortly after. Most films are reviewed immediately after they are released, and popular books are reviewed within a few months. If you have trouble finding reviews of a book, you should check at least three years after publication dates since publication of reviews of certain books, especially scholarly ones, may be delayed that long. To find information on historical subjects, keep in mind that events are sometimes not written about for some time after they occur; some events are of course kept from the public by people who do not want them to be known. For example, most people did not know about many of the events surrounding the Watergate affair until more than two years after they had occurred. If you were researching the role that presidential aides played in the Watergate scandal, you would not find much in periodical indexes for the year 1972; rather, you would need to consult indexes for 1973 and 1974, the years during which the story was gradually told in the press. In order to research news accounts of such events, you would need to find out when they were announced or when media coverage began, as well as when they occurred. To find the dates of the reporting of the events of the Watergate affair, check an encyclopedia article. The *New Columbia Encyclopedia* gives a good summary with dates. Once you find the dates of coverage in the *New York Times*, you can usually refer to approximately the same dates for coverage of the same events in other papers. An article in a newspaper, magazine, or professional journal will be listed only in the index for the year it was published. If that same article is reprinted, it will be listed again in the index for the year in which it was reprinted.

Making Source Cards

Plan to make two kinds of cards from the beginning: *source cards,* for all the information you will need to prepare your bibliography, and *note cards,* for material that you plan to use in writing the paper. Before you begin to make source cards, study the forms for reference citations in chapter 9.

As soon as you find the titles of books or articles on your topic, you should make a card for each reference that seems promising. You may be tempted to jot down all the references you find on a single sheet of paper, but it is better from the beginning to use a single card or sheet for each source. Why? Quite simply because it is easier and more efficient in the long run to have a single slip or card for each. There is room on a card to add call numbers and other information. You may later want room to jot down a note about what someone has told you about a source or a comment to indicate how you have actually used a source. This can be helpful later, since your instructor may ask you to annotate your bibliography, that is, to indicate after each item in your list of sources how you have actually used it. In addition, individual source cards are easy to alphabetize or otherwise organize for the final list of sources.

When you first find a reference to a book that you want to consult, note the author, title, and—if you have found it in the card catalog—the call number. Leave room for publication information of the edition that you actually use. (Note the first example on the next page.) Later, when you have the source in hand, you can double-check the spelling of the author and title and then add the place and date of publication and the publisher. Keep in mind that there may be more than one edition of a book in your library, and you may use a different edition from the one you first found cited in a catalog or bibliography. In any case, before you make your first source card, find out from your instructor which documentation style you should use, and record the information as it will appear on your list of sources.

A SAMPLE SOURCE CARD

> Lash, Joseph. *Eleanor* *and* *Franklin.*
>
> New York: Norton, 1971.

In summary, source cards can be used in the following ways:

1. To record all the information you need to find a source and to document it for your bibliography
2. To note the value and content of a source
3. To indicate how you have actually used a source
4. To alphabetize for your final list of sources

Source cards that have been used for these purposes can be very helpful to an instructor who wants to monitor your progress.

A SOURCE CARD NOTING CONTENT

> Woolf, S. J. "A Woman Speaks Her Political Mind."
> New York Times 8 April 1928: 3.
>
> Good quotes from a speech by E. Roosevelt.

When you make a source card for an article in a periodical—newspaper, magazine, or journal—record all the information needed for the citation in your list of sources. Include date, volume number, and page number, as well as author, title of article, and complete title of the periodical. Consider the following example:

> Roosevelt, Eleanor. "Why Democrats
> Favor Smith." North American
> Review 224 (1927-1928): 472-475.

Taking Preliminary Notes and Classifying Sources

Although most of your note taking will take place later, there will be times even in the earliest stages of your research when you will want to record dates, facts, statistics, or ideas as you read general reference works or skim periodicals or books. You probably will not quote from an encyclopedia or cite it later, since you will seek far more specialized sources dealing with your topic, but writing out a summary of an encyclopedia overview can contribute to your understanding of a topic. When you take notes, identify the source of the note with the first item from the source card—either the author or, when there is no author, the title—followed by the page number (see chapter 6). If you should jot down a complete sentence or even a phrase written by someone other than yourself, make sure that you put quotation marks around it (see p. 77). Make separate cards for notes you expect to use for writing your paper, and put only one note on a card.

It will be easy to measure your progress by classifying your source cards as you go along. Put them in three stacks or mark them with Roman numerals indicating which of three categories they belong in:

1. Sources that you have found and hope to use
2. Those that you hope to find, either by recalling them from users of your own library or by borrowing them from other libraries
3. Those that you do not expect to be able to find

Adding a note now to each reference about its availability and possible usefulness can be helpful later.

Consider the notes on this source card:

Strouse, Jean. "Toni Morrison's Black Magic."
Newsweek 30 March 1981: 52-57.

Interesting facts about her life
Details about her work as an editor
Good quotations

Use for introduction

Evaluating Sources

Before you spend very much time studying a book or an article you have found, you should try to decide how reliable it is. Try to answer the following questions:

1. Is it up-to-date? An article on drug use among teenagers written in 1960 will not tell you much about the drug culture that developed a few years later, though it could be quite illuminating in contrast. An encyclopedia article on computers that lists a bibliography from 1965 and earlier will be worthless to someone studying current computer technology. Keep in mind that current editions of standard encyclopedias often include out-of-date material. The dates on the sources at the end of an article will usually let you know if the article is current, but not all articles include a list of sources. The difficulty of knowing if some encyclopedia articles are up-to-date is only one reason for their limited usefulness.

2. What are the author's credentials? You may be able to learn about an author's background and other publications from *Contemporary Authors*. You can often find information about authors with an academic background—usually established scholars who have published with a university press—in the *Directory of American Scholars* or *American Men and Women of Science*. An author's academic or institutional affiliation is often listed on the title page or the jacket of a book. You should be wary, however, of accepting the evaluation of a book found on its jacket or sometimes on pages inserted before the title page. These comments, often called blurbs, may have been solicited from the author's friends; and those quoted from published reviews are of course selected because they are the most favorable.

3. Is a journal or newspaper known to be generally fair, or is it biased in some definite way? You might try looking it up in Farber's *Classified List of Periodicals for the College Library* or Katz's *Magazines for Libraries*. Both of these publications evaluate periodicals and indicate those that have a particular bias.

4. Does the source seem adequately documented? You may be surprised to learn that some books and articles have less documentation than you will be required to have in your paper. Most reliable books, however, will have at the very least a comprehensive list of sources, either after each chapter or at the end of the book. Others will include notes as well. Articles in popular magazines are less likely to indicate their sources than are those in scholarly journals, which will almost always include precise information about sources. You need not necessarily discard a source simply because it lacks a bibliography. A personal memoir, for example, is often based on notes and diaries recorded by the author. Eleanor Roosevelt's account of her career as

a social activist would of course be a valuable source, but one that should be treated for what it is: a personal account that is based on memory and private records and that presents the author in the way that she wants to be remembered.

5. In the case of controversial topics, does a source give a balanced or a one-sided view? If you know that a topic is controversial, you can usually determine whether a source acknowledges both sides of an issue. For example, an article on the future of nuclear power that fails to mention that many people see nuclear power as a serious threat to the environment would clearly be biased. You may, however, be unaware of the controversial aspects of a topic. For example, if you were doing research on the conviction of Alger Hiss and you consulted only sources that assumed his guilt, you might never know that there are people who insist on Hiss's innocence. By beginning with objective sources—encyclopedia articles or other reference works—at the beginning of a project, you can usually discover the controversial aspects of a topic and judge your sources accordingly. Comparing the material in two or more encyclopedia articles can be helpful.

6. It is not always easy to decide whether a source is reliable, particularly when you first study a subject. In addition to the other suggestions given here, you should also determine if a source uses vague language or misleading statistics. Beware of the following:

• Vague, nonspecific use of language, such as the word "average." A statement that the average annual income for a group of first-year college graduates is twelve thousand dollars is meaningless unless we know whether that figure refers to the arithmetic average of all the salaries added together (the mean average); whether it means that half the group makes more than that and half makes less (the median average); or whether more people make twelve thousand dollars than any other amount (the modal average).

• Percentages given without evidence that they are based on representative samples. An article in a college newspaper that notes that 90 percent of the students would prefer to play video games rather than attend a good play is meaningless unless the interviewers questioned a representative group of students—some in the student center's game room, others outside the game room, and perhaps others attending a play.

• Percentages given without an indication of the size of the sample taken. The statistic "25 percent of the students polled" may be based on a sample of a hundred students or only four.

Misleading graphs or pictures. Can you detect deception in the way a graph is drawn or bias in a picture?

For a detailed and amusing treatment of the misuse of statistics, see Darrell Huff, *How to Lie with Statistics* (New York: Norton, 1954).

7. Is a book published by a respected publishing house? This is sometimes difficult for the beginning student to discover. If you have never heard of the publishing house, you might ask your instructor about it, find other books by the same publisher and see if you can judge their quality, or look the publishing house up in a book like *Writer's Market* for the current year.This reference work will tell you what a particular house usually publishes, who its target audience is, and what its standards for accepting new work might be.

8. How was the book reviewed? (See *Book Review Digest* and other book review sources mentioned in the annotated list of references in the appendix.) Checking reviews can also give you some idea of what the book contains and how it might be useful in your research.

Reading Effectively

Reading an article or a book for research is rarely a matter of beginning with the first page and progressing steadily from beginning to end, word for word. There are times when you will read that way, but even then you will probably first skim through the text, noting its length, chapter or paragraph headings, and sometimes its conclusion. Let us consider various ways of learning from a text, beginning with a short article and ending with a substantial book.

Many articles found in popular periodicals can be skimmed quickly with attention to facts or ideas relevant to your topic. One technique is to read the introduction and the conclusion; a second is to read first sentences of paragraphs; a third is to look for headings, graphs, illustrations, or a summary. Depending on the content of an article, one or more of these approaches may be adequate for you to decide if you want to read more carefully.

Similar techniques apply to skimming a book. A detailed table of contents can tell you a lot, as can a good index. You may also want to look at the introduction and the conclusion of a book. Sometimes books are organized in such a way that you can learn much about their content by reading the beginning and concluding paragraphs of each chapter.

A helpful device for a thorough reading of a paragraph, an article, a chapter, or a complete book is known as the PQRST method.[1] When you decide that you really want to master the facts and ideas of a particular text, you may want to follow these steps:

---

[1] The PQRST method has been used for years to teach study skills (I learned it from my high school English teacher). Recent versions can be found in these texts: Ellen Lamar Thomas and H. Alan Robinson, *Improving Reading in Every Class*, 3rd. ed. (Boston: Allyn and Bacon, 1982); George Spache and Paul Berg, *The Art of Efficient Reading*, 3rd ed. (New York: Macmillan, 1978).

P: Preview
Q: Question
R: Read
S: Summarize
T: Test

To *preview* a text you can follow the appropriate steps described for skimming: looking at the table of contents, the introduction, conclusion, beginning sentences, illustrations, and index. You may then want to make a list of *questions* that you expect or hope the text will answer. You then *read* the text with those questions in mind. When you finish reading, try to *summarize* what you have read, either by telling someone about it or by writing it down. The final step is to give yourself a *test*: Try to answer the questions that you posed in the beginning. Good readers often apply this method unconsciously. You may be one of them. Perhaps you examine a book, looking for clues to its content; you think of questions you hope it will answer; you read carefully, summarize what you have read, and finally test yourself—and the book—for answers. Even so, if you would like to be a better reader, you might want to apply the PQRST method consciously.

There will be times when the process stops during the third step. You may approach a text you have examined with an open mind, looking for answers to questions, only to discover that it does not really treat the topics you are researching or answer the questions you are asking. No matter how interesting it is, you should lay it aside for now.

Keeping an open mind is an important part of effective reading. Good researchers may expect or look for certain answers, but they must be open to other possibilities. If you approach a book expecting to find particular answers, you run the risk of misinterpreting it, of finding only what you want to find, of ignoring qualifications and alternative points of view. Just as we can put words in the mouth of another person, so we can misread a text, taking statements out of context and even seeing words that are not there. The best way to avoid misreading is to be aware of the possibility of its happening and to keep an open mind as to what the author is actually saying.

Returning to the Library

Most students will use library resources throughout the stages of reading, note taking, and drafting a paper. By scheduling work time in the library, you can easily look up the new people, places, words, and events that you encounter in your reading. To identify reference works that you may want to consult once your research is underway, study the descriptions of reference materials in the appendix of this book.

The actual business of conducting research is never quite as systematic as might be inferred from the guidelines of this book. A step-by-step procedure suggests a formula that, if followed carefully, will result in a polished, finished product; but the reality of asking questions and seeking answers —the essence of meaningful research—is often messy and erratic. You may find yourself wandering down a dead-end road or digressing to a subject that leads away from your topic. The steps suggested here can help you stick to a manageable number of questions and to reach realistic, if qualified or tentative, conclusions.

EXERCISES

A. Practice the PQRST method as you study the next chapter in this book. Preview, raise questions, and read carefully; then summarize the main points in a single paragraph. After you have finished the summary, test yourself by looking back over the chapter to see if you left anything out or if you raised questions that you cannot answer.

For students with research in progress

B. Make a list of the questions you hope to answer through your research.

C. Try to reduce those questions to a single statement beginning with "I want to know."

D. Study the annotated list of reference works in the appendix of this book and mark those that you think may be useful to your project. Make a list of those you have marked, putting them in the order in which you expect to consult them.

E. Design your own search strategy by listing the steps you expect to follow to find library material on your topic and those that will take you beyond the library. (See the next chapter.)

F. After consulting bibliographies, periodical indexes, and the card catalog, record on index cards the sources that you expect to consult, including all the information that you will need to document your final paper.

G. Choose at least one book on your list and consult *Book Review Digest* to find out how it was reviewed. Write a paragraph summarizing the reviews you find there.

5

SEARCHING BEYOND THE LIBRARY

You may prefer using books and periodicals to find out what you want to know about a topic, but some questions simply cannot be answered by reading. Sometimes first-hand information is more current than anything you can find in print. Certain types of information change constantly. Consider the following questions: What is the current interest rate? How are property taxes computed in a community? What services are available at a public health facility? How many members are there in a political organization? To answer such questions, you would probably want to ask an expert —a banker, a tax assessor, an administrator of a public health organization. An expert, unlike a book, can talk back to you, correcting misperceptions, making connections between things you have learned, and suggesting further avenues for you to explore. Often public interest groups and charitable organizations provide topical and up-to-date information that is not available elsewhere. The League of Women Voters, for example, usually has current information about political candidates, and the Better Business Bureau offers basic information about companies—how long they have been in the community and how well they deal with consumer complaints. Even if people with special knowledge do not have time to talk to you, they may be able to provide or recommend reading material or suggest other people who can talk to you.

Some research requires that you question people directly; other research will depend largely on exploring printed material. All research, however, will be more meaningful if you can talk about it with someone else. Even if you expect that your research will be conducted mainly in the library, it is a good idea to try to find someone else who has an interest in your topic—a teacher, a family member, or a friend.

Deciding When to Ask Questions

Many topics are suited to extensive oral research. The following list will give you an idea of the kind of topics that would be enriched by talking to people and asking them questions:

1. The value of services provided by public facilities—a public health department, a drug rehabilitation center, a public school, the food stamp program
2. Job opportunities in particular fields—nursing, computers, the military
3. The function and impact of a business or industrial organization in a community
4. The problems of elderly people confined to nursing homes
5. Public responses to a historical event—the day John Kennedy was killed, the end of World War II, the release of the Iranian hostages

Students researching topics like these might spend much of their time asking questions, but others researching topics that depend mainly on written materials can also learn in this way. Michael Gold, for example, had read about the James Dean cult, but it became real to him when he talked to people who were teenagers during the time it flourished. Carol Garcia studied statistics about the benefits of heating with the sun, but she did not know that people who heat their homes with the sun feel they are doing something important until she interviewed an expert who talked about how solar energy contributes to the quality of life for future generations.

Just as you should not write a research paper using a single book, you should not base your conclusions on what you learn from one person. If you were researching careers in the military, for example, you would want to talk not only to recruitment officers but to people who have been recruited as well.

Contacting People

There are many different ways to ask questions: writing letters of inquiry, making phone calls, or posting notices; arranging an appointment in someone's office, dropping by an office unannounced, or stopping people on the street; arranging a formal interview or asking one or more people to fill out a prepared questionnaire. There are no set rules to tell you which approach is best. Every time you want to learn from other people you will have to consider their personalities, their situations—how busy they are or how free to talk—as well as your relationship with them. Your history teacher, for example, may have encouraged you to stop by during office hours whenever you have a question; the academic dean of the college may be willing to answer your questions if you write a letter explaining what you want to know; and the admissions officer may make an appointment to see you, but may not be specific about what is actually required for admission.

The suggestions and examples in this chapter will serve as a guide to your own research. Some suggestions may be helpful, and others may seem irrelevant to the kind of research you are conducting. In seeking information from people, however, you should observe these rules in every case:

1. Be respectful of the time and needs of anyone that you question. Never be late for an appointment.
2. Remember that no one is obligated to answer your questions, and that even though many people may be happy to talk to you, they do so as a courtesy.
3. Be courteous in return, even if you are angered by a response.

POSTING NOTICES

In a college community, it is often easy to find people who know about a subject that you are researching. A proven way to make such contacts is to post notices on bulletin boards in the student center, dormitories, or other appropriate places. The notice may include your telephone number and a request that interested people call you, or it may include a space for them to write their names and telephone numbers. The following list suggests the kinds of notices that may yield results:

1. Wanted: people who are willing to talk about their experiences in the Vietnam War.
2. I am interested in talking to students who have feminist mothers. Do you, or do you know anyone who does?
3. I am collecting campus folklore. Please telephone me if you know any stories about strange or funny happenings on this campus.
4. I am trying to construct a profile of the typical college student's eating habits. Will you help?

FINDING ORGANIZATIONS TO CONTACT

If you live in a city, you have many places to visit where you will find people with special interests, but even small towns have organizations that exist to inform the public. Students researching some aspect of business may want to visit the chamber of commerce. Those studying a foreign country may want to contact a consulate, cultural organization, language school, airline, or even a restaurant connected with or run by people from that country. For almost any topic that you research, someone in your community probably would like to talk about it. If you are exploring the role of unions in a factory town, consider calling the local chapter of the AFL-CIO. If you are studying some aspect of early childhood development, you may be able to visit a Montessori school. For students of medical topics, there are public service organizations—Alcoholics Anonymous, the American Diabetes Association, the American Heart Association—that provide information to the public. Other organizations, such as mental health associations or councils that deal with drug abuse or children's issues, exist primarily to educate the public. In many communities public service agencies can help you identify specific organizations that may be helpful. If you are looking for a nursing home to visit, contact the local community council on aging. The yellow pages of the telephone book list a variety of such organizations under "Social Services." In some communities, the United Way has an information and referral service that directs people with specific questions to appropriate organizations.

REACHING THE RIGHT PEOPLE

Identifying appropriate people to question requires more thought for some topics than for others. If you are researching an event that has occurred in the last fifty years, you may want to talk to people who remember the event; but to choose the right ones, you will want to consider how old they were at the time of the event. For example, a man who was in college when the depression hit will remember it much differently than will someone who was a child at the time. People who were in their teens in the 1960s will respond differently to questions about hippies or the antiwar movement than will people who were in their fifties. A woman who was twenty when she learned of the bombing of Pearl Harbor will probably have different memories of that day than will someone who was thirty years older.

Age is only one consideration in determining a person's ability to answer a question. A person of appropriate age with little interest in politics might talk about Truman, but probably will not remember Henry Wallace. A person who actually fought in the Vietnam War probably will not be a good source for information about the antiwar movement; some people who survived Nazi concentration camps might feel reluctant to discuss the Holocaust, while others may want to share their experiences.

It is important to try to find out how people have learned what they know. Are they amateurs or professionals? Do they have a vested interest in a subject? Do they have personal experience or second-hand knowledge? Someone who sells cameras may not be as good a resource as a person who uses a camera professionally or for whom photography is a serious hobby.

CHOOSING AN INTERVIEW METHOD

Once you have identified the people who are willing to talk to you, you still have to decide what approach to take. Should you ask them to fill out a questionnaire, to answer a series of prepared questions, or to answer questions as they come up in conversation? Sometimes a written questionnaire can help you to identify what a person is likely to know or be willing to talk about, but generally questionnaires have a limited use, and it is usually best to follow up a written questionnaire with a face to face conversation. Some people—particularly government officials and administrators who speak for an organization or bureau—will only answer prepared questions to which they have agreed in advance.

Questionnaires that rely on short answers often lead to false or meaningless conclusions. In his study of *Rebel without a Cause*, Michael Gold might ask a number of people who were teenagers when the movie first came out to fill out a questionnaire about their memories of the movie in which they would indicate whether or not they thought the movie influenced them. But people who said yes would not really tell Michael very much unless he knew what kind of influence they were referring to. Did they wear red nylon jackets? rebel against their parents? engage in delinquent behavior? To find out, Michael would have to ask people to explain their answers.

WRITING LETTERS

There will be times when you will want to ask questions by writing a letter. Many important people—government officials, politicians, writers, and even entertainers—employ people to help them handle their mail. While such people are not likely to grant you an interview, they may answer a letter. Remember that the mails are often slow; for that reason, you should write letters as soon as possible, always indicating the time restrictions of your research. The following example may serve as a model:

```
                                        Box 5012
                                        Brooklyn, N.Y. 11210
                                        February 21, 1983
```

```
Mr. Michael Swank
Swank Motion Pictures
201 S. Jefferson
St. Louis, Missouri 63103
```

```
Dear Mr. Swank:
     I am writing you at the suggestion of Mr. Jay Harriman, who
works in the media center at Brooklyn College. I am currently
engaged in a research project about the film Rebel without a Cause,
which was directed by Nicholas Ray. Since your company distributes
```

the film to colleges, I thought you would be able to tell me about the frequency with which the film is shown. Could you let me know how often you distribute the film? Is there less of a demand than there was five years ago?

Since I have a limited amount of time to complete the research, I would be very grateful if you could answer within ten days. Enclosed is a stamped self-addressed envelope for your convenience.

Sincerely yours,

Michael Gold

Michael Gold

When you write an administrator of a charitable organization, an editor, a writer, or other individuals, you should always include a self-addressed stamped envelope. There are no fixed rules about when to include postage, but usually government offices have a budget for answering mail. In general, you should think about the convenience of the person from whom you are requesting information.

There may be times when you will write a letter to request an interview. In addition to your address, you may want to include your telephone number along with the times when you can be reached or a time when you will call the person. Often people who have received a letter informing them of the purpose of your research and what you want to know will be receptive to a call. Consider the following example:

217 Manchester Ave.
Atlanta, Ga. 30300
January 16, 1983

Mr. Dennis Creech
Georgia Solar Coalition
1103 Euclid Ave.
Atlanta, Ga. 30307

Dear Mr. Creech:

I am a college student considering a career in architecture and am currently researching passive solar design for houses. I have already done considerable reading about the subject, but I have several unanswered questions. I would appreciate it very much

if you could talk to me. I estimate that you could answer my
questions in twenty to thirty minutes. I will call you on Monday
morning to see if it would be possible to arrange an interview.

                                              Yours truly,

                                          Carol Garcia

                                              Carol Garcia

MAKING TELEPHONE CALLS

Whenever you telephone someone to obtain information, remember to be
considerate of that person's time and privacy. If you go through a secretary,
identify yourself, explain briefly why you have called, and ask when it
would be convenient for the person to talk with you. The experience of
Sara Maxfield, the student researching Alice Walker's *Meridian*, a novel
dealing with the problems encountered by civil rights workers in the sixties,
serves as a good example. When Sara discovered that one of her professors
had participated in the civil rights movement, she called him and opened
the conversation as follows: "Professor Bradford, this is Sara Maxfield, one
of your students. I am researching the problems of civil rights workers in
the sixties, and I wonder when you would have time to answer a few questions about your experiences." Professor Bradford was able to talk for a few
minutes on the phone. He talked about what life was like for college students in those days, and since he had read *Meridian*, he was able to give
first-hand information about some of the historical events mentioned in the
book. The information he gave Sara does not appear in the final paper, but
her time was by no means wasted. Her conversation with Professor Bradford gave her a much better understanding of the central concerns of her
research.

There may be times when you will make phone calls to ask questions
requiring short answers: Do you employ part-time help? How large is the
book collection in your library? Do you offer training in computer program-
ming? When is the next meeting of the National Organization for Women?
How many organizations does the United Fund support in this community?
In cases when you need a quick answer, it is best to ask the question,
express your appreciation, and hang up.

MAKING APPOINTMENTS

Whenever you ask people for favors, it is best to do so at their convenience.
That means making appointments. On a college campus, most faculty

members who post office hours expect students to drop by or call during those hours. If you have more than a few brief questions, however, ask for an appointment. If you have trouble getting in touch with someone, leave a message with his or her secretary or a note on the office door. Simple courtesy and consideration of other people will lead you to the best way to arrange an interview. Most people in a college community will cooperate with an interview request if they have time and feel that they can be of help to you—and if your request is courteous and appropriate.

Conducting a Successful Interview

Before you begin an interview, whether on the telephone or in person, be prepared to record what you want to remember, either by writing it down or by tape recording it. At the very least, you should have a pencil and note pad with you to jot down brief notes. You do not want to borrow a pencil, of course, or keep someone waiting on the telephone while you look for a piece of paper. There are instructions at the end of this chapter for recording information you receive by talking to people. In addition, the different kinds of note cards described in chapter 6 can be adapted to oral research. There may be times when you want to quote a person directly, paraphrase a response, or summarize a whole interview.

ASKING THE FIRST QUESTION

A very specific question at the beginning of an interview can limit the whole process by locking the interviewer into a narrow focus. Usually when you are interviewing people, you want to ask initial questions that are general enough to allow them to reveal their attitudes and special interests. You also want to ask questions or make simple observations that invite a response.

Sometimes finding just the right opening is a matter of luck. That was the experience of a student in Wyoming who was investigating the legends of hardship that circulate among the rangers. He arranged to talk to an old man who was in his youth during one of the worst winters of all times. His opening question, "Could you tell me about how many cattle died in the winter of nineteen eleven to nineteen twelve?" led only to "Nope, no idea." The student was lucky enough to get a second chance, and the next time he came at the subject indirectly by observing, "Sure has been a hard winter." That was all that was needed to stimulate the old man's memory. "Bad? You don't know anything about bad. You should have been around in the the winter of nineteen twelve. . . ." An hour later the student had what he wanted: a first-hand account of the hardships of that year, including a tall tale or two.

Usually, however, if someone has agreed to talk to you about a topic, you should state in a straightforward way what you want to know. Explain your project, and then ask a general question to begin.

LEADING PEOPLE TO TALK

In most cases, you will learn more from people by leading them to talk than by rigidly sticking to a prepared list of questions. Keep in mind that people are individuals and that they have unique experiences as well as specific information they can give you. The following questions and responses are often productive:

> What can you tell me about . . . ?
> What do you remember about . . . ?
> Can you explain that to me?
> Tell me what you mean.
> Can you help me understand?

This last response may be helpful if you encounter hostility or when people tell you that you cannot possibly understand what they mean. In the long run, one way to ask questions will work for you, and others may seem strange. You want to find a way to say "talk to me" to the person you want to learn from, and you want to say it in a way that is natural to you and appropriate to the situation. Usually, if you can lead people to talk about a subject that interests them, you will be able to get them to tell you what you want to know.

DEVELOPING PATIENCE

Hearing what people have to say, rather than what we want to hear them say, is not always easy. Discovering the special interests of others and uncovering the significant experiences that have informed their lives calls for care and sensitivity. Learning to recognize what people are willing or able to talk about takes practice, and you may have a few failures before you succeed. One of the most difficult tasks is to know when and how to respect people's privacy. If you are too cautious about asking personal questions, you may never learn anything from others; on the other hand, if you probe too deeply or too quickly into private matters, you may alienate some people. To find out if an issue is too personal for an individual, you may ask, "Do you object to talking about . . .?" And indeed some people do. Here are some final suggestions that may help you in speaking with people:

1. Listen carefully for details and ask the person to elaborate on those that seem important.

2. Avoid interrupting with your own suggestions.
3. Use requests like "tell me more about that" when you want the person to focus on a detail.
4. Try to ask questions in a neutral way that does not indicate what you think.
5. Assume the attitude of a willing student. Do not be afraid to show your ignorance.
6. Do not push when someone seems reluctant to answer a question. You can always come back to subjects later if the person becomes more open with you.
7. Keep an open mind.

Recording Oral Responses

There are three common ways of recording and storing information from oral sources. One, appropriate to brief interviews, is to listen carefully and then to write down what you want to remember immediately afterward. The second is to take notes during the interview; the most accurate is, of course, to make a tape recording. You will have to decide which method is most appropriate for each situation.

TAKING NOTES

For very short interviews and for times when people object to the use of a tape recorder, you may choose to jot down notes as you listen. Notes are particularly useful for proper names that you want to remember and for questions that you want to come back to. For more extensive note taking, you may plan in advance how to organize what you hear. One way is to divide a sheet of paper in half—one side for generalities, the other for details. If you think you will quote what someone says, make sure you have an accurate record. If possible, have the person read and verify what you want to quote.

MAKING A TAPE RECORDING

An audio tape recording is easy to make. You simply ask permission to make the tape, set up the recorder in a convenient place, and turn it on at the beginning of an interview. The only disadvantage of using a recorder is that some people may not speak as frankly in the presence of a recorder as they would otherwise. Most people, however, are not troubled by a recorder and soon forget that it is there. When you want to make a recording, you should consider the following:

1. It is best to ask permission for the taping in a positive way. You might simply say, "I would like to record our conversation. Is that all right with you?" When asked this way, most people will agree.
2. Plan ahead: Make sure that you have enough tape and either an extension cord to assure easy access to an electrical outlet or a battery-powered recorder.
3. Label your tapes carefully.

A video recorder is much more difficult to use, and many people are considerably inhibited when they are being videotaped. If you have access to a video recorder, however, there may be times when you will want to use it. For example, your media department may provide videotaping services of lectures by visiting speakers, including the question-and-answer session afterward. It is a good idea to get written permission from a lecturer before making a recording.

TRANSCRIBING A RECORDING

If you decide to write out a recorded interview, you may be surprised at how long it will take. If your side of an interview has consisted of short questions and responses, an hour of tape may turn out to be as many as twenty typewritten pages. Often when we talk, we repeat ourselves, sometimes three or four times, so you may want to listen to the tape once, and then go back to select what you want to copy down.

A Sample Interview

Carol Garcia learned much about solar energy by talking to people. When she chose her topic, she had never even seen a solar house, but by the time she finished her research, she had talked to an expert and toured solar homes. She began by talking to a friend's parents who had recently built a solar greenhouse. They invited her over to see it and told her about the Georgia Solar Coalition, an organization that promotes solar energy mainly by education. Carol arranged an interview with Dennis Creech, director of the organization. She began by writing a letter (see p. 65) explaining that she was a student researching passive solar design, that she wanted to ask him a few questions, and that she would call his office in a few days. When she called, Mr. Creech invited her to visit the coalition's office and to browse in the library. He explained that he would arrange time to answer a few questions.

Before she went for the interview, Carol read about solar energy, limited her topic to passive solar design, and outlined the major points she wanted to make. She was then able to prepare questions in advance of the interview. The answers she got helped her understand more clearly what she had read. The following is a summary of the interview:

CAROL GARCIA: I'm confused about how long it takes for people to get back the money they put into solar components in a house. Suppose I had a typical three-bedroom house and I wanted to add a solar greenhouse—how much money could I save? Would it pay for itself?

DENNIS CREECH: Unfortunately, there are not any simple answers to those questions. During the useful life of a home, the investment will be paid back several times. However, the savings for a solar installation vary from one house to another, and they depend on several factors: the materials used, the size of the sunspace, how it is used, and how much a person is spending on heat before the greenhouse is built. If a greenhouse is used for living space, then some of the heat it produces must be used to heat it; if it is used strictly for heating, all of the heat can be brought into the house. The most I can say is that the savings will depend on the cost of the greenhouse and the amount of previously used heat that it can provide. We can be much more specific about the savings from a solar hot water heater, which will provide up to 80 percent of a family's hot water needs. That means that a family spending two hundred dollars a year could save as much as one hundred sixty dollars.

GARCIA: If I had one thousand dollars to spend, what could I do to heat my house more efficiently?

CREECH: The first thing you should do is get better insulation, weatherstrip windows and doors, and caulk any air leaks. Then if you have a south facing wall that connects with living space, you might install a convective loop collector. If you do the work yourself, a three-by-eight-foot collector will cost you about sixty dollars. One collector will heat a small room on sunny days, but several may be needed for larger rooms. If you only have money for one room, you should probably choose the one that is most frequently used in the daytime.

GARCIA: Most of what I read about solar houses uses the word *glazing* rather than *glass*. Why is that? Are some windows and transparent walls made of plastic?

CREECH: Several different materials are used for both windows and walls. Each has advantages and disadvantages. Glass is nice when you want to be able to see out, but it is fragile. Plastic provides privacy and is more durable, but ultraviolet radiation causes plastic to yellow.

GARCIA: I have been studying about the different kinds of solar radiation —ultraviolet, infrared—and I wonder if it is necessary to use those terms to explain how the sun can be used to heat a house.

CREECH: No. What is important is that sunlight must come through glazing, hit a mass, and be absorbed as heat; and in rooms that use a convective loop, it must have a way of moving into the living space.

GARCIA: I understand how Trombe walls work in winter by setting up a convective loop, but I do not understand what happens in the summer. Why don't they heat up a room in the summer?

CREECH: It is very important for a Trombe wall to be shaded in summer. This is usually accomplished with an overhang that blocks the high summer sun. The space in front of the Trombe wall will receive heat from the outside by conduction through the glass. For this reason, we recommend high and low vents to the outside to exhaust the heat. These, of course, are closed in the winter.

GARCIA: The more I learn, the more I believe that every new building ought to include some passive solar features. Is that true?

CREECH: Yes. Any building that doesn't have passive solar features is obsolete the day it is built. Just the way a building is positioned on a lot—and the placement of the windows—can save 20 percent or more on heating and cooling.

GARCIA: As director of the Georgia Solar Coalition, what is the single most important idea—other than the importance of conservation—that you want to get across when you talk about solar energy?

CREECH: Orientation of glazing. If it is not facing south, there will not be enough sun in winter and there will be too much in summer.

GARCIA: What do you tell people who ask you about the benefits of building homes with passive solar features?

CREECH: I tell them that they will save money, that they will have a more livable home, and that they will make a contribution to society and to the quality of life of future generations.

GARCIA: Are you successful? Are people going solar?

CREECH: Yes, we are having some success. People are willing to save energy, but they need help. There are the energy tax credits, which help some people, but that's not enough. Most people need more information; they need to understand how passive solar energy works. And lower- and middle-income people need help with financing. They need to be able to borrow money for solar remodeling at reasonable interest rates. Many people have learned to put the sun to work for themselves, but for the actions of individuals to have a big effect, more people must be educated.

EXERCISES

A. Explore the resources of your community by looking through the yellow pages of the telephone book. Consult the following headings and make a list of places you would like to visit:

Art galleries
Athletic organizations
Bookstores
Libraries
Political organizations
Restaurants
Special schools for children
Social service organizations
Theaters
Colleges and universities

B. Make a list of subjects that you think you might be able to learn more about by talking to people.

 1. For each item on your list identify at least one person whom you could interview.
 2. Experiment with interviewing techniques by selecting a few of the items and making a list of questions about them.

C. Choose one subject you would like to know more about, and make a list of questions to use for an interview.

 1. Conduct an interview.
 2. Write a paper based on what you learn.

For students engaged in a research project

D. Think of someone who would be able to give you information about your topic that you cannot find in other sources. Write a letter to that person in which you explain the purpose of your research project and request information.

E. Think of some aspect of your topic that you might learn about through an interview and make a list of the questions that you would like to have answered. Then think of a person who could help you; try to arrange an interview.

6

RECORDING INFORMATION

The early stages of research include three kinds of activities: choosing and narrowing a topic, collecting sources, and making notes. To explain how to go about accomplishing these tasks, it is helpful to present them as steps that follow one after another. But in reality these steps overlap. You may find when you are making notes that you need more sources; and as you evaluate your notes, you may discover that though you have narrowed your topic, you must focus it even more. You will be a more successful researcher if you allot sufficient time, after you have collected sources, to alternately skim and read material, take and classify notes, go back to your sources, and, when necessary, gather new material.

Making Notes

Making notes is an essential part of learning, studying, and researching; but it is not always easy to know when to make notes or how much to record. The way you make notes is to some extent a personal choice and depends on your study habits and how you learn. For example, some students are able to listen more attentively to a lecture if they make notes throughout, taking down most of what the speaker says; others prefer to jot down a few key words and phrases that they later use to reconstruct or summarize a lecture. In some cases, you may want to take down only what you do not know; in others, you may want a record of whatever a particular person says. The same is true for reading. Some students prefer to record main ideas as they read, others to make a few jottings and to summarize the whole at the end. At times, you may simply want to jot down only the facts that you do not already know about a specific topic. Making notes for a research project can help you learn about a topic as well as provide a record of the facts and ideas to be used in a final report of that research.

Remember that you will have two kinds of cards for recording information. You will have a set of *source cards*, one for each source with all the information needed for documentation exactly as it will appear in your list of sources at the end of your paper. You will also have a set of *note cards*. Keep your source cards with you for easy reference, so that when you begin to take notes, you can identify the source of each with the first item of the source card—the author's name or the title when there is no author.

You may not take all of the kinds of notes described in this chapter, but you probably will find most of the suggestions helpful. There are, however, a few rules that should be followed by all student researchers:

1. Document each note, clearly indicating the source on each card at the top. You will be taking too many notes to be able to remember where each came from.
2. Stop before making each note and ask yourself if it is really relevant to your topic.
3. Before you make a note from a passage, decide whether you need to quote it entirely, whether you can paraphrase it effectively, or whether it should be included in a summary.
4. Clarify with proper punctuation or abbreviations whether a note is a direct quotation, a paraphrase, an original observation, or a fact of general knowledge.
5. To save time and insure accuracy, you may want to photocopy passages of more than a few lines.
6. Pause from time to time and evaluate your progress: Sort your notes into categories, consult your bibliography cards to identify which sources you have not read, and make a list of what you still have to do.

Photocopying

Copying machines make it possible for you to have your own copies of articles or passages from books, and at times you will find it very convenient to have an exact copy of material that you expect to use. You can, however, waste time and money by copying material before you are sure that you will use it. After you have sufficiently narrowed your topic and identified most of your sources, you may want to consider what you would like to photocopy. Most libraries have machines that will copy directly from microform materials such as newspapers on microfilm. Since it can be particularly tedious to copy by hand from microform materials, you probably will want to have copies made for articles and passages that are crucial to your research. You may also find it helpful to photocopy magazine or journal articles that you would like to be able to study carefully or come back to when you are working outside the library. Once you have made a copy, be especially careful to record on the copy itself all the details necessary to identify the source, as well as the page numbers.

Documenting Notes

To document your sources in a final paper is to cite—with a list of sources at the end of a paper, with parenthetical or numerical references within a paper, or with endnotes or footnotes—the books, articles, interviews, or other sources you have used to obtain information. It is important that you document each note as you make it by indicating both the source and the page number. Since your bibliography cards include complete documentary information—author, title, place of publication, date, etc.—you do not need to repeat it on your note cards. All you need is an identifying word or two and a page number. For many sources, you can simply use the last name of the author. When there are two works by the same author, you may choose to use both the author's last name and a key word from the title; if there is no author, a shortened version of the title is adequate.

Identify your own ideas as well as facts of general knowledge with an appropriate code. For example, if you use your initials for your own observations and GK for general knowledge, you will later know exactly what conclusions you have reached independently, what seems to be generally known, and what is the unique property of another author.

Other precautions will help you avoid confusion when you begin to write your paper. You will find it helpful to have only one reference per card. Each card should have a general subject heading as well as a reference to the source:

Use conventional quotation marks along with large marks in the margin of a card to avoid mistaking a direct quotation for a paraphrased passage.

In the beginning, you may be tempted to copy everything that interests you, but it is important that you select very carefully which material you want to record and what is the best form for each note. You will probably make cards for the following: quotations, paraphrases, interpretations, summaries, lists, statistics, facts of general knowledge, and original ideas and conclusions. In the early stages of research, you are more likely to quote directly; as you learn more about your subject, you will know how to assimilate and paraphrase material; and toward the end, you will probably interpret your sources and reach some conclusions on your own.

Quoting

To quote is to reproduce exactly someone else's words. Always put quotation marks around quoted matter, including short phrases and key words. In addition, large quotation marks in the margin of a quotation card serve as a double precaution against accidental plagiarism—mistaking someone else's ideas, information, or manner of expression for your own thoughts or conclusions.

Personal   Roosevelt, E.

                                                   My Story

                                                   p. 308

"In all our contacts it is probably the sense of being really needed and wanted which gives us the greatest satisfaction and creates the most lasting bond."

It is very easy to misquote—to leave out a word or phrase or to write the wrong word—when you are copying a passage. It is a good idea to double check each quotation after you have finished transcribing it. For particularly long passages, you may want to have photocopies on hand to verify the quotations as you prepare the final draft.

In a research paper, it is best to use only a few quotations, selecting those that are expressed in a highly imaginative way, that are particularly characteristic of the person you are quoting, or that for any other reason you want to preserve in the original. No one, for example, would want to paraphrase John Kennedy's famous words in his inaugural address: "And so, my fellow Americans, ask not what your country can do for you; ask what you can do for your country." No paraphrase could be so concise and memorable. Another example of words that should not be changed is this moving appeal in *You Learn by Living*, by Eleanor Roosevelt: "You gain strength, courage and confidence by every experience in which you really stop to look fear in the face. . . . You must do the thing you think you cannot do."

A few direct quotations, carefully placed, can contribute authority to your paper and can make it more lively and interesting. You should certainly quote striking and memorable statements such as the two examples mentioned above. In other cases, however, when you are considering using a direct quotation, ask yourself what purpose the quotation will serve and whether it would be better to express the idea in your own words.

Some writers make the mistake of stringing together a series of quotations that they have not fully understood. If you find that most of your notes are direct quotations, you need to stop and decide how you are likely to use them. Try putting some of the quotations that you think you will use into your own words, explaining what they mean and what conclusions they have helped you reach. Before you write your first draft, sort your note cards and decide which direct quotations should be kept in their original form and which should be incorporated into your own prose. Make sure that you know exactly what each quotation means and how and why you are using it.

Paraphrasing

To paraphrase is to reproduce the exact sense of a written passage or oral statement in your own words: to convey accurately the ideas, facts, or attitudes of someone else in words that are natural to you. A paraphrase may be clearer or more concise than an original passage or statement. Paraphrasing is a necessary skill for reporting research findings, but it is more than that. You paraphrase in your own mind as soon as you finish reading a passage and try to review what you have read; and you paraphrase when you tell someone about an article you have read or a lecture you have heard or when you answer a question on a history test based on information your instructor has given you in class. In each case, you are restating someone else's ideas. The skill with which you paraphrase is a measure of what you know. If you read a paragraph and are easily able to put the ideas in your own words, then you have a good understanding of what you have read.

In the course of a research project, you will often want to restate in your own words the exact meaning of a passage. Paraphrasing helps to clarify ideas as well as identify the material you expect to use in your final research report. And by recording facts and ideas in your own words, you develop your own style: a form of expression that is natural to you.

In the beginning, you may find it difficult to paraphrase, but the more you know about a subject, the easier it is to assimilate and restate what you read. At first, you may have trouble putting unfamiliar words, names, and concepts in your own words. Rather than quoting long undigested passages, it is better simply to make a note indicating a passage you think you will want to paraphrase when you know more. Note the following example:

> Lash, _E + F_, 280-282
>
> Discussion of Eleanor's involvement with the Women's Trade Union League.
>
> Come back to this later.

You also may want to make a photocopy of material that seems important, but which you are not ready to paraphrase.

Once you are familiar with a subject, you will probably be able to write effective paraphrases of significant passages, but even then it is not always easy to know when to take the time to record a passage in your own words and when to make yourself a note about where certain information can be found. To avoid wasting time and effort trying to assimilate and paraphrase material that you will never use, when you come to a passage in your reading that seems important, ask yourself if it is really relevant to your topic. If so, you may want to take the time to record it clearly and fully in your own words while remaining absolutely faithful to the meaning of the original.

You may want to introduce a paraphrase with an identifying transition:

```
Eleanor Roosevelt believed that . . .
In his study of children, Robert Coles found that . . .
According to Lash, . . .
John Mack argues that . . .
```

Below are excerpts from books followed by accurate paraphrases. Note how each paraphrase avoids using even a phrase from the original source.

Original passage from Robert Cole's *The Moral Life of Children:*

Children know and favor the concrete. An abstract moral issue is hard for them to comprehend as thoroughly real and pressing. Thus it was that Sue did her best to make some concreteness for herself, for me—that unforgettable painting.

Paraphrased note:

Original passage from Joseph Lash's *Eleanor and Franklin:*

Among the organizations she turned to in the hope of being able to help improve the world was the League of Women Voters, the successor to the National Woman Suffrage Association. Its leaders had emerged from the long suffrage struggle as militant advocates of better working conditions for women, children's rights, reform of the political process, and peace.

Paraphrased note:

> organizations)   Look 353
>
> The League of Women Voters, one of the organizations Eleanor Roosevelt joined, evolved from the National Woman Suffrage Association. Its leaders, who had all been engaged in the fight for woman's suffrage, took on new causes: improved conditions for women in the workplace, political reform, rights of children, and peace.

Original passage from Alice Walker's *In Search of Our Mothers' Gardens:*

During the sixties, political assassinations, the Civil Rights Movement, and the Vietnam War turned many people away from concern about atomic weapons and toward problems they felt they could do something about.

Paraphrased note:

> nuclear threat   Walker 343
>
> Alice Walker argues that in the sixties, political upheavals, social injustice, and the war in Vietnam — problems they felt they could do something about — absorbed the attention of many people, distracting them from the problems posed by nuclear weapons.

Original passage from Douglas T. Miller and Marion Nowak's *The Fifties:*

Three classic youth-problem films of the fifties were released in 1954–55: *The Wild One* with Brando's moving portrayal of the tough but sensitive motorcycle gang leader; *Rebel without a Cause,* the James Dean vehicle that took delinquency films out of the slums and into the suburbs, and *Blackboard Jungle,* which unequivocally associated delinquency with rock music. Although these films vaguely hint at larger social ills, they fail to explore them, and imply . . . that serious rebelliousness has no real cause but can be attributed to individuals.

Consider how this note card combines paraphrase with a quotation:

Effective paraphrasing requires concentration and practice. You may have to write more than one draft to capture the substance of a passage entirely in your own words. At some point, however, you may be surprised to discover that you can write a paraphrase that is actually clearer than the original. In his research on *Rebel without a Cause,* Michael Gold found he had to understand a passage fully in order to put it in his own words. His own paraphrases sometimes made more sense to him than the original. In the following example, he decided that he had also improved on the source:

Original passage:

Dean's appeal   Astrachan, 17

"But in each of the Dean roles, the distinguishing
elements are the absence of his knowing who he is,
and what is right and wrong. Dean is always
mixed-up and it is this that has made him
so susceptible to teenage adulation."

Michael's version:

Dean's appeal   Astrachan, '7

James Dean always played a
character who is unsure about his own
identity and about moral issues.
Teenagers are particularly attracted to
this young man's portrayal of doubt
and confusion.

Sometimes you may want to quote a word, phrase, or clause within a paraphrase as in the following note:

Public life

Roosevelt, E.
My Story
297

Although she was slow to become a public person, and even slower to take up the cause of women's rights, she eventually referred to herself as an "ardent citizen and feminist."

Paraphrasing often overlaps other forms of note taking, such as interpreting—making sense out of a statement or passage—and summarizing—reducing a longer work to its main points. The more you know about a topic, the more you will be able to interpret what you read.

Interpreting

Interpretation begins as soon as you start to say what something means, to draw conclusions from facts, to explain why certain information is significant. For example, in Tamara Hareven's *Eleanor Roosevelt: An American Conscience*, Roosevelt is quoted as follows: "I don't have any more energy than anyone else. But I never waste any of it on regrets." This statement could be interpreted to mean that Roosevelt was driven to work and to do what she conceived of as her duty. It also might be used as evidence of her determination always to look forward to possible accomplishments rather than backward to failures.

The way we interpret a person's words often depends on what else we know about that person and about the time in which the statement was made. The following example is from the first chapter of Robert Lindner's *Rebel without a Cause . . . The Hypnoanalysis of a Criminal Psychopath.*

Michael Gold first chose to copy it word for word:

> History has assigned to this country and her allies the task
> of cleansing civilization of the predatory creature whose
> typical history is presented in this volume. Psychological
> science has provided us with an instrument to study him
> closely and at first hand; to examine him thoroughly as we
> would a virulent bacillus; to dissect him and obtain his
> measure; perhaps even--assisted by those great social forces
> which are beginning to clear the slime and muck of
> underprivilege and economic expediency--to make of him a good
> citizen in a new world.

Later, Michael interpreted this quotation in the following note:

> Robert Lindner's Rebel without a Cause was published in 1944,
> a year when the whole world was all too aware of the evil--in
> the form of Adolf Hitler--that the psychopathic mind could
> create. Lindner was an idealist; he thought of
> his work as a contribution to the fight against fascism, and
> he hoped that his study would help change the social
> conditions that create the psychopathic personality in the
> first place. He wanted to change society by changing its
> individual victim: "to make of him a good citizen in a new
> world. . . . "

To reach this interpretation of the original passage, Michael had to note the copyright date, 1944, and to infer that the book was written during World War II. He then associated "the predatory creature" with Hitler and fascism and concluded from the last sentence that Lindner was a social reformer. It is always a good idea to know the date of your sources, and sometimes that knowledge will be essential to interpretation. Our appreciation of a book, a film, a political statement, or a psychological theory usually is increased if we are aware of its context. Michael Gold's understanding of *Rebel* grew as he learned something about the time in which it was made; and Sara Maxfield's reading of *Sula* and *Meridian* was enriched by her investigation of the historical background of the novels—both of the times when they were written and the times when they took place.

Summarizing

Summarizing, like paraphrasing, is a process of putting someone else's material in your own words. Rather than the careful rewriting of an original passage, a summary may be jottings, sentence fragments, or a loose outline of the main ideas of anything from a short passage to an entire book. After reading a dense paragraph, the introduction or conclusion to a book, an essay, or a magazine or newspaper article, you may want to condense what you have read by writing down the main points.

The following note is a summary of a newspaper article that reported the main points of a speech that Eleanor Roosevelt gave in 1929:

> Women   "Mrs. Roosevelt
>   Prepares,"
>   2
>
> Eleanor Roosevelt advised women who want to enter politics that they must work up through the ranks, rigorously educate themselves, and be willing to work a little harder than men. Women should seek office only because they are competent to do the job, not because they are women.

The ability to summarize—to restate concisely the main facts, ideas, or episodes of a longer work—is a useful skill for all kinds of learning, and it is essential for writing research papers. Whenever you summarize, you must choose what is essential and what can be omitted. In most cases, you will delete illustrations, examples, and analogies; and you will discard passages intended to attract the reader's attention, to entertain, or to persuade. As with all note taking, you should stop and ask yourself if a passage is relevant to your topic before you take the time to summarize. To summarize, you may choose one of the following forms:

A list of words or numbers
A series of phrases or clauses
Several loosely connected sentences
An informal paragraph
A polished paragraph
A series of paragraphs

Summaries may require several note cards. To avoid confusion, number each card directly above the source in the upper right corner.

Collecting Data: Lists and Statistics

Making a list is a way of recording information in an abbreviated form. There will be times when you will want to make a list from a single source —the main points of a book or, from an encyclopedia article, the titles and dates of publication of a novelist's major works. But not all lists will come from a single source. The information in the note below was gathered from three sources:

you have been advised to put only one note on a card, there may be times when you want to consolidate facts from different sources on a single card (as in the previous note), indicating the sources in order in the upper right corner or in parentheses after each item. Students doing many kinds of research jot down lists: of organizations Eleanor Roosevelt belonged to and positions she held; of important films of the 1950s; of psychologists who have studied the movement from youth to adulthood; of types of solar heating equipment; of novels by black Americans.

You may want to use a separate card for noting numerical data:

Bachman study   Beardsley and Mack,
                                                  p. 83

Male high school seniors who
say they often worry about the nuclear
threat :

1976: 7.2%
1982: 31.2%

You have been advised to beware of the misuse of statistics; used properly, however, statistics can help you make sense of what you learn. One of the most common kinds of statistical studies is the sampling of a group of people to determine their behavior, opinions, or income. The results of such studies are usually expressed in percentages. Assuming that they are based on reliable sampling, statistics are significant to certain studies and essential to others. The list below gives examples of research topics and statistical information that might be significant to them.

1. The Future of the Women's Movement: the percentage of women who actively support the movement
2. The Economics of the Rock and Roll Record Industry: the percentage of recordings that are on pirated tape recordings
3. Interpreting the Gross National Product: the percentage that is related to true productivity and that which is generated by illness and catastrophe

4. The Popularity of Movies about Teenagers: the percentage of moviegoers who are under twenty-one
5. Energy Costs: the percentage of homes and buildings that are inadequately insulated

Recording Original Observations and Conclusions

Throughout the process of research, you will want to make cards on which you record your own thoughts and observations. The note below, for example, is an effort to explain contradictory statements in different sources. The student, Linda Orton, has used her own initials to indicate that the ideas are hers:

E. Roosevelt's motives   L.O. 2/9/82

The articles in Ency. Americana and Brittanica state that ER entered public life to help FDR. Both she and Lash say that she was urged to work to keep the Roosevelt name before the public while FDR recuperated. However, as a public person ER pursued her own interests and not necessarily those of her husband. Perhaps she used her husband's illness as an excuse or defense for doing what she really _wanted_ to do anyway.

If you date each card right under your own initials, you will have a record of the evolution of your own thoughts about your topic. Some students find that their research leads them to conclusions different from what they had originally expected; others discover evidence that supports their original ideas about a topic. For example, Michael Gold expected to find that the success of *Rebel without a Cause* was due to the personal charisma of James Dean and the attraction that he held for teenagers who grew up in the conservative 1950s. But in fact he discovered that the success of the film was much more complicated and depended on the contributions of a number of people. On the other hand, very early in her research Carol Garcia expected to find that solar energy could contribute significantly to the heating of homes, and she discovered that she was right.

Stating General Knowledge

You do not need to cite a source for notes recording information that most people already know or information that is found in a number of books and articles on a subject. That Eleanor Roosevelt was the wife of Franklin Roosevelt, the niece of Theodore Roosevelt, and the mother of five children are all facts of general knowledge. The following note gives another piece of general knowledge:

GK

Eleanor Roosevelt was First Lady for twelve years, from 1933 until 1944.

From time to time, you will make cards to remind you of facts that you have absorbed from a number of sources, which you assume that anyone with a basic understanding of your topic would know and which can read-ily be found in general reference books. Many students have difficulty deciding what is general knowledge and what must be documented with the appropriate source. Before making a note of general knowledge, ask yourself the following questions: Is this information available in a variety of sources? Would most people familiar with the topic know this information?

The list below should help you distinguish between statements of gen-eral knowledge and paraphrased information that must be documented. The first item under each number is a statement of general knowledge; the second, a paraphrase with the source indicated in parentheses; and the third, a full citation for the source.

1. a. Rachel Carson wrote *Silent Spring*. [General knowledge]
   b. Forty states passed legislation restricting the use of pesticides within two years of the publication of Rachel Carson's *Silent Spring* in 1962 (Hodgson 402).
   c. Hodgson, Godfrey. *America in Our Time*. 1976; rpt. New York: Vintage, 1978.
2. a. President Truman dismissed General Douglas MacArthur as commander of the Korean forces. [General knowledge]
   b. In the early days after Truman fired MacArthur, mail to the White House indicated that for every one person who approved Truman's action, twenty opposed it (Manchester 562).
   c. Manchester, William. *The Glory and the Dream*. 1974; rpt. New York: Bantam, 1979.
3. a. Betty Friedan, author of *The Feminine Mystique* and *The Second Stage*, is associated with the beginning of the women's movement. [General knowledge]
   b. Betty Friedan and other moderate feminists recommended working for change through the established political and legal channels (Hodgson 411).
   c. See 1 c above.
4. a. Many people in the late sixties questioned the wisdom of American involvement in Vietnam. [General knowledge]
   b. Among the many young men who attempted to avoid the draft during the Vietnam War were some 172,000 conscientious objectors, most of whom worked for two years in an alternative public service (Baskir 41).
   c. Baskir, Lawrence M. and William A. Strauss. *Chance and Circumstance*. New York: Vintage, 1978.
5. a. Japan bombed Pearl Harbor on December 7, 1941. [General knowledge]
   b. One of the consequences of the bombing of Pearl Harbor and the subsequent declaration of war by the U.S. was the detention of tens of thousands of Japanese Americans in relocation camps (Kelly 786).
   c. Kelly, Alfred H. and Winfred H. Harbison. *The American Constitution*. 5th ed. New York: Norton, 1976.

Avoiding Plagiarism

To plagiarize is to take the language, ideas, or conclusions of another person and to represent them as one's own. Plagiarizing, paraphrasing, and documenting need to be understood in relation to each other; most people

never have to be concerned with plagiarism as long as they learn to paraphrase correctly, to distinguish general knowledge from information that
must be documented, and to document with care.

Some students come to college confused about what plagiarism is. Perhaps in grammar school they dutifully copied an article from an encyclopedia, turned it in to the teacher as a report, and received an A. Even in high
school, they may have written papers that included phrases, sentences, or
even paragraphs that were copied from books or articles without using
quotations marks and citing the sources. At the college level, this is absolutely unacceptable. You must always make perfectly clear which of the
words and ideas that you are using were taken from someone else.

You should also avoid plagiarizing accidentally. Some students think
that they are paraphrasing correctly when in fact they have retained the
sentence structure of the original source or even a phrase or an unusual use
of a word. At times, people plagiarize accidentally when they sincerely
forget what was their own idea and what they learned from other people.

You will never plagiarize accidentally if you observe these rules:

1. Document all material from other sources, including direct quotations, paraphrases, summaries of facts, statistics, lists, charts, and
   illustrations.
2. Exempt from documentation only material of general knowledge
   and your own thoughts and conclusions.
3. Review your note cards and sources after you have finished your
   paper to make sure that you have not unconsciously confused someone else's ideas with your own.
4. Put a pair of large quotation marks on either side of a quotation note
   so that there will be no confusion in your mind about which notes
   are quotations.
5. In your final paper, carefully observe the conventions for quoting
   (enclose short quotations in quotation marks and set off longer ones)
   so that there will be no question about where a quotation begins and
   ends.
6. Paraphrase and summarize by completely casting information and
   ideas in your own words and style, inserting quotation marks within
   your paraphrase or summary whenever a unique word or phrase is
   retained from the original source.
7. Observe all the rules of the particular documentary style that you
   use.

EXERCISES

A. Photocopy an article—about a page long—from a general or specialized encyclopedia on a subject that interests you.

1. Choose a paragraph from the article and paraphrase it.
2. Reword part of the same paragraph, but retain the author's wording in a phrase or clause. Be sure to indicate this wording with quotation marks. Remember that whenever you use an author's words without giving credit, you are plagiarizing.
3. Make a list of the main points of the article.
4. Summarize the article in a single paragraph.
5. Note any statements in the article that are general knowledge. Remember that statements of general knowledge do not have to be documented in a research paper.
6. Note a phrase, clause, or sentence that you would quote in a research paper.

B. Read the short paper on Eleanor Roosevelt that begins on page 125. Using a light pencil, put a "q" beside each quotation, "gk" beside statements of general knowledge, and "c" by any original conclusions of the author. Indicate in the margin how many sources are used in each paragraph.

C. Study the four sample papers in chapters 11, 12, 13, and Appendix A.

1. Note how each uses quotations. Which uses the most? Which the least?
2. Select a quotation from one of the papers and paraphrase it, trying to retain the sense of the original.
3. Write a brief summary—approximately one hundred fifty words—of Carol Garcia's paper (see p. 216).

For students who have already started taking notes

D. Choose one of your notes that is a direct quotation.

1. Paraphrase it by objectively restating it in your own words and retaining the tone of the original, carefully avoiding any expression of your own opinion.
2. Using the same quotation, or selecting another, write a paragraph in which you combine paraphrase with interpretation.

E. After you have finished taking notes from all the sources that you have collected, stop, take stock, and evaluate your progress. The process of reading, taking notes, questioning people, and perhaps reading again may have led you to rethink your original intentions. Follow the steps on the next page to determine whether you need to redefine your topic:

1. Check each note card and make sure you have recorded all the information you need to identify the source in your paper.
2. Look over your note cards and make a list of the possible approaches to your topic.
3. Sort your cards to determine which aspect of your topic you have learned the most about.
4. Make a list of questions that you still need to answer.
5. List your next steps.

7

ORGANIZING MATERIAL

There are many different ways to organize knowledge, and the process of studying a topic is always a struggle to make connections and to discover relationships. When you first try to order facts and ideas, you will probably discover for yourself what you actually know about a topic. You then have the task of trying to organize what you have found to make it clear to others. Working carefully in the preliminary stages of organization will help you to write a final paper that is clear and logical.

Sorting Note Cards

When you have finished collecting materials, talking to people, reading, and taking notes, you will want to stop and evaluate what you have done. A good way to begin is to spread out your notes and other sources on a large surface and to sort them into categories. Michael Gold began his study of *Rebel without a Cause* intending to learn about the success of the film and the contribution that James Dean made to it. When he categorized his note cards, he discovered that in addition to material about Dean and the film's success, he had learned about the people who made the film—the director, the writers, the actors. He had learned about the James Dean cult; and he had also discovered that although many people associate the film with Dean, he was actually only one of many people who brought *Rebel* to fruition.

Sometimes students sort their notes only to discover that they have a miscellaneous collection of facts; if this happens to you, you should select the category that most interests you and return to your sources for more information or, if necessary, collect more sources. One student spent several days reading and taking notes on the subject of running. When he stopped to sort his note cards, he found that they fell into these categories:

Sprinting
Recreational jogging
Competitive running
The benefits of jogging
The Boston Marathon
Famous runners

After examining the categories, he discovered that he really had a little information on several different aspects of a large subject and that none of the categories related to each other in a meaningful way.

This student could have strung his notes together haphazardly, beginning with recreational jogging and ending for no particular reason with the Boston Marathon or famous runners. But the result would have been little more than a mishmash of facts. So, instead, he looked at his sorted cards and chose the category that interested him the most: the benefits of jogging. He then went back to his sources and found additional information on that more limited topic. After discarding the irrelevant notes and taking new ones, he found that he could sort the notes he now had into four main categories: weight control, muscular development, psychological health, and cardiovascular fitness. Note the balanced outline (p. 102) that he eventually made.

Testing Your Hypothesis

Most people begin a research project with some idea of what they will find. Michael Gold, for example, expected to find that the success of *Rebel without a Cause* was due to the charisma of its leading actor, James Dean, but he discovered that many other factors contributed to the film's success. This discovery led him to discard a single hypothesis, to raise a number of questions, and to keep an open mind. Carol Garcia went into her research with a question about how homes can be heated and cooled efficiently, and she had in mind a number of possible answers to that question, answers that might also be called hypotheses. She wondered, for example, if the solution might be building more nuclear power plants to provide energy for homes, or whether woodstoves, windpower, or active solar systems would solve the problem. Each of the possible answers to the question was a tentative hypothesis, and in the beginning Carol considered each. She gradually discarded her other hypotheses, and concluded that incorporating passive solar design features in building homes would be the most efficient way to control temperature.

Before you begin to outline your findings, you should pause and ask yourself whether you still have one or more working hypotheses or a preliminary thesis that you think your findings will demonstrate. If so, write it out, and then go back to your sorted notes and test it. If Michael Gold had written out his original hypothesis—that *Rebel's* success is due to its leading actor—then he would easily have seen that his research could not support that statement. It is a good idea to make a list of any preconceived ideas you have and to test them against your notes to make sure that you do not distort your findings in order to prove yourself right. Ask your self the following questions:

1. What did I expect to find when I began research?
2. What did I actually find?
3. If these two are different, what led me to change my mind?
4. If they are the same, have I ignored any evidence that might suggest a different conclusion?

It is possible that your original expectations and your conclusions will be the same, but most researchers find that their original ideas are altered more than once. This of course does not always happen in the systematic way suggested by the list of questions above, since a single article or even a sentence in a text may change your way of thinking.

Developing a Controlling Idea or Thesis Statement

You will be able to control and shape your material more effectively if you can explain in a sentence or two exactly what your paper will be about. This statement of what you intend to demonstrate in your paper is the thesis, and everything in your paper should contribute to that goal.

THE THESIS STATEMENT

After you have sorted your note cards and decided that you have enough material to write a report, you may want to write out what you think will be your thesis statement, the controlling idea of your paper. Again Michael Gold's experience provides a helpful example. After he sorted his notes and before he made an outline, Michael wrote: "*Rebel without a Cause* was created over a period of years, developing from the dedicated collaboration of many people who brought different points of view and experiences to the project, and it influenced the behavior and feelings of a large number of young people who were united by their infatuation with James Dean." By keeping this statement in mind both when he outlined his material and when he started writing his first draft, Michael was able to decide which notes were relevant and which, though they were interesting, should be set aside. Trying to stick to a controlling idea made it easy for Michael to discard notes concerning Dean's irrational behavior and his similarity to Marlon Brando.

After he wrote a first draft based on this controlling idea, Michael examined what he had written, revised it—bringing the information about the Dean cult to the beginning—and wrote a new thesis sentence: *"Rebel without a Cause* was really the product of the imagination, the creative energy, and the plain hard work of a group of people—the director, writers, actors, and technical experts—who compose the community of a film." This thesis allowed Michael to use the information about the Dean cult in his introduction, to qualify it in the fifth paragraph, and to focus in the remainder of the paper on the various people who contributed to creation of the film. He was able to use the information about the film's interpreters in a final section leading up to the conclusion.

Not everyone is able to identify a controlling idea after sorting note cards. Some students need to write out an introductory paragraph before they can identify a single thesis or main idea that directs the progress of the finished product. Others discover a controlling idea only after they have begun writing. That is what happened to Sara Maxfield, who had to write several pages about the two novels she had studied before she was able to identify this controlling idea: Toni Morrison in *Sula* and Alice Walker in *Meridian* explore the early life and young adulthood of a female character by examining how her development is determined by her society, her personal relationships, her historical context, and the options open to her.

Some students, like David Harris, cannot reduce their findings to a single sentence, and they have to settle for a summary paragraph. The process of trying to get down your first ideas may help you to discover an approach to your topic and a way of relating the different aspects of your study to each other. The first draft of an introductory paragraph may simply be a way to get started. After you have written it, you may be able to sketch out a preliminary outline. Later you may want to revise it and incorporate it into a more polished introduction.

EXPOSITORY OR PERSUASIVE THESIS

The controlling idea or thesis statement of a research paper may be expository or persuasive, or a combination of the two. An *expository* thesis simply states what the paper is about in a sentence that suggests that what follows will be interesting and informative. A *persuasive* thesis also states what the paper is about, but in a manner that shows that the author is taking a stand, making an argument, hoping to change the reader's beliefs or move the reader to action.

Linda Orton's thesis statement in her paper about Eleanor Roosevelt is expository: "Her many activities included work to improve the lot of disadvantaged women and to help all women develop their potential." This precise statement alerts the reader that the rest of the paper will provide information about Eleanor Roosevelt's work for women.

Carol Garcia's thesis statement is also expository: "The simplest, most economical, and most effective way to use the sun's energy is to design houses that capture and retain the sun's heat in the winter and exclude it in the summer." The rest of her paper explains how this is done.

David Harris's thesis statement is the first step in his attempt to persuade his readers to take a particular point of view: "Child psychiatrists, pediatricians, educators, and legislators are becoming increasingly aware that the world's children are paying a price for the arms race in their own psychological welfare, and many have concluded that they must do something and encourage others to respond to the problem. Although there is much to learn about how to deal with children's fears of a nuclear disaster, those responsible for the welfare of children must act now to educate themselves and to provide children with the information and reassurance they need to grow up in the nuclear age." This more complex statement of intent sets up the argument that will follow as David brings forth the evidence to persuade his reader that there is a problem and that action must be taken to solve it.

Michael Gold's thesis is a combination of persuasion and exposition. "*Rebel* was really the product of the imagination, the creative energy, and the plain hard work of a group of people—the producer, director, writers, actors, and technical experts—who compose the community of a film." In his paper Michael Gold puts together the story of all the people who helped to create the film, and at the same time he argues against the idea that James Dean himself was responsible for the film's success.

Many good research papers have both expository and persuasive elements, but there can be dangers in overemphasizing either mode. By writing a purely expository paper, you may leave your reader thinking "So what?" Some students work very hard researching a topic, but they fail to present the material in a way that convinces readers of its importance. Their papers are nothing more than a collection of facts. Carol Garcia, however, does more than simply lay out the facts; she makes it clear that what she has to say is important and that her readers should be interested. If you are genuinely interested in a subject—as were all the students whose papers are in this text—then you will be able to make that subject interesting to your readers.

On the other hand, in an excessively persuasive paper you may give the impression that you are on a soap-box proselytizing for your favorite cause. Persuading people to see things as you do is often a difficult task; to do so in writing is especially difficult. Although you may be able to convert someone to your point of view with an emotional appeal, lasting persuasion usually depends on a convincing presentation of evidence based on what seems to be undeniable fact. Almost all successful persuasive writing requires careful research and thoughtful presentation of research findings.

There are some dangers to conducting research with the intention of using it to write a persuasive paper. You may be tempted to oversimplify a complex subject, to select only the evidence that proves a thesis and ignore the rest. You probably should not begin a persuasive paper until you yourself have been persuaded by what you have found.

Writing an Introduction

There are no hard and fast rules about when you should write the introduction to a paper, but some students who have difficulty organizing material find that the effort to write an introduction results in a kind of unconscious organizing. The draft of an introduction may serve as a skeleton outline that, as you review your notes, you can elaborate and develop. It is usually a good idea to draft an introduction very early on, to analyze the main points in an introduction, and then to determine what should be eliminated and what needs to be expanded. Give yourself time for this process to take place. After you have reviewed and sorted your note cards, and perhaps even after you have constructed what you think is your thesis sentence, take a clean notebook and go off by yourself and begin writing. What comes out may surprise you and may help you shape your paper. A preliminary draft of an introduction can be useful even if you discard it later and write another.

Although you may use more than one paragraph for the introduction to your paper, your first paragraph must do double duty. It must help announce what the paper is about, and it must get the reader's attention. Readers will probably continue to read if they are convinced that what they will learn from the paper is both interesting and important.

Following the Standard Outline Format

The standard outline format that is used in most disciplines is simple and logical. It alternates between numbers and letters, using Roman numerals for major categories of a paper, capital letters for the subheadings under the major categories, Arabic numbers for details under the subheadings, and lower-case letters for any breakdown of the details. Each subordinate heading is indented, beginning immediately under the first letter of the first word of the larger category. You should be able to adapt this pattern (shown on the following page) to any topic.

    I. [First major category]
       A. [Subheading]
       B. [Subheading]
   II. [Second major category]
       A. [Subheading]
          1. [Detail]
          2. [Detail]
             a. [Breakdown]
             b. [Breakdown]
       B. [Subheading]
  III. [Third major category]

Many topics can be organized using only one level of subdivisions under the major categories. An outline that includes even minor details is more than a plan; it is really a distilled version of a complete paper that will later be cast in readable prose. A very detailed outline sometimes requires as much work as a rough draft.

OUTLINING YOUR MATERIAL

There are different ways of thinking about outlining. For some writers the outline is a strict plan carefully structured before drafting of the paper begins. For others, outlining is a process of discovery that changes as they draft and revise. Michael Gold and Sara Maxfield combined the process of drafting and outlining, David Harris worked out his paper in complete sentence outline before he began his first draft, and Carol Garcia wrote a tight topical outline that she followed strictly. Instructors vary in their requirements about outlines. Some teachers may not even ask to see your outline, some may want only the final outline, and still others may want to check the drafts of outlines in order to advise you as you organize the paper. Keep in mind that an outline is a tool to help you shape your material, not a hurdle that you must get over to meet a requirement. If you are having trouble making an outline, you may need to reconsider your thesis statement and to reexamine your sources to find out what you have really learned.

CONSTRUCTING AN OUTLINE

An outline is both an organized description of your research findings and a plan for the report you will write about your research. An outline of what you have found may reveal irrelevant material or point to aspects of your topic that need more research. A final outline of what you intend to write about may go through several stages as your ideas develop. Most people are able to construct an adequate plan using words or, at most, phrases to indicate the main points or topics they plan to cover. A sketchy topical outline allows you to develop ideas as you compose, whereas a detailed sentence outline requires that you develop your ideas primarily in the outlining process. Some people, however, do prefer to organize their material in complete sentences before they begin to compose.

The kind of outline you use should be determined by the subject you have researched, the amount of factual evidence you have to support your points, and the nature of your own thought processes. For most people, there is an interaction among writing, thinking, and organizing. As you proceed with the writing of a paper, you will probably revise your outline more than once, rearranging the order of topics, adding evidence, deleting irrelevant material.

BALANCING AN OUTLINE

Your paper will probably be more effective if you try to present your findings so that the different parts are about the same length. If you are researching two books, for example, you should give approximately the same space to each. The student who once had such a hodgepodge of miscellaneous material on the subject of running eventually focused his study and constructed this perfectly balanced outline:

THE BENEFITS OF RUNNING

    I. Weight Control
        A. Aids self-control
        B. Expends calories
        C. Suppresses appetite
        D. Encourages a healthy diet
   II. Muscular Development
        A. Improves tone
        B. Enhances contours
        C. Increases strength
        D. Improves endurance
  III. Psychological Well-Being
        A. Aids sleep
        B. Inhibits depression
        C. Increases strength
        D. Intensifies vitality
   IV. Cardiovascular Fitness
        A. Strengthens heart
        B. Lowers blood pressure
        C. Changes blood lipids
        D. Improves circulation

The parts of an outline are often not as symmetrical as they are here, where each category has an equal number of subcategories. Research findings may not fall into categories with equal and parallel subheadings, and it is a serious mistake to try to force your material into a neat outline. To do so is to distort your findings and to suggest a false logic and even false conclusions. It is much better to have a sketchy, unbalanced outline that is an accurate reflection of your findings than a neat but misleading one. But an outline that is very unbalanced may indicate serious problems in organization.

Some topics can be planned from the beginning in such a way that the findings will necessarily suggest a balanced outline. For example, a student who wanted to learn something about jazz and who decided to study two representative musicians from four cities where jazz has flourished constructed the following outline:

THE MANY FACES OF JAZZ

    I. New Orleans
       A. King Oliver
       B. Sidney Bechet
   II. Chicago
       A. Tommy Dorsey
       B. Glenn Miller
  III. New York
       A. Dizzy Gillespie
       B. John Coltrane
   IV. San Francisco
       A. Gerry Mulligan
       B. Chet Baker

This outline is geographical in that each main category is a city where jazz was important, but there is also a chronological principle at work: jazz began in New Orleans, moved up the river and on to Chicago, then became popular in New York, and finally emerged on the West Coast. Often, as with the jazz outline, the best organizing principles for research findings are inherent in the topic and in the way the research is conducted. An anthropologist studying the economic significance of various animals in a peasant community might naturally order her findings by reporting on one animal at a time, moving from the least important to the most important. Many students, however, begin to explore a subject without a fixed idea of what they want to find out; and in such cases, it is best to keep an open mind about how to organize research findings, allowing, as Michael Gold and Sara Maxfield did, the material itself to suggest its own order.

USING AN ORGANIZING PRINCIPLE

There is usually more than one way to organize the same material. You might, for example, shape your findings by ordering events as they happened, by showing how two or more elements are alike and different, by making general statements and then supporting them with concrete evidence, or by setting up a problem and demonstrating solutions. With the exception of the opening paragraphs that deal with the cult that developed after Dean's death, Michael Gold largely organized his material chronologically, telling the story of the making of *Rebel without a Cause* as it happened. Sara Maxfield chose to compare and contrast novels by Alice Walker and Toni Morrison, treating first their similarities and then their differences, using a point-by-point comparison. David Harris ordered his paper according to logic, moving from an explanation of the problem to a discussion of the solution. Carol Garcia, on the other hand, first set up a problem—the high cost of energy—and then explained the solution, ordering the design elements of passive solar design according to their relative importance. Your organizing principle may emerge unconsciously as you struggle with your material, and a carefully constructed thesis will usually call for one or another treatment. Michael Gold's research focused on a process and therefore invites a temporal ordering, whereas Sara Maxfield's examination of two novels suggests a comparative treatment.

REVISING AN OUTLINE

Michael Gold organized his study of *Rebel without a Cause* rather easily. He first watched a videotape of the film and read the book that gave it a title. After a period of reading, taking notes, photocopying articles, and marking relevant passages, Michael categorized his notes and wrote his first preliminary thesis sentence: "*Rebel without a Cause* was created over a period of years, developing from the dedicated collaboration of many people who brought different points of view and experiences to the project, and it influenced the behavior and feelings of a large number of young people who were united by their infatuation with James Dean." He decided that he could organize his paper chronologically, telling the story of the creation of the film from beginning to end. He then sorted his cards into stacks representing those people who contributed to the film's production, those who were influenced by it, and those who have interpreted it. He arranged them chronologically and made the following outline:

THE COMMUNITY OF A FILM: REBEL WITHOUT A CAUSE

I. The Beginning
  A. Robert Lindner's Rebel without a Cause

  B. Warner Brothers' purchase
  C. Lindner's contribution
 II. The core community
  A. The director
  B. The producer
  C. The musical director
 III. The screenwriters
  A. Problems
  B. Leon Uris
  C. Irving Shulman
  D. Stewart Stern
 IV. The actors
  A. James Dean
   1. Relationship with Ray
   2. Improviser
  B. Natalie Wood
  C. Supporting actors
 V. Influence
  A. The original fans
  B. The Dean cult
  C. The interpreters
  D. Conflicting views
  E. Problems of evaluation

When revising the first draft based on this outline, Michael decided to rearrange his material. By moving the information about the Dean cult to the introduction, Michael could stress that what many people know about the film—James Dean and his impact—is only part of the story. Studying his outline, he retitled the other categories and rearranged the material, emphasizing the different stages of the film's development in a more effective way. His new outline looked like this:

 I. Rebel's followers and creators
  A. Rebel's impact
  B. The Dean cult
  C. The creators
 II. A collaborative effort: the beginning
  A. Robert Lindner and Warner Brothers
  B. Nicholas Ray
 III. The writers
  A. Odets and Uris
  B. Shulman
  C. Stern

    IV. The actors
        A. James Dean
        B. Natalie Wood
        C. Others
     V. The Interpreters
        A. Conflicting views
        B. Problems of evaluation
    VI. Rebel's place in film history
        A. Appropriate categories
        B. Need for reevaluation

Sara Maxfield organized what she wanted to say by comparing Toni Morrison's vision with that of Alice Walker. In the main part of her paper —Roman numeral III—she uses a point-by-point comparison, considering *Sula* first and then *Meridian*. Although Sara developed a controlling idea, she did not construct this outline until after she wrote a rough draft. Having gathered her ideas, she then tried to organize them as follows:

     I. Introduction
        A. Questions raised
        B. Answers: Two contemporary novels
    II. Similarities
        A. Narrative technique
        B. Content
        C. Authors
   III. Differences
        A. Personal and public
           1. Sula
           2. Meridian
        B. The individual and history
           1. Sula
           2. Meridian
        C. Choice and change
           1. Sula
           2. Meridian
    IV. Conclusion
        A. Morrison's vision
        B. Walker's vision

Writing and outlining helped Sara discover what she wanted to say by trying to say it. Once she outlined the main points embedded in a rough draft of some seventeen pages, she was able to cut her paper and to revise it using the outline as a guide. She eliminated material that was not related to the main points of her outline, and she improved her writing by making her point as clearly and simply as possible. Her final step was to write a concluding paragraph.

OUTLINING WITH NOTE CARDS

Sara's experience was very different from that of Carol Garcia, who began to write a first draft only after she had constructed a successful outline. After considerable background reading in the field of solar energy, Carol decided to focus on passive solar design—architecture that uses features of the building itself to capture the heat of the sun. She gathered information and expanded her understanding of her topic by reading, talking with experts, and visiting solar houses. When she sat down to organize the notes she had made, she found that she was able to sort them easily into categories and to sketch the following outline:

   I. Introduction
       A. High cost of energy
       B. The sun: An affordable source of energy
  II. Three properties of heat
       A. Radiation
       B. Conduction
       C. Convection
 III. Four passive solar features
       A. South-facing windows
       B. Thermal storage walls behind glazing
       C. Attached sunspaces
       D. The convective loop collector
  IV. Other design considerations
       A. Shape of building and room placement
       B. Features of site
   V. Heat retention in winter
       A. Seals for air leaks
       B. Insulation for walls and roof
       C. Earth-shelter
  VI. Heat reduction in summer
       A. Earth-shelter
       B. Shade
       C. Ventilation
       D. Reflection
 VII. Conclusion
       A. Psychological benefits
       B. Economic benefits
       C. Social benefits

WRITING A SENTENCE OUTLINE

At his instructor's suggestion, David Harris wrote a sentence outline, an exercise that was very helpful since he was forced to think through his entire paper before he wrote the final draft. By putting down his main points in complete sentences, David was able to gain control over a very complex subject:

I. The psychological effects of the nuclear threat on children are considerable.
  A. A significant number of children experience serious worry about nuclear weapons.
  B. The psychological effect of the nuclear threat varies with age, social class, and parental attitudes.
  C. Children in countries with nuclear weapons and those from non-nuclear nations seem to have comparable levels of concern.
II. The fear that children experience is a normal, appropriate emotional response to danger with serious consequences for some.
  A. Some live with a sense of futurelessness.
  B. Futurelessness causes some to live for the moment.
  C. Living for the moment may result in self-destructive behavior.
  D. It causes others to live a double life.
III. Children need help from responsible adults in dealing with the nuclear threat.
  A. Children lack defense mechanisms to deal with fears.
  B. They are holding adults responsible.
  C. They must be given hope.
IV. There is no single solution to the nuclear threat or to the problems it creates for young people, but one significant aspect of any set of solutions must be education.
  A. Young people want more information.
  B. Educators and other responsible adults must end their own denial of the problem and learn more about the effects that living in the nuclear age is having on today's children.
  C. Adults must begin by sharing knowledge with the young.
  D. Although further research is needed, educators and parents must act on what is already known.

EXERCISES

A. Read the short paper about Eleanor Roosevelt at the end of chapter 8 and sketch out an outline of the main points.

For students who have finished taking notes:

B. Sort your note cards into categories and eliminate those not obviously related to your topic.

C. Is there more than one way to organize your cards? Choose the one that seems best and sketch out an outline of your findings.

D. Write out a statement of what you intend to demonstrate in your paper. Do you expect to write an expository or a persuasive paper?

E. If you plan to write a persuasive paper, sort your note cards, choosing those that will most effectively advance your argument.

8

COMPOSING AND REVISING

You begin writing your paper the first time you paraphrase a written source or jot down a summary after an interview. By the time you sit down with a clean sheet of paper, several stacks of notes, and an outline, you will already have written drafts of small parts of your paper. Nevertheless, the task of taking this raw material and crafting it into smooth, readable prose lies ahead. Even though you may have an outline that seems orderly enough, you still must arrange the bits and pieces that you have collected into logical sentences and paragraphs, creating a coherent pattern. Shaping your material requires constant attention to the way one sentence relates to another, as well as to how each relates to the whole. From the beginning, it is good to make your points as clearly as possible, using all the transitions, definitions, and explanations that are necessary for meaning.

Getting Started

Before you start to write, try to have the materials, the space, and the time you need to write at least three hundred words—a good beginning.

Many writers like to compose first drafts in longhand, using a pencil for easy erasure. If, however, you write best with a favorite pen, by all means use it. A long legal pad is good for drafts because you can use every other line, leaving space for revision, and still have several sentences on a page.

Find a surface—a large desk, a dining room table, or a card table—where you can line up your note cards, stack books, and lay out your writing materials. You will save time if you find a place where you can leave these materials until your paper is complete; but if roommates, family members, or others are likely to distract you, it may be best for you to pack up and head for the library.

You will probably get more done if you can allot at least three hours for a writing session. If possible, allow yourself a little more time than you think you will need and plan to take a break after about an hour and a half or when you get tired.

COMPOSING ON A TYPEWRITER

A portable typewriter is a valuable research tool that you can use at your own desk or in designated sections of most libraries. If you are a good typist—or even just a fair one—you may prefer to compose your first draft on a typewriter, triple spacing to provide adequate space for revision. Even if you mark through passages as you compose, a typed draft is more legible than a handwritten one. Many writers combine handwritten composition with typing, from time to time jotting down sentences by hand and then incorporating them into a typescript.

USING A WORD PROCESSOR

If you have access to a word processor or personal computer and know how to use it, you may want to compose your paper on it, revise on it, or both. Some people who are skilled in using a word processor still have difficulty composing on it and prefer to write out their first drafts in longhand. They may then use the processor for second drafts and final revisions. Others use it from the beginning. If you have your paper typed by a professional typist who uses a word processor, he or she may provide a typed copy for you to revise and then a clean copy incorporating your revisions.

Imagining the Reader

All writers need to consider for whom they are writing. Scholars who write for professional journals assume that their readers are people like themselves, specialists who share a vocabulary and a common body of knowledge. Microeconomists, behavioral psychologists, or medieval historians might report their research in a way that only others in their fields can read with ease. In the course of your research, you may have found articles or books that you could not make much sense out of simply because their authors used many words you did not understand.

Most students, however, do not write up their research findings for specialists. Unless your instructor specifies a reader for you, it is usually advisable to think of your audience as someone who wants to learn about your topic, but who knows little about it. You may find it helpful actually to imagine a particular person who fits that description, a classmate or family member who is interested in what you are learning but who has no context or special vocabulary for understanding it. Michael Gold, for example, does not write for movie buffs only, but for anyone who has even a slight interest in movies. He imagines a reader who may not even have seen *Rebel without a Cause*.

BEING CONSISTENT

From the beginning, you want to strive for consistency—selecting a verb tense, a level of word choice, and a tone that you carry throughout your paper. You should also be consistent about the mechanics of writing. When there are variant spellings of a word, for example, choose one and use it consistently; or when you are documenting your sources, choose one style of documentation and use it throughout the paper.

DEVELOPING A READABLE STYLE

Your main consideration when you choose your words and construct your sentences should be readability. You want to write so that others can understand what you have to say as easily as possible. Some students are tempted to use a specialized vocabulary or long but obscure words because they want to sound intelligent; but it is best to concentrate on communicating what you know clearly rather than on showing off what you have learned.

What you write will be more readable if you create a voice that is natural to you, so that when you read what you have written, it sounds like you when you are trying to explain something that is important. Of course you will not use slang, which is often natural to informal speech, but which is also often vague and imprecise. One way to test the voice of what you have written is to read out loud or, even better, into a tape recorder. If your voice sounds pretentious or insincere, you will probably want to work on your style. Once you have completed a portion of your paper, read it carefully and ask yourself the following questions:

1. Have I used long words where shorter ones would have been just as effective?
2. Have I been general where I could have been specific?
3. Have I tried to show off what I know rather than to say clearly and precisely what I mean?

If the answer to even one of these questions is yes, you probably need to try more consciously to compose sentences and paragraphs that others can read with ease.

Planning Ahead

Budgeting time is important at every stage of research, and it becomes crucial as you begin to write. Not only do you need time for composition, revision, and typing, but you need adequate time in between these steps. When your first draft is finished, it is a good idea to set it aside before you revise it. When you come back to a draft after some time, you will usually be able to see where it needs improvement. The time required for writing papers varies enormously, but the schedule below is adequate for most people writing a paper of approximately ten pages.

1. Writing the first draft: two to three days or five three-hour sessions
2. Laying the first draft aside: one day
3. Revising and typing the second draft: one day
4. Laying it aside: one day
5. Revising and typing the finished paper: one day

Writing the First Draft

Whether you write in longhand, use a typewriter, or compose on a word processor, writing your first draft should be a process of trying out alternatives, marking some out, and starting over again and again. Even if you are working from a detailed outline, you will probably experiment with different ways of presenting your research as you write. A handwritten or typed first draft should in fact be messy, reflecting numerous efforts to improve your writing—to say it better—as you compose. The way in which you introduce your sources and give credit for information can, however, help you present your findings and argue your thesis.

WRITING IN YOUR OWN VOICE

Think of your paper as being mainly written in your own voice. You are explaining in your own words what you have learned and what you have concluded. Whenever you paraphrase or summarize the words of the writers whose articles and books you have studied, you must try to do so in a way that is natural to you, in words that you might use, while being careful to indicate your sources in the text of your paper so that it is perfectly clear which are your thoughts and ideas and which are those of others.

CITING SOURCES AS YOU COMPOSE

From the beginning, cite each source as you use it and make sure that you have all the information needed for a complete citation in the bibliography.

Every quotation, every paraphrase, every fact that you have learned in your research should be identified in the text of your first draft. Sometimes you may want to begin a paragraph or a sentence with the name of the author or authors of a source you are using:

```
Joseph Lash concludes that . . .
Tamara K. Hareven offers another view.
Bernard Bailyn et al. explore . . .
Davidson and Lytle demonstrate that . . .
```

Always cite the page number when you refer to a part of a source rather than the whole and place the page number of the source at the end of a clause or sentence as you compose:

In _Eleanor and Franklin,_ his best-selling Pulitzer Prize-winning biography, Joseph Lash explains Eleanor Roosevelt's role in the League of Women Voters (355).

As Eleanor Roosevelt has written, ''It is probably the sense of being really needed and wanted which gives us the greatest satisfaction and creates the most lasting bond'' (308).

When you do not mention the author's name in the text, include it in the parenthetical reference along with a page number:

During Franklin's convalescence, Eleanor assumed the responsibility of keeping the Roosevelt name before the public (Hareven 20).

Always make it clear where a paraphrase ends by putting the page number at the end of several sentences or a paragraph taken from the same part of a source. See first paragraph on page 126.

Note how sources are cited in the sample paper at the end of this chapter, and see page 132 for further examples of ways to introduce sources.

If you are writing a paper using the APA style or the simple number system of documentation, you will include other information in the text of your paper as you compose—date of publication for APA and a number for each source in the number system. See chapter 12 for APA and chapter 13 for the simple number system.

The rules on the following page assume that you are using the documentation style recommended by the Modern Language Association, but the principles apply to other styles of documentation as well. These rules should help you with the technical aspects of integrating sources into a coherent text. For examples, see the marginal notes in the short paper at the end of this chapter.

1. Make perfectly clear the exact source of all material except facts of general knowledge and your own ideas and conclusions.
2. Indicate sources within the text when you can do so smoothly and always when you need to clarify which are your own ideas and which you owe to someone else. When you refer to material from a particular page number of a written text, you will have to give the page number—in parentheses or in a note.
3. After direct quotations either indicate the source in parentheses or with a note number that will correspond to a note at the bottom of the page or on the endnote page or to an item in your list of sources.
4. Place references after paraphrased material in such a way that there is no doubt about the source. In paragraphs that depend entirely on a few pages of a single source, cite the source at the end of the paragraph.
5. When you use two or more sources in a paragraph, use as many citations as are necessary for clarity.

PROVIDING FOR NOTES AS YOU COMPOSE

If your paper requires either explanatory or documentary footnotes or endnotes, indicate in your draft where you expect to place the note, using an asterisk, a circle, or some other code. In the margin, place the page number and any other information necessary to write a complete note later. Since revising often includes rearranging, you should number the notes only when you are ready to type the final copy.

INTEGRATING QUOTATIONS WITH YOUR OWN WORDS

Learning how to combine your own words with someone else's is more difficult than learning the technicalities of documentation. The best guide for doing this effectively is again your own voice. Quote only when it is important to capture another person's voice or exact words, and know enough about your subject so that you can smoothly move from your own ideas and words to those of another person. Remember, this is *your* research paper. The sources you use and the quotations you include are intended to back up and explain your thesis. You are not just compiling data—you are interpreting and reporting your findings.

You may choose to quote a word, a phrase, a sentence, or several sentences, but in any case, you should retain the exact spelling and punctuation of the original. When you use quotations, it is important that you do so smoothly, making sure that your sentence is grammatically correct and that any quoted material appears exactly as it does in the original. Short quotations—not more than four lines—should be incorporated into the text of your paper. They may be integrated in a variety of ways:

At the beginning of a sentence:

''The very best of human possibilities,'' according to George
Eliot in <u>Daniel Deronda,</u> is ''the blending of a complete personal
love in one current with a larger duty'' (685).

Following an introductory clause:

A character in George Eliot's <u>Daniel Deronda</u> refers to marriages
as ''all the wondrous combinations of the universe whose issue
makes our good and evil'' (812).

With an introductory clause followed by a colon:

Joseph Lash stresses the complexity of Eleanor Roosevelt's
character: ''She was the teacher, the moralist, the dreamer, but
she was also highly practical'' (386-387).

Combined with paraphrase in the same sentence:

Lash argues that because of Franklin's career, Eleanor's
''proddings and probings had to be carried on in a way that would
not embarrass him politically'' (387).

Note how short quotations are integrated into the sample paper at the
end of this chapter.

Long quotations of more than four typed lines are usually set off with a
colon with no quotations marks and indented ten spaces from the left margin. The right margin does not change. Do not add extra space before or
after the quotation, but simply double-space throughout. If the long quotation is all from one paragraph, do not indent further (see the long quotation on page 126), but if you are quoting two paragraphs, indent the first
line of each three more spaces:

Dickens's descriptive power is evident in the opening lines of
<u>Little Dorrit</u>:

> Thirty years ago, Marseilles lay burning in the sun,
> one day. A blazing sun upon a fierce August day was no
> greater rarity in southern France then, than at any
> other time. . . .
>
> There was no wind to make a ripple on the foul water
> within the harbour, or on the beautiful sea without. The
> line of demarcation between the two colours, black and
> blue, showed the point which the pure sea would not
> pass; but it lay as quiet as the abominable pool, with
> which it never mixed.

AVOIDING PADDING

You may be tempted to pad a research paper, to put in all the interesting bits of information you have found, even when they do not directly relate to the main idea of the paper. If your instructor has asked for a paper of a particular length—perhaps ten pages—you may at first feel that you cannot possibly write so much on your topic and that you therefore will have to use all your notes. Before she focused her topic on passive solar design, for example, Carol Garcia read about active systems of heating with the sun. When she organized her note cards, Carol discovered that she had several notes on solar collector panels, hot water heating, and other features of active solar systems. Carol discarded the notes about active solar energy and wrote an outline and first draft limited to passive solar design. Even then, she had more than enough material, and at her instructor's suggestion, she cut her paper from twelve to six pages. If you have adequately researched your topic, you will probably find that you can write far more than the minimum required length.

Revising

By writing every other line on long sheets of paper—such as legal pads—or by triple- or at least double-spacing a rough typed copy, you will have adequate space for revising sentences and words, but revising paragraphs and the overall structure will sometimes require rewriting on separate paper and cutting up the sheets you have written and rearranging them. Every time you read through your paper, you will probably make minor changes in words and sentences, but the larger structural changes need to be made systematically.

EVALUATING ORGANIZATION

Once you have written a first draft, you should examine it to see if it really reflects what you intended to say. The first step is to compare your preliminary outline—the one you made before you began to write—with an outline of what you have written. The surest way is to go through your draft and to write down in abbreviated form—words and phrases—what you have actually written, making a new outline of the draft itself. Then consult your original plan. Are they the same? Which is better?

REARRANGING THE PARTS

Rearranging may require drastic methods: taking a paragraph from the middle and putting it in the introduction, for example. Sometimes you can indicate changes in the margins, but often you will want to make the change by cutting up your manuscript and pasting or taping sections on new sheets, leaving space for writing transitions to connect one part to another. Even if you are working with a word processor, you will often find it easier to do major rearrangement on your printed copy in this fashion before entering it onto your disk or tape. Numbering the pages of your draft, even though you know these will not be the final page numbers, makes it easier to change or add material during revision. If, for example, you write a paragraph that you want to insert in the middle of page 12, number it 12a and place it after the original page 12, indicating clearly in the text where you want to insert it.

ELIMINATING UNNECESSARY MATERIAL

You may be reluctant to strike through sentences and paragraphs that you have worked so hard to write, but most rough drafts include extra words, sentences, and even larger units that you later admit are really not necessary. You may have to force yourself to mark through repetitive or irrelevant passages. Tell yourself that your writing will be more effective if it is not repetitious and if each part contributes to the whole. Then read through your draft looking for what you can strike through without weakening your meaning. Notice how Michael Gold cuts the passage below from forty to twenty-two words:

Original: According to Kreidl, it was Leonard Rosenman, the musical director of Rebel, who suggested the thirty-one-year old Stewart Stern as a replacement for Shulman. At last, Ray had found a collaborator with whom he could work until the film was finished.

Revision: Leonard Rosenman, the musical director of Rebel, suggested the thirty-one-year old Stewart Stern, who worked with Ray until the film was finished.

Since Michael's preceding paragraph ends with a statement about the break between Shulman and Ray, there is no need to repeat it, and nothing is lost with the other cuts (see p. 178).

Carol Garcia cut her paper by eliminating material that was not directly related to the topic of passive solar design. In the following paragraph, she cut out a complete sentence:

There is, however, an unlimited source of energy available to us in the form of sunlight; and the simplest, most economical, and effective way to use the sun's energy is to design houses that capture and retain the sun's heat in the winter and exclude it in the summer. The pattern of energy use in this country can be changed radically simply by building new houses so that they can

be heated with the sun and by remodeling old houses to include
solar features. To create buildings that maximize solar heat
collection in cold months and minimize it in the summer, it is
necessary to understand how solar heat may be collected,
transferred, and stored.

CLARIFYING MEANING

Ask yourself if you have expressed what you want to say as clearly as possible, and then reread your paper from the point of view of an interested reader who does not know very much about your topic. Sometimes what is clear to you may not be clear to someone else. Because you have become familiar with a topic, you may find it difficult to imagine whether what you have written makes sense to someone who has not studied the same material. Sara Maxfield found after rereading her first draft that she needed to include a brief statement of the main action of *Sula* and *Meridian*, so that what she said about the two books would make sense to someone who had not read them.

IMPROVING PARAGRAPHS

The goal of all revision is clarity. When you examine a paragraph to see what improvements you can make, first identify the main idea and then decide if you have developed it as clearly as possible. Do you need more explanation? Is there irrelevant material that belongs elsewhere or not in your paper at all? Is the order effective? Sometimes when you have doubts, you may want to write another version and choose between the two.

IMPROVING SMALLER UNITS

Although you will probably change some sentences and words as you revise the larger units of your paper, it is advisable to go through it at least once just to improve diction (word choice) and sentence structure. The following list suggests a procedure for revising that you may find helpful:

1. Examine the length of your sentences. If most are approximately the same length, try to achieve more variety either by combining short sentences or breaking down long ones.
2. Check for active voice. Whenever possible, structure sentences so that the subject is followed by an active verb. Note the following example from Michael Gold's paper:

Original: Rebel was directed by Nicholas Ray.
Revision: Nicholas Ray directed Rebel.

You can easily locate passive verbs by looking for "is," "was," and other forms of the verb "to be." (But the passive voice is not taboo. It can be used effectively both to vary sentence structure and to emphasize the object rather than the subject—as I have done in this sentence. Instead of beginning another sentence with "You can use," I decided to emphasize the passive voice.)

3. Note whether you have stretched out your sentences with unnecessary clauses or phrases. If so, these examples may help you revise:

Original: The difficulty of dealing with screenwriters who are uncooperative often delays the production of a film.
Revision: Uncooperative screenwriters often delay film production.

Original: James Dean's fans were characterized by an excessive degree of sentimentality regarding his memory.
Revision: Dean's fans sentimentalized his memory.

4. Decide if the verb forms are unnecessarily complex, as in the following sentence:

Original: Rebel without a Cause was to have been based on a book by Robert Lindner.
Revision: Robert Lindner's book was the original inspiration for Rebel without a Cause.

5. Look out for excessively long or vague words. Whenever you can, substitute a short, easily understood word for an unnecessarily long or obscure one.

Original: Eleanor Roosevelt endeavored to improve living conditions for indigent people who were deprived of the benefits of society.
Revision: Eleanor Roosevelt worked to improve the lives of the poor.

6. Check for repetition. Do you use certain words repeatedly? If so, search for good synonyms to provide some variety. You may find a thesaurus, a dictionary of synonyms, or a regular dictionary helpful to remind you of other appropriate words. But, of course, you should never use a word unless you are confident that its meaning will be clear to your reader.

Revising for the Last Time

Ideally, you should consolidate your revisions in a second draft, preferably a rough typed copy. If you set this second draft aside for a day and then come back to it, you will certainly find that there are more changes you want to make. Once again you will want to examine the organization, the transitions, the paragraphing, the sentences, and the choice of words, making changes directly on the draft. Some students run into difficulty at this stage. They are unable to complete their revisions because they feel there is always more to be done, always something more they can do to improve their paper. While it is true that no writer ever produces the perfect paper, there must come a time when you realistically judge that you have done all you can to improve the paper in the time allowed. Three important steps in revision remain:

1. Check and correct spelling, looking up any words of which you are unsure.
2. Check and correct punctuation, reading through once concentrating on punctuation and capitalization. Use the rules in chapter 10 for guidance.
3. Make final alterations in the documentation. If you are using documentary notes—a number after each reference corresponding to an endnote placed after the main body of your paper or to a footnote placed at the bottom of the page—you are ready to put in the numbers as soon as you are sure that there will be no more rearranging, deleting, or adding of material. This is usually one of the last steps before you type the final copy. It is also a good idea to check your sources against your note cards to see if you have made any errors in page numbers, quotations, or other details.

Examples of Revision

The following passages show the process of revision. The typed passages were taken directly from rough drafts, and the revisions are indicated in longhand.

1. From Michael Gold's paper:

~~It was~~ Leonard Rosenman, the musical director of <u>Rebel</u>,

~~who~~ suggested the thirty-one-year-old Stewart Stern *who* ~~as a~~

worked with
~~replacement for Shulman. At last~~ Ray ~~had found a collaborator~~
film was finished, bringing
~~whom he could work with~~ until the end. ~~Apparently it was Stern~~
together the ideas of previous writers with his own.
~~who synthesized the various ideas that fed into the finished~~

~~script.~~

Note how Michael has reduced the number of words, simplified the language, and generally made the original passage more readable.

2. From Sara Maxfield's paper:

The characters of Morrison and Walker relate differently
~~Another difference in the two novels lies in the~~ way the

~~characters relate~~ to time and their place in history.
Both are relatively short novels made up of a
~~Neither novel is long, and both are constructed from a~~
brief chapters,
series of ~~short individual parts that form the chapters. Both~~
                                      using   *a*
~~are~~ told in the third person, and ~~use~~ the name of ~~the~~ female
character
~~protagonist~~ for the title.

Note how Sara changed her first clause from negative to positive, reduced the number of words, and simplified the whole sentence.

3. From David Harris's paper:

is no single solution to the nuclear threat or to
There ~~must be many approaches to solving~~ the problems
it
that ~~the nuclear threat~~ causes for children and adolescents,
but significant aspect of any set of solutions)   *Although*
~~and~~ one ~~solution~~ must be education. ~~There are those who think~~
some people argue
that ~~young people~~ should be shielded from the horrible facts

of the nuclear threat ~~and of what a nuclear war would be like~~,
                                          even small children
~~but~~ most people realize that it is impossible to shield ~~them~~

from that knowledge.

Note how David has clarified his argument.

4. From Carol Garcia's paper:

One way to bring sunlight into a building is

~~The simplest method of passive solar heating is called~~

~~direct gain. Heat radiation from the sun enters a living space~~
a method known as direct gain.

~~directly, preferably~~ through south-facing windows ~~and is~~

Sunlight passes through the windows and is absorbed
~~absorbed~~ by objects ~~in the building~~ or parts of the building,

Effective solar buildings usually
which convert it into heat. ~~To make effective use of direct~~

~~gain, building designs must~~ have ~~at least~~ one of these

features: heavy walls constructed of brick or masonry, floors

Containers of
made of brick or tile over concrete, or large ~~receptacles~~

~~containing~~ water ~~and placed~~ within the living space.

Note how Carol has clarified this passage by being more direct.

A Sample Short Paper

COMPOSITION

Linda Orton was asked to write a short documented paper of no more than four pages on some aspect of the life of Eleanor Roosevelt, focusing on a single interest or achievement. With only two weeks to complete the assignment, Linda knew that she had to choose a topic quickly and to concentrate on material related to that topic. After reading the article on Eleanor Roosevelt in the *Encyclopedia Americana*, Linda chose to study her early accomplishments before she became First Lady. She consulted the card catalog under "Roosevelt, Eleanor" and found three books that contained considerable material on this period; and with the help of the *New York Times Index*, she found several articles about her work for women. Linda decided to concentrate on Roosevelt's efforts to help women: her work for charities, her attitude toward suffrage, and her involvement in women's political groups.

This decision helped Linda direct her reading, but when she finished her research, she found that she had taken notes in several areas that did not directly relate to her chosen topic. Yet she still thought she might be able to use some of that very interesting information. Her first rough draft included information about Roosevelt's parents and her education, as well as speculation about what motivated her to live as she did. This first draft was too long and unorganized.

Linda decided to cut the parts about Roosevelt's childhood and her psychological development. She was then able to concentrate on Roosevelt's public accomplishments. Her second draft, however, was still not focused enough.

REVISION

Revision often involves excluding information that may be very interesting, but that is really irrelevant to the research topic. The passages below show one student revising by eliminating material that is not directly related to her topic.

Original: Among the young men who were attracted to Eleanor was Franklin Roosevelt. Soon they were secretly engaged. Their engagement coincided with Eleanor's increasing interest in social reform, which resulted in her going to work in a settlement house in one of New York's slum districts.

Revision: In 1902, at about the time she became involved with Franklin, Eleanor began to work as a volunteer at the Rivington Street Settlement House in one of New York's slum districts.

Original: For some years after she was married, Eleanor's life was filled with raising her five children, meeting the demands of her domineering mother-in-law, and running a complicated household.

Revision: For some years after she was married, Eleanor was occupied with family obligations.

Linda finally decided to outline the main points that had to do with Eleanor Roosevelt's public activities in behalf of women. When she did this a clear thesis sentence emerged: "Her many activities included work to improve the lot of disadvantaged women and to help all women develop their potential."

Linda Orton
Professor Kearns
English 102
January 29, 1984

Eleanor Roosevelt: Blazing a Trail for Women

Eleanor Roosevelt was the First Lady of the United
States for some twelve years, but she was much more than
that. Long before she became First Lady, she was working
for a better society: Her many activities included work
to improve the lot of disadvantaged women and to help all
women develop their potential. In 1902, at about the time
she became involved with Franklin Roosevelt, she began to
work as a volunteer at the Rivington Street Settlement
House in one of New York's slum districts. There she
taught young women who could not regularly attend school
due to their long working hours. This experience,
Eleanor's first extended contact with poverty and its
demands, helped shape her social conscience, according to
Joseph Lash (E&F 98); it also exposed Franklin to real
poverty for the first time (E&F 135).

For some years after she was married, Eleanor was
occupied with family obligations. As Franklin's career
developed, she assumed more of the responsibilities of the
wife of a government official. During this time, she did
not join the widespread movement to help women get the
vote. Even when Franklin voiced his support for women's
suffrage in 1911, Eleanor "considered men superior
beings" (E&F 173), and she remained--in Joseph Lash's
words--"anti-suffragette, and vigorously so" (E&F 168).

Thesis sentence

Note short quotations integrated into paraphrase

World War I offered Eleanor the opportunity to re-enter public life. As head of the Naval Department knitting project, she supervised more than forty groups of women who knitted woolen clothing for soldiers (E&F 213). In the first volume of her autobiography, This Is My Story, Eleanor writes that it was her war work and her activities immediately following the war that caused her to change her ideas about women's suffrage: "Soon after [ratification of the Nineteenth Amendment] I undertook work which proved to me the value of the vote. I became a much more ardent citizen and feminist than anyone . . . would have dreamed possible" (297).

Note use of ellipsis to indicate omission from quotation

After the war, Eleanor took projects specifically concerned with bettering the lot of women and helping them develop their full potential. Her interest in education led her to purchase Todhunter, a school for girls. There she taught a variety of subjects and struggled to help her students see beyond their own narrow world (E&F 306-308). During this time, she continued to work for social reform, specifically for shorter working hours and better working conditions for women. Her concern for women's welfare and an increasing recognition of her abilities helped her to rise rapidly to responsible positions in several organizations, including the Women's Trade Union League and the League of Women Voters (E&F 281).

Eleanor found that the various parts of her rich life enhanced each other. Through her work in women's organizations, she made friends and learned skills that proved invaluable in her later work:

Quotation of more than four typed lines is indented 10 spaces

   Eleanor not only made friends but she learned
   by doing, a title she used in one of her last

books. These friendships and activities did not
replace but supplemented her life at home,
running a large household and bringing up five
children to whom she had to be father as well
as mother. (<u>Love</u>, <u>E</u> 85)
This incredibly competent woman, however, was more than
teacher, social reformer, and homemaker.

After Franklin contracted polio in August 1921,
Eleanor's activities took a pronounced political turn.
During his convalescence, she assumed the responsibility
of keeping the Roosevelt name before the public (Hareven
20). But she did not give up her work to help women play a
significant role in society.

Eleanor began to see suffrage as a means for
achieving specific goals: Having gained the vote, women
now had the duty to work for political power and to work
for social reform through the system. In 1921 Eleanor
joined the women's division of the New York Democratic
State Committee. Other members quickly recognized her
organizational abilities, and she soon headed the
division's finance committee (Hareven 26–29).

Joseph Lash concludes that by 1924 Eleanor Roosevelt
was one of the leading politicians of the state of New
York (<u>Love</u>, <u>E</u> 86). On 16 April of that year, the <u>New York
Times</u> reported that she had helped win the fight for the
right of women to choose their own representatives at the
state convention ("Democratic Women Win"). She also
worked to incorporate issues of concern to women in the
New York State Democratic platform (<u>Love</u>, <u>E</u> 88). The
following year, Eleanor took part in the fight before the
New York State legislature for a forty-eight-hour work
week for women ("Women at Odds"), and she continued to

Only a single
parenthetical ref-
erence needed
since all facts in
paragraph are
from the same
source

battle industrial lobbyists on this issue in 1926 and
1927 (E&F 310).

During these years, Eleanor Roosevelt worked to
increase women's involvement in national politics. In
1924 she led the struggle to include women's issues in
the Democratic platform at the National Convention
("Democratic Women to Help"). In 1928 she headed the
bureau of women's activities of the Democratic National
Committee and directed the national women's campaign for
Al Smith, the party's nominee for president ("Mrs. F. D.
Roosevelt").

In 1928 Franklin was elected governor of the state
of New York, and Eleanor found herself with new
responsibilities as the wife of the governor. While she
felt that she should no longer hold official positions in
certain organizations, especially within the Democratic
party, Eleanor continued to work for women's rights and
social reform (Rice 5). On a national radio broadcast in
1929 called "Women in Politics," she advised women to
get involved in politics and to "work a little harder
than men" since they "have a new trail to blaze" ("Mrs.
Roosevelt Prepares").

Eleanor Roosevelt is widely recognized for her
aggressive and creative approach to her responsibilities
as the wife of the president of the United States. A

Final paragraph is Linda's own conclusion

little investigation reveals, however, that she was an
independent thinker and a leader in her own right. She
blazed many trails through the wilderness of social
injustice; her work with women and for women formed one
of those trails.

WORKS CITED

"Democratic Women to Help on Platform." New York
    Times 31 March 1924: 2.
"Democratic Women Win." New York Times 16 April
    1924: 2.
Hareven, Tamara K. Eleanor Roosevelt: An American
    Conscience. Chicago: Quadrangle Books, 1968.
Lash, Joseph P. Eleanor and Franklin. New York:
    Norton, 1971. Referred to in the text as
    E&F.
----------. Love, Eleanor. Garden City, N.Y.:
    Doubleday, 1982. Referred to in the text as
    Love, E.
"Mrs. F. D. Roosevelt Urges Peace Work." New
    York Times 4 Aug. 1928: 4.
"Mrs. Roosevelt Prepares to Unite Democratic
Women." New York Times 9 Nov. 1929: 25.

Roosevelt, Eleanor. This Is My Story. New York:
    Harper Bros., 1937.
Rice, Diana. "Mrs. Roosevelt Takes on Another
    Task." New York Times 2 Dec. 1928, sec. V:
    5.
"Women at Odds on 48-Hour Bill." New York Times
    26 Feb. 1925: 23.

EXERCISES

A. Note the thesis sentence of Michael Gold's paper on *Rebel without a Cause* beginning on page 172. How much can you cut out of the paper that does not directly relate to the thesis? Practice your revision skills by trying to shorten this paper.

For students who have organized their notes

B. Write a paragraph—perhaps one that would be appropriate as an introductory paragraph to your research paper—which explains the main findings of your research. Set it aside and come back later to revise it.

C. Write a sentence that reduces your findings to a single controlling idea.

D. Imagine your readers. Write a paragraph in which you indicate the kind of readers you are writing for—how much they know about your topic, how interested they are, and what you will need to explain for your research to make sense.

E. Write or type a rough draft, skipping lines to leave room for revision.

For students who have finished a draft

F. After setting your draft aside for at least a few hours, go over it and mark passages that need to be reorganized, sentences that can be improved, and words that should be replaced.

G. Go through your draft and cut unnecessary words and shorten lengthy sentences.

H. Reread the section on revising in this chapter, make a check list for revising your own draft, and go through your paper again, doing all you can to improve it.

9

DOCUMENTING SOURCES

There are different ways to document written reports of research findings, but all have the same purpose: to make the source of such findings perfectly clear to the reader. The differences in documentation styles are mainly small details of capitalization, underlining, and spacing, but it is important that you use a style that is appropriate for your subject and acceptable to your instructor. It is also important to use only one style for each research paper and to be consistent about the smallest details so that your reader will know exactly what each item means.

Choosing a Documentation Style

The style used in this chapter—known as the MLA style since it is recommended by the Modern Language Association—is appropriate for papers in English, philosophy, history, and other disciplines in the humanities; and it will be acceptable to some instructors whatever your topic might be. For his paper on *Rebel without a Cause*, Michael Gold followed the style recommended by the Modern Language Association. He compiled a list of sources and cited all references in an abbreviated form in parentheses in the text of his paper. Sara Maxfield also followed the MLA style, but at the request of her instructor, she used both a list of sources and documentary footnotes. Because she frequently quoted from two novels, Sara cited each novel with an abbreviation and gave the page number in the text itself.

When necessary, other instructors will direct you to a style commonly used by researchers in the particular subject you are studying. David Harris followed the author/date system recommended by the *Publication Manual of the American Psychological Association*. David also provided a complete list of references at the end of his paper—with some slight differences of details from those used by Sara and Michael. He identified the author, the publication date, and, when appropriate, the page number in the text of his paper, using parentheses when needed. Carol Garcia numbered her sources, listed them alphabetically at the end, and identified each by appropriately placing its number in the text. Carol followed the simple number system used in many scientific disciplines and adapted it to her own needs. When she used a source several times, she included in the textual citation the page number as well as the number of the source.

All four students were careful to be consistent, that is, to cite the same kinds of sources in the same way each time they were used. If you understand the conventions used in all four papers, you will have two valuable skills: the ability to document appropriately any paper you write and the ability to interpret the documentation of articles and books that you read.

Deciding What to Document

As you write your paper, you should keep in mind from the beginning that literally everything you take from your sources must be documented. Not only must you make perfectly clear to your readers the exact source of quotations and paraphrases of your sources, but also where you have found ideas, concepts, and the smallest facts. You must give credit for a concept like the relationship of a film to the culture that produced it as well as for a fact like the particular kind of sports car that James Dean drove. The only material that does not need documentation is information that most people would consider to be general knowledge—widely known facts, such as the fact that Dean was a famous movie actor.

PARENTHETICAL AND TEXTUAL DOCUMENTATION

A list of works cited at the end of the paper must be supplemented by references both in the running text of the paper and in parentheses at the end of sentences and paragraphs. How you cite sources within your paper should be determined by what you want to stress, the need to make your references as clear and concise as possible, and your effort to vary sentence structure to avoid boring repetition. Sometimes you may choose to mention the author's name at the beginning of a sentence or paragraph; at other times, you may place the author's name along with the page number of a source in parentheses at the end. Place the parenthetical reference at the end of a clause or sentence. When all of the information in a paragraph comes from the same part of a single source, you may place the parenthetical reference at the end of the paragraph.

In every case, you should make it clear which source you are citing. For example, if there is only one work in the bibliography by an author, then you need only cite the author's name and a page number. If there are two sources by the same author, however, you must include both the author's name and the title—or shortened title—of the work to which you are referring. For each source you cite, the parenthetical citation combined with any information in the text identifying the source should be as brief and unambiguous as possible, making it perfectly clear to the reader which item in the bibliography is being cited. The first item in a bibliographic citation—author, editor, translator, speaker, performer, director, title, or some other entry—must appear either in the text or in parentheses in order for readers to find it easily.

The following sentences suggest various ways to document your sources within the text of the paper.

1. Author's name in the text:

> Stephen B. Oates goes even further in exploring the consequences of childhood experiences on Martin Luther King, Jr.'s development (1–17).

Note: When there is only one work by an author in the list of works cited, it is not necessary to mention the title in the text.

2. Title and author's name in text:

> In Eleanor and Franklin, his best-selling, Pulitzer Prize-winning biography, Joseph Lash explains Eleanor Roosevelt's role in the League of Women Voters (355).

Note: To stress the importance of a source, use the title in the text.

3. Author's name in a text using more than one source by that author:

> Joseph Lash concludes that by 1924 Eleanor Roosevelt was one of the leading politicians of the state of New York (Love, E 86).

Note: When there are two or more sources by the same author in the list of works cited, indicate the title, or an easily understood abbreviation of the title, in the parenthetical reference.

4. Author's name in text preceding a quotation:

> The film has what Kreidl calls "a disparate smattering of different vocabularies from different sources" (86).

5. Author's name in parenthetical reference:

> Once the actors went to work, the script continued to
> evolve, with James Dean, in particular, creating as he acted
> (Kreidl 86).

6. Author's name in parenthetical reference when there is more than one citation by the author:

> After the publication of her first book, it became clear
> that Eleanor Roosevelt would have considerable influence on
> women's efforts to gain political power (Lash, E&F 517).

7. Author's name introducing an indented quotation:

> Ezra Goodman wrote of the public response to the death of
> James Dean:
>> The U.S. is currently in the throes of a movie fan
>> craze for a dead man that surpasses in fervor and
>> morbidity even the hysterical mass mourning that
>> attended the death of Rudolph Valentino in the dim
>> past of the movies. The object of this posthumuous
>> adulation is James Dean . . . who died at 24 in the
>> wreck of his Porsche sports car a year ago this
>> month. (75)

8. Volume number mentioned in text:

> In the fifth volume of Children of Crisis, Robert Coles
> tells the story of a young girl who had the habit of staring
> absently at a cemetery (549).

9. Volume number is parenthetical reference:

> Robert Coles tells the story of a young girl who had the
> habit of staring absently at a cemetery (5: 548–551).

10. More than one author's name in text:

> Davidson and Lytle note the difficulty historians have
> explaining the decisions that led to the bombing of Hiroshima
> (353).

Note: For sources with three authors, use all three last names; for more than three authors, use the last name of the first followed by et al., as in the list of works cited.

11. More than one author's name in parenthetical reference:

> Historians attempting to explain the events leading up to
> the bombing of Hiroshima are faced with a formidable task
> (Davidson and Lytle 319-353).

12. A work listed by title:

> Eleanor Roosevelt took part in the fight before the New
> York State legislature for a forty-eight-hour week for women
> ("Women at Odds").

Note: There is no need to include the page number for articles that are only one page long since the page is included in the bibliography or for alphabetized sources, such as dictionaries or encyclopedias.

13. An article listed by title from a periodical mentioned in the text:

> On 16 April of that year, the New York Times reported
> that she had helped win the fight for the right of women to
> choose their own representatives at the state convention
> ("Democratic Women Win").

14. An entire work:

> In the first volume of her autobiography, This is My
> Story, Eleanor Roosevelt explains how she changed her mind
> about suffrage and became an advocate for women's rights.

Note: To cite an entire work rather than a particular part, it is preferable to use the author's name in the text. In such cases, there is no need for a parenthetical reference.

15. More than one work in a single parenthetical reference:

> In recent years, scholars have examined the place of
> Rebel without a Cause in American film history (Biskind; Cook
> 427).

Note: Cite each work exactly as if it were cited alone; separate citations with a semicolon.

The List of Sources or Bibliography

The following form for the list of sources—also called the bibliography—is based on the MLA Handbook (1984). For advice on using the APA style (1983), turn to chapter 12. For the scientific number system, turn to chapter 13.

WHAT TO INCLUDE

To decide what to include in a list of sources, sort your bibliography cards into three stacks: (1) those you actually cited in the text of your paper; (2) those that helped you understand your topic, but that you did not actually cite; and (3) those that you either did not consult or that were not helpful. Eliminate the third category. In some cases, you may decide to list only those works you actually cited; and in others you may want to include the second group, whether as part of a single alphabetized list or as a separate list, by dividing your sources into "References Cited" and "Other References Consulted."

HOW TO ARRANGE YOUR SOURCES

Sources should be listed alphabetically by the last name of the author or, when there is no author, by the first word of the title, excluding *a*, *an*, or *the*. When you have more than one work by the same author, give the name in the first entry only. For his or her other works, substitute ten hyphens and a period for the name and arrange the titles alphabetically. Occasionally, you may be instructed to separate your sources according to books, articles, and other sources; to arrange them chronologically according to publication date; or to present them in the order that they appear in the text.

PLACEMENT AND FORMAT

A list of sources is placed at the end of a research paper—after the notes or, for papers that do not have endnotes, immediately after the last page of the text. Begin the list on a new page with a title two inches from the top. Skip three lines, and start each entry flush with the left margin. Lines after the first of each entry are indented five spaces, and the entire list is double-spaced. Do not number the items unless you are consistently following the scientific number system (see chapter 13).

A complete list of sources placed at the end of your paper will allow you to clarify your sources simply by placing a shortened form of the citation—the author's last name, a brief title, or an abbreviation—in parentheses in the appropriate place in the text of your paper.

When you quote frequently from the same text, you may want to use an abbreviation: *S* for *Sula* or *MSND* for *A Midsummer Night's Dream*. Indicate this abbreviation at the end of the bibliographic citation: "Referred to in the text as *MSND*."

Compiling a List of Sources

Every book in your list of sources should include any of the following information that is available: author, title, place of publication, publisher, and date of publication. Many sources will require additional information such as multiple or corporate authors, the name of an editor or translator, the edition, the part of a work cited, or other particular information needed to identify the exact source used. In addition to books, you may need to list portions of books, periodicals, other written sources, and non-print sources as well. The following list of examples should provide you with a model for documenting any item you need to include in your list of sources.

BOOKS

1. A book with one author:

   Abrams, M. H. The Mirror and the Lamp. New York: Oxford UP,
        1953.

2. Two or more books by the same author:

   Lash, Joseph P. Eleanor and Franklin. New York: Norton,
        1971.

   --- Love, Eleanor. Garden City, NY: Doubleday, 1982.

   Note: If the author of one book is also the first of two or more authors of a following book, you must repeat the name, since the three hyphens stand only for the author of the preceding source:

Ellmann, Richard. <u>James Joyce</u>. 2nd ed. New York: Oxford UP,
    1982.

---, ed. <u>The New Oxford Book of American Verse</u>. New York:
    Oxford UP, 1976.

Ellmann, Richard, and Robert O'Clair, eds. <u>The Norton
    Anthology of Modern Poetry</u>. New York: Norton, 1973.

3. A book with two authors:

Davidson, James W., and Mark Lytle. <u>After the Fact</u>. New
    York: Knopf, 1982.

4. A book with three authors:

Kahn, Herman, William Brown, and Leon Martel. <u>The Next 200
    Years</u>. New York: William Morrow, 1976.

5. A book with more than three authors:

Bailyn, Bernard, et al. <u>The Great Republic: A History of the
    American People</u>. Lexington, MA: Heath, 1977.

Note: The abbreviation "et al." stands for "and others."

6. A book with a corporate author:

U.S. Department of Energy. <u>An Assessment of Thermal Insulation
    Materials</u>. Washington, DC: GPO, 1978.

Note: GPO is an abbreviation for Government Printing Office.

7. A book with an anonymous author:

<u>Writers' and Artists' Yearbook, 1980</u>. London: Adam and Charles
    Black, 1980.

8. A book with an author using a pseudonym (a fictitious name):

Innes, Michael [J. I. M. Stewart]. <u>Going It Alone</u>. New York:
    Dodd, 1980.

Note: The author's real name may be supplied in brackets.

9. A scholarly edition:

```
Dickens, Charles. Oliver Twist. Ed. Kathleen Tillotson. The
    Clarendon Dickens. Oxford: Clarendon, 1966.
```

Note: If the work of the editor is being discussed, this should be cited as follows:

```
Tillotson, Kathleen, ed. Oliver Twist. By Charles Dickens.
    The Clarendon Dickens. Oxford: Clarendon, 1966.
```

10. A work in a series:

```
Reiman, Donald H. Shelley's "The Triumph of Life": A Critical
    Study. Illinois Studies in Lang. and Lit. 55. Urbana: U
    of Illinois P, 1965.
```

11. A single work published in more than one volume (with continuous pagination):

```
Johnson, Edgar. Sir Walter Scott: The Great Unknown. 2 vols.
    London: Hamish Hamilton, 1970.
```

12. A book that is part of a multivolume work with a single title:

```
Kettle, Arnold. An Introduction to the English Novel. 2
    vols. London: Hutchinson U Library, 1953. Vol. 2.
```

13. A book that is part of a multivolume work by one author when each volume has a separate title:

```
Coles, Robert. Privileged Ones. Vol. 5 of Children of Crisis.
    5 vols. Boston: Little, 1977.
```

14. A book that is part of a multivolume work when each volume has a separate title and author:

```
Stewart, J. I. M. Eight Modern Writers. Vol. 12 of Oxford
    History of English Literature. 12 vols. Oxford: Oxford
    UP, 1963.
```

15. A book with different authors for each chapter and a single editor:

    Hoffman, Daniel, ed. <u>Harvard Guide to Contemporary American
        Writing</u>. Cambridge, MA: Harvard UP, 1979.

16. A reprint of an older edition:

    Stead, Christina. <u>The Man Who Loved Children</u>. 1940. New
        York: Holt, 1965.

17. A paperback reprint of a hardback edition:

    Brown, Rosellen. <u>Civil Wars</u>. 1984. New York: Penguin, 1985.

    Note: The date, but not the publisher, of the first edition is given
    immediately after the title.

18. A revised edition:

    Ellmann, Richard. <u>James Joyce</u>. 2nd ed. New York: Oxford UP,
        1982.

19. A revised version of a work of literature:

    Fowles, John. <u>The Magus</u>. Rev. version. Boston: Little,
        1977.

20. A translation:

    Homer. <u>The Iliad</u>. Trans. Richmond Lattimore. Chicago: U of
        Chicago P, 1951.

    Note: If the work of the translator is being discussed, this should be
    cited as follows:

    Lattimore, Richmond, trans. <u>The Iliad</u>. By Homer. Chicago: U
        of Chicago P, 1951.

21. Sacred writings:

    Bible
    Bible, Revised Standard Version

```
Old Testament
Talmud
Koran
Song of Solomon
```

Note: Sacred writings are neither underlined nor placed in quotation marks. Unless otherwise indicated, references to the Bible or books of the Bible are assumed to refer to the King James Version. Indicate the particular book, chapter, and verse of the Bible in parentheses in the text of your paper:

(Gen. 20:1–17)

PARTS OF BOOKS

1. An article, essay, chapter, or other part of a book with a single author:

```
Lessing, Doris.  "The Temptation of Jack Orkney."  In Stories.
    New York: Knopf, 1978.  564-625.
```

2. An introduction, afterword, preface, or foreword to a book written by someone other than the book's author:

```
Walker, Alice.  Afterword.  I Love Myself: A Zora Neale Hurston
    Reader.  Ed. Alice Walker.  Old Westbury, NY: The Feminist
    Press, 1979.  297-313.
```

3. A previously published essay or article from a collection of writings by different authors:

```
Abrams, M. H.  "The Correspondent Breeze."  Kenyon Review  19
    (1957): 113-30. Rpt. in  English Romantic Poets.  Ed. M.
    H. Abrams.  New York: Oxford UP, 1960.  37-54.
```

4. An essay or article from a collection of works not previously published:

```
Brutus, Dennis.  "English and the Dynamics of South African
    Creative Writing."  English Literature: Opening up the
    Canon.  Selected Papers from the English Institute, 1979,
    New Series 4.  Ed. Leslie A. Fiedler and Houston Baker,
    Jr.  Baltimore: Johns Hopkins UP, 1981.  1-14.
```

5. A short story or poem from an anthology:

```
Herbert George.  "The Flower."  Seventeenth-Century Prose and
    Poetics.  Ed. Alexander M. Witherspoon and Frank J.
    Warnke.  2nd ed.  New York: Harcourt, 1963.  857.
Pope, Alexander.  "The Rape of the Lock."  The Norton
    Anthology of World Masterpieces.  Ed. Maynard Mack et al.
    5th ed.  2 vols.  New York: Norton, 1985.  2: 305-326.
```

6. A novel or play from an anthology:

```
Morrison, Toni.  Sula.  In The Norton Introduction to the
    Short Novel.  Ed. Jerome Beaty.  New York: Norton, 1982.
    581-660.
```

7. Afterword, preface, introduction, or other editorial comment on individual pieces in a collection:

```
Beaty, Jerome.  Afterword to Sula.  In The Norton Introduction
    to the Short Novel.  Ed. Jerome Beaty.  New York: Norton,
    1982.  661-66.
```

8. An unsigned article in a widely known reference work:

```
"Solar Energy."  The New Columbia Encyclopedia.  4th ed.
    1975.
```

9. A signed article in a widely known reference work:

```
Suber, Howard.  "Motion Picture."  Encyclopedia Americana.
    1981 ed.
```

10. An article in a specialized, less familiar reference work:

```
Monro, D. H.  "William Godwin."  The Encyclopedia of
    Philosophy.  Ed. Paul Edwards.  8 vols.  New York:
    Macmillan, 1967.  3: 358-362.
```

PERIODICALS

1. A signed article from a daily newspaper divided into sections paginated separately:

Benjamin, Milton R.   "U.S. Is Allowing Argentina to Buy
      Critical A-System."   <u>Washington Post</u> 19 July 1982: A1+.

Note: For newspapers divided into sections with the section designa-
   tion used as part of the page number, give the page number as it
   appears on the page (see number 1 above). For newspapers that
   are paginated continuously, give date, edition if there is one, and
   page number (see number 2 below). For newspapers divided
   into numbered sections, give date followed by a comma, then
   the abbreviation "sec." and the section number, a colon, and
   page number (see number 3 below).

2. A signed article from a daily newspaper paginated continuously:

Lelyveld, Joseph.   "V. S. Pritchett, in Step with the Years,
      Writes On."   <u>New York Times</u> 16 Dec. 1985, natl. ed.: 4.

Note: Some newspapers are published in more than one edition, and
   the pagination varies from one to another. Indicate the edition if
   it is specified on the masthead at the top of the first page.

3. An unsigned article from a daily newspaper:

"Soviet Group Presses for Broader Arms 'Dialog.' "   <u>New York
      Times</u> 5 Sept. 1982, Sec. 1: 16.

4. A signed article from a weekly magazine or newspaper:

Bettelheim, Bruno.   "Reflections: Freud and the Soul."   <u>New
      Yorker</u> 1 March 1982: 52+.

Note: Use "+" for an article that begins in one part of a periodical and
   continues elsewhere.

Lewis, James.   "Jobless Reality Fails to Impress Thatcher's
      Cabinet."   <u>Manchester Guardian Weekly</u> 5 Sept. 1982: 3.

5. An unsigned article from a weekly publication:

"Computers."   <u>Time</u> 2 Aug. 1982: 72.

6. A serialized article:

> Broad, William J.   "Science Showmanship: A Deep 'Star Wars'
>   Rift."   New York Times 16 Dec. 1985, natl. ed.: 1+.   Pt.
>   2 of a series begun on 15 Dec. 1985.

Note: If author and title are the same for all the articles in the series,
give only one citation, indicating the dates and pages at the end.
With the same author and different titles, give separate citations,
using three hyphens in place of the author's name for all citations after the first. With different authors, give separate
citations.

7. A signed editorial:

> Smith, Gerard.   "Toward Arms Control."   Editorial.   New York
>   Times 29 June 1982: A23.

8. An unsigned editorial:

> "Tuition Subsidies Are Not Benign."   Editorial.   New York
>   Times 3 July 1982: 20.

9. An article from a monthly magazine:

> Greider, William.   "The Education of David Stockman."
>   Atlantic Dec. 1981: 27-54.

10. An article in a journal with pages numbered continuously through
each volume:

> Gelfant, Blanche H.   "Mingling and Sharing in American
>   Literature: Teaching Ethnic Fiction."   College English
>   43 (1981): 763-72.

Note: The numbers after the title of the journal refer to the volume
number, the date, and the pages of the article cited.

11. An article in a journal that numbers pages separately for each issue:

> Sprague, Clare.   "Dialectic and Counter-Dialectic in the
>   Martha Quest Novels."   Journal of Commonwealth Literature
>   14 (1979): 39-52.

Note: Where there is no volume number, treat the issue number as though it were a volume number.

Biskind, Peter. "Rebel without a Cause: Nicholas Ray in the Fifties." Film Quarterly 28.5 (1974): 32-38.

Note: The numbers following the journal title refer to the volume (28) and issue (5).

12. A signed review with a title:

Berger, Peter L. "A Woman of This Century." Rev. of Hannah Arendt: For Love of the World, by Elizabeth Young Bruehl. New York Times Book Review 25 April 1982: 1, 20-21.

13. A signed, untitled review:

Harrison, John F. C. Rev. of The Age of Capital, 1848-1875, by E. J. Hobsbawm. Victorian Studies 20 (1977): 423-25.

14. An unsigned, untitled review:

Rev. of The French Lieutenant's Woman, by John Fowles. Times Literary Supplement 12 June 1969: 629.

15. A letter to the editor:

Flint, R. W. Letter. New Republic 18 Feb. 1957: 23.

16. A response to a letter or letters:

Lemann, Nicholas. Reply to letters of Roger Williams and Virginia K. Williams. Atlantic Dec. 1984: 14.

17. A speech or address for a special occasion printed in a periodical:

Morrison, Toni. "Address to the American Writers Congress." 9 Oct. 1981. In Nation 24 Oct. 1981: 396-412.

18. An article from *Dissertation Abstracts* or *Dissertation Abstracts International:*

Webb, John Bryan. "Utopian Fantasy and Social Change, 1600-1660." DA 43 (1982): 8214250 (State U of New York at Buffalo).

19. An article from a volume of abstracts:

> Johnstone, John W. C. "Who Controls the News." <u>American Journal of Sociology</u> 87 (1982): 1174-81. Abstract from <u>America: History and Life</u> 20. A (1983): no. 2120.

20. An article from a newsletter:

> Cliggott, Douglas. "Proposed Tax Reform Will Have Negative Effect on Capital Investment." <u>Business Executive Expectations</u> Third Quarter 1985:2.
>
> "Mathematics Credit for Computer Courses." NCTM News Bulletin. 22.2 (1985): n pag.
>
> "Report of Recent Events." <u>American Studies International Newsletter</u>. Aug. 1985: 1.

Note: Newsletters may not include volume and issue numbers, dates, or even pagination. Some, like the first item above, are only one sheet, so there is no need to indicate the absence of pagination as in the second citation. In cases where a publication does not employ the usual conventions needed for a citation, adapt what information you have to a form as close as possible to that of a conventional periodical citation, making sure that you provide enough information for readers to find the source. For example, the first citation uses "Third Quarter" to indicate the particular issue since there is no volume number or specific data given.

OTHER WRITTEN SOURCES

1. The published proceedings of a conference:

> <u>Conserving the Historical and Cultural Landscape</u>. Proc. of the Conference of the National Trust for Historic Preservation, Western Region. 2-3 May 1975. Denver, CO Washington, DC: Preservation Press, 1975.

2. A government publication:

> Office of the Federal Register. <u>United States Government Manual, 1980-81</u>. Washington, DC: GPO, 1980.

3. A legal reference:

Brown v. Board of Education of Topeka.   347 US 483.   US Supreme
    Court, 1954.

4. A pamphlet:

Saltman, Jules.   Teenagers and Alcohol: Patterns and Dangers.
    New York: Public Affairs Comm., 1983.

Note: A pamphlet is treated like a book.

5. A volume of published letters:

Wilson, Elena, ed.   Edmund Wilson: Letters on Literature and
    Politics, 1912-1972.   New York: Farrar, 1977.

6. A letter printed in a volume of collected letters:

Wilson, Edmund.   "To William Faulkner."   25 Sept. 1956.   In
    Letters on Literature and Politics: 1912–1972.   Ed. Elena
    Wilson.   New York: Farrar, 1977.   540.

7. An unpublished letter from a collection:

Stevenson, Adlai E.   Letter to Ralph McGill.   11 May 1954.
    Ralph McGill Papers.   Emory University, Atlanta, GA.

8. Personal letters:

Paley, Grace.   Letter to author.   30 July 1981.

9. A dissertation:

Gray, Donald Joseph.   "Victorian Verse Humor."   Diss. Ohio
    State U, 1956.

10. A document from an information service:

Delker, Paul V.   Adult Education--1980 and Beyond.   Occasional
    Paper No. 59.   Columbus: Ohio State U, 1979.   ERIC ED 189
    309.

11. A manuscript or typescript:

Crane, Hart. Manuscript of <u>The Bridge</u>. Hart Crane Collection.
Columbia University, New York.

NON-PRINT SOURCES

1. A lecture or publicly delivered paper:

Levine, George. "George Eliot's Scientific Ideal: The
Hypothesis of Reality." English Institute. Cambridge,
MA, 1 Sept. 1979.

2. A radio or television program:

<u>The Doomsayers</u>. Prod. Brian Capener. PBS Special. 8 Sept.
1982.
"Maya Angelou." Narr. Bill Moyers. <u>Creativity</u>. PBS Special,
Atlanta, GA, Ch. 30. 8 Jan. 1982.

Note: When you want to refer to a particular individual (producer,
director, narrator, or actor), cite that person's name first:

Moyers, Bill, narr. "Maya Angelou." <u>Creativity</u>. PBS
Special, Atlanta, GA, Ch. 30, 8 Jan. 1982.

3. A performance of music, dance, or drama:

<u>La Bohème.</u> Cond. James Levine. With Teresa Stratas.
Metropolitan Opera. Metropolitan Opera House, New York.
13 Jan. 1982.

Note: When you want to refer to a particular individual (conductor,
director, choreographer), cite that person's name first:

Levine, James, cond. <u>La Bohème</u>. With Teresa Stratas.
Metropolitan Opera. Metropolitan Opera House, New York.
13 Jan. 1982.

4. A film:

<u>Vietnam: An American Journey</u>. Films Inc., 1979.

Rebel without a Cause. Dir. Nicholas Ray. With James Dean,
    Sal Mineo, and Natalie Wood. Warner Brothers, 1955.

Note: When you want to refer to a particular individual, cite that person's name first:

Ray, Nicholas, dir. Rebel without a Cause. With James Dean,
    Sal Mineo, and Natalie Wood. Warner Brothers, 1955.

5. A face-to-face interview:

Creech, Dennis, Director of the Georgia Solar Coalition,
    Atlanta, GA. Personal interview. 30 Jan. 1982.

6. A telephone interview:

King, Coretta Scott. Telephone interview. 1 Nov. 1982.

7. A work of art:

Cézanne, Paul. A Modern Olympia. Louvre, Paris.

8. A work of art with a cited illustration:

Bonnard, Pierre. The Open Window. The Phillips Collection.
    Washington, DC. Illus. in Master Paintings from the
    Phillips Collection. By Eleanor Green et al. New York:
    Penghurst Books, 1981. 71.

9. A musical composition:

Handel, George Frideric. Messiah. Ed. Watkins Shaw. Novello
    Handel Edition. Sevenoaks, Eng.: Novello, n.d.

Note: Use n.d. (no date) for any undated material.

10. An audio recording:

The Police. Synchronicity. A & M, SP-3735, 1983.

11. A song referred to or quoted from an audio recording:

The Beatles. "Revolution." From The Beatles / 1967-1970.
    Capitol, SEBX-11843, 1973.

12. An audio recording when the work of the performer or performers is discussed:

> Horne, Marilyn. Orfeo ed Euridice. By Christoph Willibald
>   Gluck. Cond. Georg Solti, Orchestra and Chorus of the
>   Royal Opera House, Covent Garden. London, OSA1285, 1970.

13. A videotape or recording:

> The Nuclear Dilemma. Video recording. BBC-TV. New York:
>   Time-Life Multimedia, 1974.

14. A computer program on tape or disk:

> Ward, Richard J. The Executive Game. Computer program.
>   Bowling Green State University. Hewlett-Packard.
>   A880-2232A.

Note: Computer programs vary considerably. For this reason, you will have to adapt a citation to the information you have. When possible, you should include an author, title, place of production, company or organization producing the program, an identifying number, and date.

15. Material from a computer service:

> "Salk, Jonas Edward." American Men and Women of Science.
>   15th ed. Bowker, 1983. DIALOG 236, item 0090936.

Note: Cite material from a computer service such as DIALOG or BRS like printed material found in books and periodicals, but add a reference to the service at the end of the citation, giving the name of the service and the numbers identifying the database and the particular item from that base.

Special Cases

You will occasionally find sources that are different from any of the sample citations in this chapter. You may find, for example, a book with no date that has an author, an editor, and a translator. Privately printed material or books published in the seventeenth century may not include any publication information. To cite unusual or one-of-a-kind sources, you may have to devise your own citation, adapting the order suggested by the models above: author, title, editor, translator, place of publication, publisher, and date.

CITING MATERIAL FROM A SECONDARY SOURCE

There may be times when you will want to cite material from a book or an article that you have found in a secondary source rather than in the original. Generally, it is best to locate the original and to cite it directly; but in cases when the original is not available, you must cite the source you actually use.

For citing the source of information found in a second source:

```
Squire, James R.   The Responses of Adolescents while Reading Four
     Short Stories.   Urbana, IL: NCTE, 1964.   In David Bleich,
     Subjective Criticism.   Baltimore: Johns Hopkins UP, 1978.
     101.
```

For citing a quotation from a source other than the original.

```
Fish, Stanley E.   "Literature in the Reader: Affective
     Stylistics."   New Literary History 2 (1970): 140.   As
     quoted in David Bleich, Subjective Criticism.   Baltimore:
     Johns Hopkins UP, 1978.   122.
```

CITING TITLES WITHIN TITLES

When the title of one work is part of the title of another, you may be confused by what to underline and what to enclose in single or double quotation marks.

1. Any titles normally underlined (books, plays, films) that are part of the titles of articles are still underlined:

```
The Duchess of Malfi
"Sexual and Social Mobility in The Duchess of Malfi"
```

2. Omit underlining of titles that would normally be underlined but that are part of a book title:

```
Paradise Lost
Surprised by Sin: The Reader in Paradise Lost
```

3. Underline the titles of books that include other titles normally enclosed within quotation marks:

```
"Michael"
Ten Interpretations of Wordsworth's "Michael"
```

4. Use single quotation marks for titles normally enclosed in quotation marks that are part of the title of an article:

```
"The Drowned Man of Esthwaite"
"The Illusion of Mastery: Wordsworth's Revisions of 'The
    Drowned Man of Esthwaite'"
```

CITING TABLES AND ILLUSTRATIONS

A table or illustration should follow as closely as possible that part of the paper that it illustrates. Double-space before, after, and within tables, making ruled lines when necessary to clarify the material. Type any heading or caption at the top of the table or illustration flush with the left margin: Table 1; Fig. 1. Give the source at the bottom, also flush with the left margin:

```
Source: College English 44 (1982): 673.
```

Making an Annotated Bibliography

Occasionally an instructor will ask you to make an annotated bibliography. To do this, you simply add a brief descriptive note after the appropriate bibliographic entry. Consider the following examples:

```
Hareven, Tamara.  "Social and Political Apprenticeship,
    1920-1933."  In Eleanor Roosevelt: An American Conscience.
    Chicago: Quadrangle Books, 1968.  21-47.  This chapter is
    about Eleanor Roosevelt's initial work with social reform
    and labor groups. It outlines her development and increasing
    influence in politics and women's rights. A good, concise
    overview of these years.
Lash, Joseph P.  Eleanor and Franklin.  New York: Norton, 1971.
    A broad, reliable basis for further study, this book is a
    good place to begin a study of the Roosevelts. Lash explores
    the environments in which they were raised and covers their
    lives up until Franklin's death.
```

```
Rice, Diana. "Mrs. Roosevelt Takes on Another Task." New York
    Times 2 Dec. 1928: Sec. 5, 5. This article is based on an
    interview with Eleanor Roosevelt in which she discusses her
    coming role as First Lady of New York State. Her views on
    women in politics are particularly interesting and are
    reported in her own words.
```

USING AND INTERPRETING ABBREVIATIONS

Spell out the names of the states in the text of a research paper, but for documentation use the two-letter abbreviations recommended by the postal service (CA for California, NY for New York, for example).

Spell out the names of the months in the text of your paper, but use abbreviations in the list of works cited: Jan., Apr., Oct.

These designations are almost always indicated in abbreviated form:

AD (A.D.)   *anno Domini,* meaning "in the year of our Lord," as in AD 169
a.m.   *ante meridiem,* meaning "before noon"
BC (B.C.)   before Christ, as in 400 BC
p.m.   *post meridiem,* meaning "after noon"

The MLA recommends that in documentation you indicate publishers' names with appropriate abbreviations. Use the following samples as models:

Farrar	Farrar, Straus & Giroux
Knopf	Alfred A. Knopf, Inc.
MIT P	The MIT Press
MLA	Modern Language Association of America
NAL	New American Library, Inc.
Norton	W. W. Norton and Co., Inc.
Oxford UP	Oxford University Press, Inc.
Pocket	Pocket Books
Random	Random House, Inc.
U of Chicago P	University of Chicago Press
UP of Florida	University Presses of Florida
Viking	Viking Press, Inc.

Some of the following abbreviations are occasionally used in writing using the new streamlined MLA style; you may encounter others in your reading. It is best to refer first to the sample citations in this chapter to document your own work and to use this list for clarification and for interpreting your sources. In general, use appropriate abbreviations in documentation and brief qualifying parenthetical asides (i.e., cf., etc.). Spell out most words in the text of your paper.

abbr.	abbreviation, abbreviated
abr.	abridged, abridgment
adapt.	adapted by, adaptation
anon.	anonymous
app.	appendix
assn.	association
assoc.	associate, associated
attrib.	attributed to
b.	born
biog.	biography, biographer, biographical
bk.	book
bull.	bulletin
c. (ca)	*circa*, meaning "about" (commonly used to indicate approximate dates, as c. 1840)
cf.	*confer*, meaning "compare"
ch. (chap.)	chapter
col.	column
colloq.	colloquial (indicates informal speech)
comp.	compiled by, compiler
cond.	conducted by, conductor
(contd.)	continued
d.	died
dir.	directed by, director
diss.	dissertation
div.	division
doc.	document
ed.	edited by, editor, edition
e.g.	*exempli gratia*, meaning "for example."
et al.	*et alii*, meaning "and others." (used in citing works with more than three authors)
etc.	*et cetera*, meaning "and so forth" (Avoid using this and most other abbreviations in the text of a paper.)
ex.	example
fl.	*floruit*, meaning "flourished." (commonly used to indicate the approximate time that a person lived—usually the period of highest achievement—when birth and death dates are unknown)
ibid.	*ibidem*, meaning in the same place. (Though no longer recommended by the MLA or the APA style, this abbreviation was

	once commonly used in endnotes to indicate that a source is the same as the preceding one.)
i.e.	*id est,* meaning "that is." (Like "e.g." and "etc.," this abbreviation should be confined to parenthetical references and notes and avoided in the running text.)
illus.	illustrated by, illustrator, illustration
intro.	introduced by, introduction
l., ll.	line, lines
ms., mss.	manuscript, manuscripts
narr.	narrated by, narrator
n.d.	no date (of publication)
no.	number
obs.	obsolete
P	Press (Note UP in documentation to refer to University Press, as Oxford UP)
pref.	preface, preface by
proc.	proceedings
pseud.	pseudonym
pt.	part
rev.	revised by, revision; or review
rpt.	reprinted, by reprint
sc.	scene (used in citing passages from plays, omitted when scene and act are cited together: *Hamlet,* 2.1)
ser.	series
sic	"thus, so" (used in brackets within a quotation, or in parentheses following a quotation to indicate that an error in spelling, punctuation, or grammar is reproduced faithfully from the original)
st.	stanza
supp.	supplement
trans. (tr.)	translated by, translator, translation
U	University (note UP in documentation to indicate University Press, as Oxford UP)
UP	University Press, in documentation, as Oxford UP
v., vv.	verse, versus (vs. and vss. also used)
viz.	*videlicet,* meaning "that is" or "namely"
vol., vols.	volume, volumes
vs. (v.)	versus or against (v. is commonly used in titles of legal cases)

Content Notes

Occasionally you may want to use a note to give information that would be distracting if you included it in the text of your paper. For example, when

Carol Garcia decided to eliminate a discussion of active solar systems from her report, she could have used a content note to define active solar systems and to distinguish them from passive systems, indicating a source where further information about active solar systems could be found. Sara Maxfield includes a content note to list other works by Toni Morrison and Alice Walker; and Michael Gold notes that new technology may well change the approach of future papers on his subject.

A content note is also useful to point the reader to several sources—perhaps not included in the bibliography—where he or she can find a full discussion of a topic. Whether it occurs at the foot of a page or the end of a paper, chapter, or book, a content note is simply a note that gives information or makes a comment instead of or in addition to a normal source citation. *Warning*: Content notes should only give significant information; avoid the temptation to include interesting but irrelevant facts in notes.

EXERCISES

A. Using as a guide the MLA style represented by the examples in this chapter, write bibliographic citation for the sources below:

1. A book by Tom Wolfe entitled *The Right Stuff*, published in 1979 by Farrar, Straus & Giroux in New York.
2. An article by Dennis A. Williams entitled "Can the Schools Be Saved?" which appeared on pages 50 through 58 of the May 9, 1983, *Newsweek*.
3. A book by Douglas T. Miller and Marion Nowak entitled *The Fifties: The Way We Were*, published in New York in 1975 by Doubleday.
4. A poem by William Morris entitled "The Defense of Guenevere" in an anthology called *Victorian Literature: Poetry*, edited by Donald J. Gray and G. B. Tennyson and published by Macmillan Publishing Co., Inc., in 1976.
5. An essay by Geoffrey H. Hartman entitled "A Short History of Practical Criticism," published on pages 495–509 of volume 10 of the journal *New Literary History* (Spring, 1979).
6. A video recording entitled *Shakespeare of Stratford and London*, produced in 1978 by the National Geographic Society in Washington, D.C.
7. An article in the *New York Times* of April 10, 1983 entitled "Peking's Farm Policies Beginning to Pay Off." The article, by Christopher S. Wren, begins in column two of the first page and is continued on page 8.
8. A book entitled *The Second Sex*, written by Simone de Beauvoir,

translated by H. M. Parshley, and published in 1975 by Alfred A. Knopf in New York.

9. An article called "Alcoholics Anonymous" in the 1975 edition of the *New Columbia Encyclopedia*.

10. An article by Arnold S. Kaufman entitled "Behaviorism," which appears in volume 1 of the eight-volume *Encyclopedia of Philosophy*, published in 1967 in New York by Macmillan and edited by Paul Edwards.

B. Write a bibliographic citation according to the APA style for numbers 1,2, 8, and 10 above, consulting chapter 12 for guidance.

10

PRODUCING THE FINAL PAPER

Your final paper should be as neat and accurate as you can make it. A paper that is correct and readable is more effective than one with noticeable errors and will help persuade your reader that you have been correct and diligent in your research. After you have worked so hard, you will want your final paper to display the time and care that have gone into your entire project.

Before turning in your paper, you should complete the following steps:

1. Proofread the revised draft carefully and make the final changes. Correct any errors in grammar, spelling, and punctuation.
2. Make sure that the list of sources, the notes, and the parenthetical documentation are typed according to a single style—the MLA, the APA, or the scientific number system.
3. Type your paper neatly according to a standard format. Study the guidelines in this chapter before you begin typing.
4. Proofread the final copy carefully, correcting all errors. Make a copy for yourself if you have not used a carbon sheet while typing. Finally, submit the paper according to the instructor's directions.

Proofreading the Revised Draft

This is your last chance to make stylistic changes—to substitute a familiar word for an obscure one, to change a sentence from passive to active voice, to strike through unnecessary words. If you read your paper out loud, you may discover awkward sentences. Consult a standard handbook—there will be one in the reference room—for questions of grammar or usage. If you have any doubt about the spelling of a word, look it up in a dictionary.

Checking Punctuation

Before you check for punctuation errors, consider the following list of rules, which covers the questions that most students have about punctuating research papers.

THE PERIOD

- Use a period to mark the end of straightforward sentences and to mark the end of some abbreviations: 2:00 a.m., Ms. Check the dictionary when you are in doubt about punctuating abbreviations.
- In quotations, place the period inside quotation marks: I think I know what Lewis Thomas meant when he said, "There is really no such creature as a single individual." When a quotation is followed by parentheses, however, place the period after the parentheses: "A director shows the way. He does not manipulate his actors" (Dalton 232).
- Use a period after indirect questions: Eleanor Roosevelt's friends often asked how she was able to accomplish so much.
- Double-space after a period at the end of a sentence.
- Single-space after personal initials: J. I. M. Stewart.
- Do not space after the period within an abbreviation: Ph.D.
- Do not space before commas or other punctuation that follows an abbreviation: Sherwyn M. Woods, M.D., Ph.D.
- Place periods after numbers and letters used to itemize:

1. Exercise vigorously at least three times a week.
2. Eat a diet high in carbohydrates and low in fat.
3. Sleep between six and eight hours a night.
4. Avoid nicotine and excessive amounts of caffeine and alcohol.

THE QUESTION MARK

- Place a question mark at the end of direct questions: What does it mean to be an adult?
- Place the question mark outside quotation marks if the entire sentence is a question: Have you read a short story by William Faulkner called "The Old People"?
- Place the question mark inside the quotation marks if the quoted part of a sentence is a question, even when the sentence itself is not: Robert Lindner was in town to give a lecture entitled "Must We Conform?"
- Put a question mark inside the quotation marks if both the quotation and the sentence are questions: He turned and asked, "Have you read a novel by Horace McCoy called *They Shoot Horses, Don't They?*"

- Double space between a question mark—or the quotation mark after a question mark—and the first letter of the next word.

THE EXCLAMATION POINT

- Exclamation points are usually not effective in research reporting. If you have used one, try to find another way to stress the importance of your statement. For example, instead of "Eleanor Roosevelt was a great lady!", it would be more effective simply to write "Eleanor Roosevelt was one of the most important women of this century."
- Like question marks, exclamation points should be placed inside quotation marks if they are part of the quotation and outside if the sentence itself is an exclamation.

THE COMMA

- Use a comma after lengthy introductory phrases or clauses: Since he won the Nobel Prize, García Márquez has become increasingly popular in the United States.
- Use commas to set off modifying clauses that give extra (nonessential) information: Doris Lessing, who has written a number of powerful realistic novels, has recently written a series of novels that she calls space fiction.
- Do not use commas when such a clause is essential to the meaning of the sentence: The work of Lessing's that I find most intriguing is *The Golden Notebook*.
- Use a comma before a conjunction (and, but, so, etc.) that joins two independent clauses (complete sentences): I wanted him to write about the contemporary novel, but he chose to write about poetry instead.
- Use a comma to separate items in a series: Her computer components include two disk drives, a monitor, a keyboard, a high-speed printer, and the main computer chassis itself.
- Use a comma to set off other words or phrases that rename, contrast with, or qualify other words or phrases that are not essential to the meaning of the main clause:

1. An appositive or parenthetical phrase: Norman Cousins, the long-time editor of the *Saturday Review*, believes that if people can understand a problem, they can solve it.
2. A phrase of contrast: Swimming, not jogging, is the best sport for overall fitness.
3. Qualifying words placed in the middle of a sentence: Many people became disillusioned, seriously disillusioned, in the sixties. Ralph Nader, however, proved that an individual can influence public policy.

• Single-space after a comma, except before closing quotation marks: "Dave," he said, "what is the matter with you?"

• Place a comma inside quotation marks except when the quotation is followed by parentheses: He wanted to make a film shot through with "conflict" (Thomson 15), and he achieved that through the conflicts of real people.

THE SEMICOLON

• Use a semicolon to join closely related independent clauses: Most young people in the fifties conformed to society's expectations; most of their counterparts in the sixties rebelled.

• Use a semicolon between two independent clauses that are joined together by conjunctive adverbs like *however, nevertheless,* and *therefore:* Successful students keep up with their assignments; however, they also make time for recreation.

• Use a semicolon between items in a series when at least one includes commas: The participants in the 1982 Writers Congress included Toni Morrison, who stirred her audience by urging them to stay "at the barricades"; Meridel Le Sueur, who is as old as the century; and Kurt Vonnegut, whose novels are widely read by young and old.

• Single-space after a semicolon and place it outside closing quotation marks, as in the example above.

THE COLON

• Use a colon to introduce a list or an example, when it is not preceded by a preposition or a form of the verb *to be:* Each student should write a report on one of these artists: Mary Cassatt, Auguste Renoir, Henri Matisse, or Pablo Picasso. *Or:* Imagine a typical early painting by Picasso: large sculptural nudes, primitive African motifs, distorted faces, flattened forms. *Or:* Three kinds of music were popular among college students in the fifties: rhythm and blues, jazz, and rock and roll.

• Colons or commas may be used to introduce quotations, but colons are usually best when the introductory material is longer than a few words and when the quotation itself is fairly long, as here: The president of the senior class concluded the graduation address with the following words: "Students today face many challenges. The question is not what will the world do for us, but how can we prepare ourselves to meet the needs of a complex and demanding society."

• Use a colon to introduce a second clause that amplifies the first: Many students have unusual jobs: One of my classmates is an animal trainer and another a lace maker.

• Single-space after a colon and put it outside quotation marks.

QUOTATION MARKS

- Put quotation marks around quotations of three lines or less of verse or four lines or less of prose when they are incorporated into the text of your paper (see p. 179).
- Set off longer quotations by indenting ten spaces from the left margin. Do not use quotation marks (see p. 182).
- Enclose quotations within quotations with single quotation marks: According to one critic, "George Eliot's favorite poem was Wordsworth's 'Ode to Duty.' "
- Use quotation marks around the titles of short works: essays, poems, short stories, or songs. Quotation marks are also placed around the titles of parts of books: chapters, introductions, and afterwords.

THE APOSTROPHE

- Use an apostrophe to form the possessive as follows: Morrison's novels; an actor's life; Keats's poetry (a single-syllable word ending in "s"); Dos Passos' early work (a word of more than one syllable that ends in an "s" sound); Dumas's plays (a word of more than one syllable that ends in a silent "s"); Terence's comedies (a word ending in an "s" sound and a final "e").

THE HYPHEN

- Use a hyphen to divide a word at the end of the line. Always break the word between syllables as designated in a standard dictionary, and avoid divisions that leave only one or two letters on a line: adjust-ment, *not* ad-justment. Divide compound words between the two words: type-writer. Divide hyphenated words only at the hyphen: computer-generated, *not* computer-gen-erated.

THE DASH

- Use a dash to add information that interrupts the flow of a sentence: The growing agitation for a nuclear freeze—which seemed to go beyond mere party politics—resulted in widespread demonstrations in the fall of 1982.
- Use a dash to add extra information that is itself divided by commas: Several British rock groups—the Beatles, the Who, and the Police—continue to be very popular.
- Use a dash to set off a word or group of words that summarizes what

comes before: Among Michael's friends were drummers, pianists, vocalists, guitarists—all kinds of musicians.

- To type a dash, use two hyphens. Do not space before or after.

PARENTHESES

- Use parentheses for the same purposes that you use a dash, reserving parentheses for more radical interruptions of a sentence: Big business entered the sports world with the baseball players strike of 1981 (though financial considerations affected professional sports from their beginnings) and played havoc with football the next year.

- Do not space between a beginning parenthesis and the first letter or between the last character and the closing parenthesis: Many young people in this culture (most of them in fact) earn some of their spending money.

- When you include a complete sentence within parentheses as part of another sentence, it is not necessary to capitalize the first letter or to put a period at the end: Young people in the eighties face many serious problems (the drug culture is only one) that were unheard of by their counterparts in the fifties.

- Other punctuation follows parentheses: In the nineteenth century, mothers tranquilized their hungry babies with opium (a widely used legal drug at the time). After a long set-off quotation, however, parenthetical documentation is placed after final punctuation (see p. 182).

- A period is included within the parentheses only when the parenthetical statement is completely independent: Historians are only now beginning to try to make sense of the turbulent events of the 1960s. (An early work that tried to interpret some of the ideas and values of the youth culture in the 1960s was Theodore Roszak's *The Making of a Counter Culture*.)

BRACKETS

- Use brackets to insert an editorial comment or explanatory name or word within a quotation: One biographer has concluded that "even though he suffered from a prolonged illness, he [D. H. Lawrence] never lost his love of life."

- If you change the capitalization of a letter in a quotation, place brackets around the letter to indicate the change: Steffi Sidney has said of Nicholas Ray that "[h]e wanted the movie to come from *us*, rather than from his direction."

ELLIPSIS DOTS

- Use ellipsis dots within a quoted passage to indicate that part of the quotation has been omitted: On April 8, 1928, the *New York Times* quoted

Eleanor Roosevelt as saying that if women "expect equal political prefer-ment . . . they must study history, economics and political methods, and they must mix with their fellow human beings."

- If the omission comes at the end of the sentence, add a period before the ellipsis dots: Eleanor Roosevelt argued that women interested in becoming involved in politics "must study history, economics and political methods. . . ."

- Use ellipsis dots at the beginning of a sentence only if it is not clear that something has been left out.

- Space before, between, and after the individual ellipsis dots.

UNDERLINING

- Use underlining where italics would be used in a printed text. Under-line titles of complete works—books, films, radio and television programs, plays, operas, and long poems published as books. Underline titles of peri-odicals (newspapers, magazines, and journals) and works of art (paintings and sculptures) as well as the names of ships, aircraft, and spacecraft.

SPACING OF PUNCTUATION

- The following lists summarize standard rules on the spacing of punctuation.

NO SPACE:

1. After a period within most abbreviations
2. After a quotation mark at the beginning of a quotation or before a quotation mark at the end of a quotation
3. Before punctuation used to divide or end a sentence
4. Before or after hyphens
5. Before, between, and after hyphens used to make a dash
6. After a beginning parenthesis (or bracket) or before a closing one

SINGLE SPACE:

1. After the period following personal initials
2. After commas, semicolons, and colons
3. Before, between, and after ellipsis dots
4. Before a beginning parenthesis within a sentence
5. After a closing parenthesis within a sentence unless the parenthesis is followed by another punctuation mark

DOUBLE SPACE:

1. After a period, question mark, or exclamation point at the end of a sentence except when it is followed by quotation marks

2. After quotation marks that follow a period, question mark, or exclamation point
3. After a closing parenthesis that encloses an independent sentence and the end punctuation

Typing the Final Copy

ASSEMBLING TYPING MATERIALS

Before you begin typing, have the following materials on hand:

1. A clean black typing ribbon and a typewriter with a plain standard typeface. Avoid colored typing ribbons and unusual typefaces such as italic or script.
2. Adequate correction tape, film, or liquid—whichever is appropriate for your typewriter.
3. A supply of white 8½-by-11-inch, twenty-pound-weight typing paper. Do not use onionskin or erasable paper.
4. Carbon paper if you plan to make an extra copy as you type.

MARGINS

For the main text of the paper, use one-inch margins at the top, the bottom, and on the left side of the page. The margin on the right should be as close to an inch as possible, though it is better to have it wider than an inch than narrower. Use a hyphen to divide words that would otherwise extend beyond the margin. For the first page of notes, list of sources, and other pages with a separate title, use a two-inch margin at the top.

The page number should be one inch from the right edge of the paper and a half-inch from the top.

SPACING AND INDENTATION

Quadruple-space between the title and the first paragraph. Double-space the entire text, including quotations, notes, and bibliography.

Indent the first line of each paragraph five spaces and all lines of long quotations ten spaces. Quotations may be typed flush with the right margin.

TITLE PAGE

There are two commonly used ways to indicate the title and author of a research paper as well as the course for which the paper has been written and the date of the paper's completion:

1. On the first page of the paper, place the author, course, instructor, and date in the upper right corner. (Alternatively, type this information in the upper left corner and the page number in the upper right.) Center the title and quadruple-space before the beginning of the paper (see pp. 125, 172).
2. On a separate page, use approximately the middle five inches to center each of the following items: title, author, course, instructor, date (see p. 240).

ARRANGEMENT OF PAGES

You should begin typing each item on the list below on a separate page. Arrange the parts of your paper in the following order, whether a paper has all or some of the items. Your instructor will tell you which of these to include:

1. Title Page
2. Outline
3. Text of paper
4. Appendix
5. End notes
6. List of sources (bibliography or works cited)
7. Blank sheet for instructor's comments

This is a complete list. Some papers will simply have a title and author page or section for this information on the first page, the main text, and the list of sources.

NUMBERING PAGES

Always count the first page of the text, and number consecutively through the list of sources. Some instructors may ask you to omit the number on the first page (see p. 125). Others may ask you to place a number on all pages including the first (see p. 172). The pages of an outline inserted after the title page and before the text of the paper should be numbered with lower-case Roman numerals.

LABELING PAGES

As a courtesy to your instructor, place your last name immediately beside or under the page number. Then if the pages of your paper are mixed in with those of another paper, it will be easy to reassemble the individual papers.

APPENDICES

Tables, illustrations, photographs, and charts are often placed at the end of a paper before notes and/or the list of sources. If you think such material is important but will distract the reader if included in the main text, place it in an appendix. For each item of supplementary material, make a separate appendix. A set of drawings might constitute "Appendix I," a chart "Appendix II." Place the title of an appendix two inches from the top of the page and quadruple-space before beginning the text.

PROOFREADING THE FINAL PAPER

Proofread every page before you remove it from the typewriter. When you have finished typing, proofread it again. It is sometimes easier to find errors if you read a paper out loud including marks of punctuation. If your instructor allows you to get help with proofreading, you may want to ask a patient friend to give your paper a look. If you place a light pencil mark at the end of each line that contains an error, you can evaluate the whole paper and decide how to make corrections.

MAKING CORRECTIONS

Make as many corrections as possible on the typewriter before you remove each sheet. Once a page is removed, it is more difficult to make typed corrections. Some errors (such as minor spelling and typographical errors or two words reversed) can be corrected by covering the mistake with liquid paper or correction tape and then writing over it in black ink. But if a page contains several errors that will be difficult for you to correct, you ought to retype it.

COPYING THE PAPER

It is always a good idea to make a copy of your paper and to keep the copy separate from the original. You may want to make a carbon as you type. A photocopy can be even neater than the original since it often does not show corrections made with tape and liquid paper.

BINDING

Most instructors prefer students to bind their papers together with a large paper clip in the upper left corner. A slip of paper placed under the clip will protect your paper from being damaged by the clip.

EXERCISES

A. Go over your revised draft a final time before you type it. Check for spelling, punctuation, diction, and grammar. Make all corrections on your draft before you type the final copy.

B. After you have typed a final copy, proofread it carefully and correct all errors in black ink.

11

WRITING RESEARCH PAPERS IN THE HUMANITIES

Approaches to Research in the Humanities

The humanities include those academic disciplines that explore human beings and their cultures: art, history, literature, music, and philosophy. Each of these disciplines is subdivided into a number of categories; the visual arts, for example, include motion pictures, graphics, painting, photography, and sculpture. There is some overlap between the humanities and the social sciences: in recent years some historians have applied the methods of social science to historical topics by doing very detailed quantitative studies with the help of computers, while some literary texts are examined as sociological documents. There are many kinds of investigations that students can pursue in the humanities involving both primary and secondary materials. Doing primary research in literature, history, or philosophy involves examining original documents in these fields: in literature, for example, studying the text of a novel, letters written to and by the author, manuscripts or facsimiles of manuscripts of the literary text, or other writings by the author referring to the text. Secondary research related to the same novel would include the study of critical essays, book reviews, or other materials about the text or author written by others.

Since production of visual art predates written history, students have a vast array of material to explore spanning many centuries, ranging from the cave drawings at Lascaux in southwestern France to the subway graffiti of the 1980s. To do primary research in the visual arts you would study works themselves, usually in museums. To do secondary research, you would examine reproductions of the art (printed photographs or slides), as well as books and articles written about artists and their work. You might research the career of an individual artist—Velasquez, Vermeer, Van Gogh; the influence of an artist on others—Caravaggio on Ribera and Rembrandt; the relationship of an artist to a patron—Goya to Charles IV; an artist's treatment of a particular subject—Mary Cassatt's paintings and drawings of children; or even a single painting—Picasso's *Guernica*.

History, in some ways the broadest of disciplines since it comments on all others—the history of science, of economics, of art, literature, and ideas—involves using a great variety of resources to reconstruct the past of human experience. There are three different kinds of materials available to professional historians and student researchers: primary sources generated by events themselves—letters, government reports, newspaper accounts, video or audio tapes of events; secondary sources—books and articles produced by historians who have studied the primary materials; and tertiary sources—encyclopedia articles, textbooks, or popular histories based on the secondary sources. Students taking courses that focus on events that occurred before the twentieth century would probably rely on secondary sources, perhaps using the works of historians to explore a particular problem. For example, as a student of the Renaissance and Reformation, you might do a research project on the relationship of Erasmus to Luther. Although you would use some primary sources—the writings of Erasmus and Luther—most of your work would depend on the writing of historians who have studied the primary materials. As a student of recent history, however, you would have many more primary sources available. If, for example, you were writing a research paper on the march on Washington during which Martin Luther King gave his famous "I Have a Dream" speech, you would be able to read about the events leading up to the day in various secondary sources such as a biography of King or a history of America in the 1960s, but you could also read eyewitness newspaper accounts as well as some of the speeches that were delivered that day; you could watch videotapes and look at photographs; you could consult government records and even listen to tapes of President Kennedy and his aides discussing the events leading up to the march.

Ideas about what constitutes literature are changing to include much more than poetry, drama, and fiction written by established writers. Literary scholars now do serious research that involves examining essays, memoirs, diaries, and letters, as well as popular novels, film scripts, and even television scripts. Although writing about literature in some courses may simply involve examining and analyzing a novel, poem, or play without reference to any other sources, you may have an opportunity to do some original research. Teachers of literature who assign research projects, like instructors of other disciplines, usually are very specific about the kind of research they want students to pursue. Possibilities include synthesizing various interpretations of a work by reading and evaluating critical essays about it, researching the critical reception of a book by reading the original reviews published in periodicals and newspapers, studying published letters to discover an author's intentions in writing a work, or reading a biography to find out how a particular work relates to the author's life. In some cases, you may be asked to research some aspect of the social context in which a work was written. In a course on Victorian literature, for example, you might be asked to research child labor practices in the period and to show how particular writers—Elizabeth Barrett Browning and Charles Dickens—used their works to protest those practices.

There are many interesting research projects for students to pursue in the area of music, ranging from the life and works of one of the great classical composers to the role of music in a first-grade classroom. In a course in music theory, for example, you might study the ideas of the classical theorists and perhaps compare Plato's and Aristotle's theories of the relationship between musical tones and emotional states. In a course that relates music criticism to composition, you might research the relationship of the critical writings of Robert Schumann to the music produced in the mid-nineteenth century, focusing perhaps on the work of Johannes Brahms. In another context, you might examine the historical and critical issues surrounding Mozart's *Requiem* and its place in the development of church music. If you are studying popular culture and contemporary music, you might want to explore the public demand for censorship of lyrics of rock and roll songs.

There is enormous variety among the works of philosophers who reflect on and discuss the nature and meaning of human existence. As a student of philosophy, you might be asked to research the historical foundations of a school of thought—the development of utilitarianism; to research perennial themes such as perception and reality, the nature of the moral life, or the interplay between justice and freedom; or to examine the influence of a particular philosopher on some aspect of a culture, perhaps the influence of Kant on German education or Simone de Beauvoir on American feminism.

A Sample Paper in the Humanities

When Michael Gold's freshman English teacher asked the class to choose a topic and write a research paper in one of the disciplines within the humanities, he chose motion pictures since he had a strong interest in film. His paper on *Rebel without a Cause* draws on a variety of sources, including contemporary reviews, the book that originally inspired the film, books about the director and the actors, articles in popular magazines, and critical essays in film journals. The paper is documented with parenthetical references in the text and a list of sources at the end, the style recommended by the Modern Language Association, which is the style most commonly used in college courses in the humanities.

1

Michael Gold
Professor Sprague
English 102
November 19, 1983

Conflict and Cooperation: The Making of <u>Rebel without a</u>
<u>Cause</u>

In the 1950s movies were very different from what
they are today. The most popular were musicals, Westerns,
and comedies; and most were intended for family
entertainment. Only a few were produced primarily for a

Introductory paragraphs catch reader's attention and lead to thesis statement

teenage audience. Young people referred to them as
movies, adults as picture shows and hardly anyone thought
of going to a film--which is what movies or picture shows
are called when they are taken seriously. Occasionally a
film was made in those days that influenced future films
and that affected the way people behaved. Such a film was
<u>Rebel without a Cause</u>.

Most people who remember <u>Rebel</u> associate it with one
person, James Dean--his life, his death, and the cult
that developed among some of his more ardent fans. A few
may recall that <u>Rebel</u> was also the film that made Sal
Mineo and Natalie Wood famous. Perhaps because of the

Source indicated in parentheses; details given in bibliography

premature deaths of all three of its stars, <u>Rebel</u> feeds a
kind of nostalgia among people who first saw it in their
teens, and it continues to attract young audiences in
colleges across the country (Swank). The association of
<u>Rebel</u> with the sudden death of young people began when
James Dean was killed--clearly because of his own
recklessness--in an automobile accident before the film

2

Gold

was released in 1955. It continued in 1976 when Sal Mineo
was stabbed by an unknown assailant and again in 1981
when Natalie Wood drowned under somewhat mysterious
circumstances.

Immediately after James Dean's death, a large number
of young people became obsessed with keeping his memory
alive, their efforts soon reaching the intensity of
hysteria. For some, grief developed into a kind of death
cult. According to Life magazine, thousands of fans wrote
letters to Dean every month in which they insisted either
that he was not dead or that he was immortal (Goodman
75). In 1957, Sam Astrachan reported in the New Republic
that a whole generation of young people had adopted the
jacket, gestures, and expressions that were part of
Dean's image in Rebel (17). The Dean mania became a
profitable business: some fans were willing to pay up to
two hundred dollars for poorly done oil paintings of Dean
(Mitgang 114); others purchased life-sized casts of
Dean's head, records of ballads about his death, and
pieces of old Porsche aluminum purported to be part of
his car (Goodman 78). What Life magazine referred to as
the "Delirium over Dead Star" lasted a long time. As
late as 1969, a reporter for the New Yorker interviewed
fifty-seven-year-old Mrs. Therese J. Brandes, the founder
of the James Dean Memory Club. Mrs. Brandes, who had been
in her mid-forties when Dean died, explained that while
teenagers may have had a romantic attachment to Dean, she
and her contemporaries "loved him as a son." Mrs.

No comma
between source
and page number

Several sources
used in this
paragraph; each
requires separate
citation

Brief quoted
phrase
integrated into
sentence

3

Gold

Brandes showed the reporter two closets full of recent letters as evidence of Dean's continuing popularity ("Fan" 22).

The Dean mania has at last subsided, but the film remains part of our culture. It periodically plays in commercial theaters that book old favorites. According to Mike Swank, who distributes the film to colleges, churches, and other nonprofit institutions, Rebel "is a perennially popular title" with a "steady booking pattern." It is used for entertainment and also for teaching purposes in English, history, and social studies courses (Swank).

It is of course impossible to know what our perceptions of Rebel without a Cause would be if it were not for James Dean's untimely death, but it is obvious that the Dean mania has obscured the real story of how Rebel without a Cause came to be. James Dean made an important contribution to Rebel, but he was only one of many people who helped to make this film memorable. Rebel was really the product of the imagination, the creative energy, and the plain hard work of a group of people--the producer, director, writers, actors, and technical experts--who compose the community of a film. More than any other work of art, a film is a collaborative effort requiring cooperation and compromise. Some films--and Rebel is one--grow not only from the minds of the collaborators but out of existing social concerns and the demands of the movie-going public. Once films are

Quotation from a personal letter; see p. 64

Thesis statement or controlling idea

released, they go back into society, influencing the
feelings, behavior, and ideas of their audiences. And
finally they become subjects for interpretation, for
critics and historians who try to understand what films
mean.

The story of Rebel without a Cause began in 1944
when a young psychologist named Robert Lindner published
a book entitled Rebel without a Cause . . . The
Hypnoanalysis of a Criminal Psychopath, which was widely
read. George Mayberry, writing in the New Republic,
referred to it as a "deeply and tragically human" story
(108); and Edwin J. Lukas, in the Annals of the American
Academy of Political and Social Science, hailed it as
essential reading for professionals concerned with the
criminal personality (216). In 1947, Warner Brothers
purchased the right to make a movie based on Lindner's
book and signed the young Marlon Brando to star; when
Brando's contract expired, the project was temporarily
abandoned. Juvenile delinquency, however, was a serious
social concern, spurring Columbia Pictures to make a
successful film on the subject, The Wild Ones, starring--a
popular choice for the role of delinquent--Marlon Brando.
When Nicholas Ray became a director for Warner Brothers
in 1954, he too wanted to make a film about juvenile
delinquency, and as a consequence the Rebel project was
revived (Kreidl 91). But the film Ray wanted to do had
little in common with the content of Robert Lindner's
professional case history.

Name of author
used to introduce
quotation

5

Gold

Student's own
conclusions—no
citation needed

Some of Lindner's material was used in the film,
from the title--which would catch the imagination of a
generation of teenagers--to the suggestion that problems
within a family are the cause of antisocial behavior
among the young. Lindner's study reveals how family
conflicts lead young Harold to chronic criminal behavior;
in the film unhappy homes provoke Jim, Judy, and Plato to
pranks and illegal acts that have serious consequences.
But the details are very different. Lindner's sullen
Harold, based on an actual case history, is from an
immigrant-laborer home with few material comforts. He
engages in criminal behavior from the age of twelve,
drops out of school, is periodically arrested, put on
probation, sentenced to jail, and finally committed to a
penitentiary. Jim Stark (James Dean) is one of a group of
indulged but unhappy, privileged but rebellious teenagers
who argue with their parents, drink, and sometimes steal
cars. Their escapades end in the deaths of Buzz (Corey
Allen) in a car accident and of Plato (Sal Mineo) in a
shootout with the police, who mistakenly assume that he
is armed. For Jim Stark, however, the day ends positively,
as he gets the pretty girl (Natalie Wood) and is
reconciled with his parents.

Movie titles
underlined

When Nicholas Ray's proposal to make a film about
affluent suburban kids was merged with the studio's plan
to make a movie called Rebel without a Cause, there was
no script and no real vision of how the differences
between the original book and Ray's intentions could be

6

Gold

resolved. In fact, the seeds that would flower in the
final film were scattered in the minds of many different
people. Nicholas Ray brought them together. He chose
David Weisbart for the producer because Weisbart had two
teenage children, and Ray thought that he would have a
special sympathy with the project (Ray 70). Leonard
Rosenman, the musical director, was a good choice because
he had already worked with Dean in East of Eden (Kreidl
94).

Finding a screenwriter was more difficult. According
to Ray, there is often animosity between a writer and a
director, since each is dependent on the other and yet
each wants to make final decisions. Famous writers
present additional problems, since they often want to
follow their own ideas, while the studio requires that
they cooperate with the needs of a production. Sometimes
a studio will insist that a director use a writer who is
already under contract to the studio, even though the
writer is not suited to the project (Ray 71-72).

Ray originally approached Clifford Odets, a friend,
to do the script; but Warner Brothers had other ideas
since Leon Uris, a best-selling author and successful
scriptwriter, was already under contract to them (Dalton
225). Ray agreed to Uris' joining the project since he
was interested in the subject, had experience working
with teenage boys, and was willing to do research. But
when Uris produced a sketch of a small town plagued by
juvenile delinquency, Nicholas Ray did not like it, and

Source noted at
the end when all
information in a
paragraph is
from a single
source

7

Gold

Uris had to be replaced. Ray's account of his experience
with Uris suggests that studying and finally rejecting
Uris' work allowed Ray to refine and clarify his own
intentions. By seeing what he did not want, he perhaps
came closer to knowing what he did want (Ray 73).

The next writer to work with the Rebel crew was
Irving Shulman, a novelist and scriptwriter who had been
a high school teacher and who loved sports cars, something
that Ray hoped would provide a bond with the moody James
Dean. Although an affinity with Dean never developed and
his vision of the film proved incompatible with that of
Nicholas Ray, Irving Shulman was directly responsible for
significant features of the film. His discovery of a
newspaper article about a teenage boy who plunged to his
death off the Pacific Palisades when he failed to jump
free in a "chickie run" became the famous scene in which
Buzz accidentally drives his car off a cliff because his
sleeve is caught and he cannot open the car door to
escape. Shulman also helped develop the character of
Plato; Plato's luxurious house, self-indulgent mother,
and absent father were all his ideas. It was finally a
disagreement about the character of Plato, however, that
led to Ray's decision that he needed still another writer
(Ray 73).

Leonard Rosenman, the musical director of Rebel,
suggested the thirty-one-year-old Stewart Stern, who
worked with Ray until the film was finished, bringing
together the ideas of previous writers with his own

8

Gold

(Kreidl 93). But even Stern did not produce a final,
definitive screenplay. Although he wrote at least three
different versions, none reflects completely the dialogue
and the action of the final film. Once the actors went to
work, the script continued to evolve, with James Dean, in
particular, creating as he acted (Kreidl 86).

"Please let me do something here. Let me play with
it. Just roll it." When Dean asked to be allowed to play
a scene his way, Ray said yes (Dalton 236). It is
difficult to know what subtle character traits contribute
to a successful collaboration between an actor and a
director, but we do know that Nicholas Ray trusted James
Dean's instincts. From the beginning, Ray followed the
advice of Elia Kazan, who insisted that a good director
never tries to direct a natural actor. Ray's version of
Kazan's rule was this: "A director shows the way. He does
not manipulate his actors" (Dalton 232). Two of the more
famous scenes in the film--the opening scene with Dean
lying drunk in the street playing with a toy monkey and
the scene after the fatal car accident with Dean taking a
bottle of milk and slowly pressing it to his face--were
the actor's spontaneous performances (Dalton 236, 253).
The milk bottle scene was planned one night at Ray's
house with Dean thinking through the situation and Ray
playing the father (Houston and Gillett 184).

Nicholas Ray encouraged the other young actors to
develop their own parts. Looking back on the experience,
Natalie Wood observed: "Nick gave me a career . . . with

Note use of
direct quotation

Ellipsis dots used
to indicate words
omitted

9
Gold

Rebel. . . . Because he regarded me as an actress with a
meaningful contribution to make, I felt better of myself
and better of my work. . . . I think he did that for a
lot of people" (Kreidl 208). Steffi Sidney, who played
one of the gang members, has also testified to Nicholas
Ray's freeing his actors to develop the character of a
gang: "He wanted the movie to come from us, rather than
from his direction." When Ray felt that they were still
acting as individuals rather than as a gang, he urged
them to go out together and to do things as a group--to
go to the beach and prowl around deserted buildings at
night (Dalton 230).

The evidence is abundant: from the very beginning,
Nicholas Ray recognized that the kind of film he wanted to
make would be a community effort requiring the cooperation
of many people. He wanted to make a film shot through
with "conflict" (Thomson 15), and he achieved that
through the conflicts of real people--the producer, the
director, the writers, the actors, and others. The
conflicts among young people trying to grow up, between
the young and their baffled parents, and between the
young and the forces of authority--all are portrayed
convincingly. Ray brought together the fragments of many
people's experiences: Uris' talks with juvenile
authorities and delinquents (Kreidl 77), the newspaper
article about a chicken run, Shulman's work as a high
school teacher (Ray 74), Sal Mineo's actual idolizing of
Dean (Kreidl 82), and the ganglike, semidelinquent

10
Gold

behavior of many of the young actors (Dalton 227). Perhaps
Ray achieved a kind of authenticity and unity because he
was able to fuse the experiences of so many real people
struggling to say something about the eternal conflicts
between the young and the old.

Although there are probably very few people who
would insist today that James Dean lives, Rebel without a
Cause is still alive in the minds of people who study the
history of film. In recent years, scholars have tried to
judge the film as a whole, rather than as a showcase for
the magic that Dean created. They are studying its
values, its art, and its place in American film history.
Peter Biskind, writing in Film Quarterly, sees Rebel as a
reflection of the conservative values of mid-fifties
America. He argues that the young characters condemn their
parents' weaknesses, but that in the end the film affirms
traditional family values and remains "a profoundly
conservative film" (37). David Cook, on the other hand,
in his History of Narrative Film, sees the film as "a
definitive statement of the psychic and emotional ills
that beset America during the period" (427). Douglas
McVay considers Rebel to be Nicholas Ray's masterpiece
and one of the four best films of the fifties (24).
David Thomson, who thinks of Rebel as the work of a
director who was both a serious social critic and a "great
romantic" producing great art (15), warns of the
difficulty of ever recreating that initial response:

Note how the
student uses the
names of authors
he quotes; he
then does not
need to repeat the
name in the
parenthetical
citation

11

Gold

Long quotation
indented 10
spaces;
double-spaced
before,
throughout, and
after quotation

So Rebel is vibrant with yearning aspirations, and Ray's beautiful and brave venturing with space, decor, and faces lost in a night wilderness of screen. We can never regain the view we had of the film in 1955, when its rueful passion swept so many of us away. (16)

Even though almost thirty years have passed since audiences first settled down to watch Rebel without a Cause, evaluating its place both in film history and in American society is still not easy. A profoundly conservative film, a tragedy in the classical sense, a high romance, or scathing social comment--which is the appropriate category for this still controversial film? When we consider the many different people who contributed to its creation, we may conclude that it is all of these. It is certainly not surprising to discover that a film that has what Kreidl calls "a disparate smattering of different vocabularies from different sources" should evoke such varied responses (86).

Concluding
paragraph echoes
thesis statement:
note repeated
ideas *community*,
compromise,
cooperate

Rebel without a Cause was generated through conflict; it was finally realized when the community of people who wanted to bring it about discovered ways to compromise and cooperate. But the conflict that created Rebel is still alive in the minds of people who interpret it. A film more than a book exists in the minds of its viewers. Although some may have a videotape of the film, which they can study at their leisure, most people must rely on

12
Gold

memory.[1] The community of interpreters--those who
remember, study, and talk and write about Rebel--will
probably always be fraught with conflict both because
memories are highly personal and because the struggle
between generations that Rebel explores is constantly
being renewed.

NOTE

[1] The availability of videotape for purchase or
rental makes possible an in-depth study of films
comparable to written texts. Future responses to Rebel
may be based more on careful critical analysis than on
emotional response. Therein lies another paper.

Content note
offers a thought
of Michael's that
is interesting and
relevant but that
would distract
from the main
point if included
in the text of his
paper

13

Gold

Items in bibliography alphabetized by last name of author

WORKS CITED

Astrachan, Sam. "The New Lost Generation." New Republic
    4 Feb. 1957: 17-18.

Biskind, Peter. "Rebel Without a Cause: Nicholas Ray in
    the Fifties." Film Quarterly 28.5 (1974): 32-38.

Cook, David A. A History of Narrative Film. New York:
    Norton, 1981.

"Correspondence." The New Republic 18 Feb. 1957: 22-23.

Dalton, David. James Dean: The Mutant King. San
    Francisco: Straight Arrow Books, 1974.

When there is no author, item alphabetized by first word of title (excluding a, an, or the)

"Fan" in "The Talk of the Town." New Yorker
    2 Aug. 1969: 21-23.

Goodman, Ezra. "Delirium over Dead Star." Life 24
    Sept. 1956: 75-76.

Houston, Penelope, and John Gillett. "Conversations with
    Nicholas Ray and Joseph Losey." Sight and Sound 3
    (1961): 182-87.

Kreidl, John Francis. Nicholas Ray. Twayne's Theatrical
    Arts Series. Boston: Twayne, 1977.

Lindner, Robert M. Rebel without a Cause . . . The
    Hypnoanalysis of a Criminal Psychopath. New York:
    Grune and Stratton, 1944.

Indent second and subsequent lines of bibliographic citations five spaces from left margin

Lukas, Edwin J. Rev. of Rebel without a Cause . . . The
    Hypnoanalysis of a Criminal Psychopath, by Robert M.
    Lindner. The Annals of the American Academy of
    Political and Social Science 236 (1944): 215-16.

Mayberry, George. "Alternatives to the Novel." New
    Republic 24 July 1944: 108.

14
Gold

McVay, Douglas. "Rebel Without a Cause." <u>Films and
      Filming</u> 23.2 (1979): 16-24.
Mitgang, Herbert. "The Strange James Dean Death Cult."
      <u>Coronet</u> Nov. 1956: 110-15.
Ray, Nicholas. "Story into Script." <u>Sight and Sound</u> 26
      (1956): 70-74.
Swank, Mike. Letter to author. 1 March 1983.
Thomson, David. "Rebel Without a Cause." <u>Take One</u>
      March 1979: 15-16.

12

WRITING RESEARCH PAPERS IN THE SOCIAL SCIENCES

Approaches to Research in the Social Sciences

The social sciences are primarily concerned with how human beings, and sometimes other animals, relate to each other. There is no absolute agreement about what constitutes a social science, but generally included in the area are anthropology, economics, political science, psychology, and sociology. In some institutions, however, history might be considered one of the social sciences, while certain psychologists consider their work to be part of the biological sciences. There is some overlap in the various social sciences, and some research may be conducted by teams of researchers from various disciplines. There are many topics in the social sciences that are appropriate for college students to research, but most projects that are suitable for the time limitations of an academic term and for the resources of beginning students will involve studying and synthesizing secondary materials. Beginning students in the social sciences mainly work with the written reports of other investigators who are experts in a field they are studying and who have conducted surveys, administered questionnaires, observed behavior, and arrived at conclusions based on studies that may have extended over a period of years.

Students of anthropology tend to specialize in one of two very different areas: physical anthropology, which studies humans as a biological species, and cultural anthropology, which grows from the study of single cultural groups. In an undergraduate course in physical anthropology, you might want to research the techniques used to examine human fossil remains to determine the diet of primitive peoples or whether they were warlike. As a student of cultural anthropology, you would study the written accounts of anthropologists who have done field work by leaving their own societies behind and immersing themselves in the cultures of relatively simple peo-

186

ples. You might, for example, want to focus on the work that has been done on a particular group of people, such as the !Kung San hunter-gatherers of the Kalahari Desert in southern Africa.

The field of economics offers many possibilities for student research: in a course on the history of economic thought, the influence of a particular classical economist—John Stuart Mill, David Ricardo, or Adam Smith; in the study of macroeconomics, one aspect of the complex workings of the Federal Reserve Bank in the contemporary United States; in a course on industrial organization, an analysis of the internal structure of a specific American industry; or in the area of economic development, the strategies for industrialization (or for food distribution) in a less-developed country —Chad, Bolivia, or Turkey.

Since the systematic and therefore scientific study of governments and politics dates back to classical Greece, students studying governments and political processes have a vast historical background to explore. If you are taking a course in ancient political theory, you might want to examine how questions of justice or social responsibility are treated by certain classical authors—Aristotle and Plato, perhaps. Students taking a course in contemporary comparative governments might conduct studies of the role of government in education in two different countries, while those studying international relations could explore some aspect of international law (the battle for an international copyright law), of diplomacy (the establishment of diplomatic relations between the United States and China), or international organizations (Eleanor Roosevelt's role in the United Nations).

There are many possibilities for pursuing interesting research in the field of sociology. You might explore an historical topic, such as the work of the great social reformers of the nineteenth century, people like Robert Owen, who formed a model industrial community in Scotland and later established a Utopian agricultural community in New Harmony, Indiana, or Charles Fourier, the French social philosopher, whose dreams of social harmony resulted in the establishment of a number of colonies in the United States, including the famous Brook Farm. You might want to investigate the early history of sociology as an academic discipline as reflected in the *American Journal of Sociology*, the first academic journal to publish articles on sociological topics. In a course on that aspect of sociology called social psychology, you might study some aspect of human communication, such as the speech habits of street gangs or some other social unit. Your research in this area might lead you to studies conducted by sociologists, psychologists, and linguists. You may want to focus on some aspect of group life within a single community—an ethnic enclave, a small town, or a hospital for the mentally ill.

Like the other social sciences, psychology is rapidly expanding and becoming increasingly complex. Undergraduate students in psychology usually survey the field, taking courses in several areas, such as experimental, developmental, physiological, and abnormal psychology. Students doing research in these areas might study the process by which early investigators—Pavlov and Skinner—discovered the function of rewards in conditioning behavior (experimental), the controversy about attaching psychiatric labels to children (developmental), the role of neural mechanisms in aggressive behavior (physiological), or the theories of the genesis of schizophrenia (abnormal).

As you develop some expertise in a field, you will have more opportunity to do basic or primary research. If you take a course in experimental psychology, for example, you might conduct your own experiment, perhaps using animal subjects like mice or pigeons to investigate the effects of behavior modification techniques. As you advance in a field, you could participate in ongoing research conducted by a team of investigators. Undergraduate students could conceivably conduct primary research by doing one of the following: joining a summer expedition doing field work in cultural anthropology; interviewing people to find out about their political beliefs, voting behavior, or perception of government officials; administering questionnaires to find out about people's drinking habits, sexual behavior, or marriage plans; studying programs conducted in nursing homes, mental health clinics, or birth control clinics and then trying to find out how people value the services they receive; observing children at play in a nursery school or adolescents interacting in a drug rehabilitation center.

Making a Reference List for Papers in the Social Sciences

Most undergraduate students doing research projects in the social sciences will find adequate guidance here for making a reference list. Those who need to cite types of material not noted here should consult the *Publication Manual of the American Psychological Association* [APA] (1983). All examples and rules in this chapter are based on the style established by the APA manual.

GUIDELINES FOR TYPING A REFERENCE LIST USING APA STYLE

1. Type the first line of each reference flush with the left margin, and indent the following lines three spaces.
2. Space once after commas, semicolons, and the colon following the location of the publisher. (APA requires two spaces after a colon in sentences.)

3. Space twice after periods between elements of a citation and once after periods following initials of personal names.
4. Use a solid underline with no break between words for titles.

BOOKS

1. A book with one author:

Coles, Robert. (1986). <u>The moral life of children</u>. Boston: Atlantic Monthly Press.

2. A book with two authors:

Colarusso, C. A., & Nemiroff, R. A. (1981). <u>Adult development</u>. New York: Plenum Press.

3. A book with a corporate author:

American Psychological Association. (1983). <u>Publication Manual of the American Psychological Association</u> (3rd ed.). Washington, DC: Author.

Note: In this citation, the author and publisher are the same.

4. A book with no author or editor:

<u>Writers' and artists' yearbook</u>. (1980). London: Adam and Charles Black.

5. A translation:

Piaget, J. (1980). <u>Experiments in Contradiction</u> (D. Coltman, Trans.). Chicago: University of Chicago Press. (Original work published in 1974).

6. A book with an editor:

Erikson, E. H. (Ed.) (1978). <u>Adulthood</u>. New York: Norton.

Note: The name of the editor appears first when the whole text is cited rather than a single essay or chapter.

7. A revised edition:

Selye, H. (1978). The stress of life (rev. ed.). New York: McGraw-Hill.

Note: Abbreviate the edition as it is noted on the title page: 2nd ed. for second edition, 3rd ed. for third edition, and rev. ed. for revised edition.

8. An article or chapter in an edited book:

Rohlen, T. P. (1978). The promise of adulthood in Japan. In E. H. Erikson (Ed.), Adulthood. (pp. 129–140) New York: Norton.

PERIODICALS

1. A journal article with one author:

Rogers, C. R. (1964). Toward a modern approach to values. Journal of Abnormal and Social Psychology, 68, 160–167.

2. A journal article with two authors:

Feather, N. T., & Barber, J. G. (1983). Depressive reactions and unemployment. Journal of Abnormal Psychology, 92, 185–195.

3. A journal article with more than two authors:

Kerr, B., Davidson, J., Nelson, J., & Haley, S. (1982). Stimulus and response contributions to the children's reaction-time repetition effect. Journal of Experimental Child Psychology, 34, 526–541.

Note: Cite all authors in list of references, but in the parenthetical reference in the text, when there are more than six authors, cite the last name of the first author followed by et al.: (Rogers, et al.)

4. An article from a journal numbering pages continually throughout a volume:

Weeks, S. G. (1973). Youth and the transition to adult status: Uganda. Journal of Youth and Adolescence, 2, 259–270.

5. An article from a journal numbering pages separately for each issue:

Braddock, J. H.   (1985).   School desegregation and black
assimilation.   _Journal of Social Issues_, _41_ (3), 9–22.

6. An article written in a language other than English:

Delgorgue, M., & Engelhart, D.   Style graphique chez l'enfant:
Deux recherches sur la discrimination entre dessin d'enfant
"normal" et dessin d'enfant "pathologique." [Graphic
style among children: Two studies of differences between
the drawings of "normal" and "pathological" children].
Bulletin de Psychologie, _38_, 303–321.

Note: If the source used is an English translation, cite only the English
title, and do not use brackets.

7. An article condensed or reprinted in a journal other than its original
source:

Coleman, J. S.   (1973).   How do the young become adults?   _The_
Education Digest, _38_, 49–52.   (Condensed from _Review of_
Educational Research, 1972, _42_, 431–439)

8. A work cited in a secondary source:

Tizard, B.   (1984).   Problematic aspects of nuclear education.
Harvard Educational Review, _54_, 271–281.

Note: Cite the secondary source in the reference list, but cite both the
original and secondary sources in the text. For example, Tizard
refers to the results of an unpublished paper given at a conference in 1984. Cite that study in the text as follows: A study conducted in Sweden by Holmberg and Bergstrom in 1984 . . . (cited
in Tizard, 1984, p. 273–274).

9. The entire issue of a journal:

VandenBos, G. R. (Ed).   1986.   Psychotherapy research [Special
issue].   _American Psychologist_, _41_ (2).

Note: If there is no editor for the special issue, cite the title first, alpha-
betizing it by the first significant word in the title.

10. An abstract:

> Harding, C. & Kristiansen, C. M. (1984). Statistically
> sophisticated subjects' perceptions of the health risks of
> smoking. Journal of Social Psychology, 124 (2), 263–264.
> (From Psychological Abstracts, 1986, 73, Abstract No. 3651)

11. An article in a periodical published annually:

> Kessler, R. C., Price, R. H., & Wortman, C. B. (1985).
> Social factors in psychopathology: Stress, social support,
> and coping processes. Annual Review of Psychology, 36,
> 531–572.

12. A magazine article:

> Bettleheim, B. (1982, March 1). Reflections: Freud and the
> soul. New Yorker, pp. 52–93.

Note: APA uses p. and pp. to indicate pages of magazines, newspapers, and books, but not for journals.

13. A signed newspaper article:

> Anderson, J. (1983, July 25). Finding loving homes for
> hard-to-place children. Christian Science Monitor, p. 16.

14. An unsigned newspaper article:

> Women and gun ownership. (1986, February 24). New York
> Times, p. 18.

15. A newspaper article with discontinuous pages:

> Pear, R. (1986, February 24). Stiffer rules for nursing
> homes proposed. New York Times, pp. 1, 9.

16. An article from a newsletter:

> Staff. (1986, February 17). Effects of cocaine abuse on the
> unborn. Behavior Today, p. 3.

OTHER WRITTEN SOURCES

1. A report from the Government Printing Office:

National Institute on Alcohol Abuse and Alcoholism.   (1980).
Facts about alcohol and alcoholism (DHHS Publication No.
ADM 80-31).   Washington, DC: U.S. Government Printing
Office.

2. A report from an information or document deposit service:

Meyer, J. A., Ed.   (1982).   (Report No. ISBN-0-8447-1358-9).
Washington, DC: American Enterprise Institute for Public
Policy Research.   (ERIC Document Reproduction Service No.
ED 223 327)

3. A report of a congressional hearing:

Hearing before the House of Representatives Select Committee
on Children, Youth, and Families.   (1983).   Children's fear
of war.   Washington, DC: U.S. Government Printing Office.

NON-PRINT SOURCES

1. A video recording:

National Institute of Mental Health.   (1980).   Drug abuse
[Video recording].   Bethesda: Author.

2. A cassette recording:

Shapiro, H.   (1971).   Future of evolution (Cassette Recording
No. 010-13492).   Center for Cassette Studies.

3. A film:

Frenzini, L. R. (Producer).   (1973).   Neurotic behavior
[Film].   Del Mar, CA: CRM Educational Films.

Note: For films with both director and producer, cite as follows:
_____. (Producer), & _____. (Director).

CITING REFERENCES IN THE TEXT

The citations of references within the text of David Harris's paper provide models for the most common kinds of references. The following rules will help you cite other references in the text of your paper:

1. Separate references with more than two authors by commas and an ampersand (&) before the last: _____, _____, _____, & _____.
2. List all the names of authors for sources in the reference list. For parenthetical references of sources with six or more authors, use the name of the first author and et al.
3. Omit initials in textual citations except when there are two authors with the same last name.
4. Include all references cited in the text in a list of references at the end of the paper, except personal communications (letters or conversations) that cannot be retrieved by the reader.
5. Write out the full name of corporate authors for the first citation. You may, however, choose to abbreviate for citations after the first: American Psychological Association (APA).
6. Cite references that have no author by a shortened version of the title, usually the first two or three words, using quotation marks for articles or parts of books and a solid underline for titles of books.

A Sample Paper in the Social Sciences

David Harris wrote the sample paper in this chapter in a course in developmental psychology that focused on children and adolescents. He argues convincingly that the nuclear threat causes serious problems for some children and that responsible adults must take appropriate action to deal with these problems. David's paper illustrates the writing style and documentation method appropriate for a paper in the social sciences, following the guidelines of the American Psychological Association (1983).

Effects of Nuclear Threat
1

The Need for Education to Combat the
Psychological Effects of the Nuclear Threat on Children
David Harris
Psychology 325

Running head: EFFECTS OF NUCLEAR THREAT

Effects of Nuclear Threat

2

Abstract

A significant number of children in the United States, Russia, and some non-nuclear countries experience serious worry about nuclear weapons. The fear that they may not have a future may have harmful consequences for some, including living for the moment, engaging in self-destructive behavior, and leading a double life. These children need help from adults to deal with their fears and to regain a sense of hope; the first step in meeting these needs is for responsible adults to educate themselves about the problem and then to share appropriate knowledge with the young.

An abstract is a concise summary of the contents of the paper

Effects of Nuclear Threat

3

The Need for Education to Combat the
Psychological Effects of the Nuclear Threat on Children

A bright flash and a terrible noise followed by a
sense of dreadful loneliness in an empty, desolate
plain--then a child wakes crying and afraid from a
nightmare that is all too common among children. Child
psychiatrists, pediatricians, educators, and legislators
are becoming increasingly aware that the world's children
are paying a price for the arms race in their own
psychological welfare, and many have concluded that they
must do something and encourage others to respond to the
problem. Although there is much to learn about how to
deal with children's fears of nuclear disaster, those
responsible for the welfare of children must act now to
educate themselves and to provide children with the
information and reassurance they need to grow up in the
nuclear age.

That significant numbers of children suffer from
fears of a nuclear catastrophe has been known for some
time. In the wake of the threats to use nuclear weapons
at the time of the Berlin crisis in 1961 and the Cuban
missile crisis in 1962, two researchers, Escalona (1965)
and Schwebel (1965), independently undertook studies in
U.S. high schools to discover how young people are
affected by living in the nuclear age. Both concluded
that the majority of high school students are seriously
worried about the danger of nuclear war. At the time that

Opening sentence catches reader's attention

Introduction

Thesis sentence

Second paragraph gives background

Use last names of authors followed by date

Effects of Nuclear Threat

4

these studies were published, there was little public
response to the problems they exposed, and it was not
until the late 1970s that researchers resumed
investigation into the psychological effects of the
nuclear threat on children. Inspired in part by the
accident at the Three Mile Island nuclear reactor plant
and further spurred by recent findings that a nuclear war
would create a "nuclear winter" with devastating effects
on plant and animal life (Turco, Toon, Ackerman, Pollack,
& Sagan, 1983), increasing numbers of researchers in
psychiatry, the social sciences, and education, as well
as legislators, have undertaken investigations to discover
what children know and think about the issue and how
their perceptions may affect their lives.

    A number of studies conducted in the last decade
reveal that significant numbers of children are profoundly
concerned about nuclear weapons. As part of a report
published by the American Psychiatric Association,
Beardsley and Mack (1982) prepared an article entitled
"The Impact on Children and Adolescents of Nuclear
Developments," in which they reported the results of a
study based on 1,151 questionnaires administered to three
diverse groups--one made up of grammar school students,
two of high school age youth--in three U.S. cities. This
study revealed that a sizable number from all groups were
"deeply disturbed about the threats of nuclear war and
the risks of nuclear power" (p. 88). When asked what the

For more than two authors but fewer than six, use names of all authors for first citation

This paragraph presents data and builds argument

Effects of Nuclear Threat

5

word "nuclear" brings to their minds, the respondents
came up with largely negative images: "Dead wildlife and
humans . . . cancer . . . people dying, buildings ruined,
society demolished . . . stars, planets, space, darkness
. . . the world's final demise" (pp. 75–76). In a study

Include page numbers for quotations

based on lengthy interviews with thirty-one high school
students, Goodman, Mack, Beardsley, and Snow (1983) found
that "although some try not to dwell on it, while others
claim that they worry constantly, all 31 of the
adolescents assert that the existence of nuclear weapons
impinges upon their lives on a daily basis" (p. 510).
There is also evidence that the number of young people
who worry about this issue is increasing. Bachman (1983)
studied the attitudes toward the military of graduating
high school seniors every spring from 1976 to 1982 and
found that the percentage who said that they often
worried about the nuclear threat rose steadily from 7.2
percent in 1976 to 31.2 in 1982.

Most of the studies reveal that a significant number
of youth are seriously worried, and they also suggest
that a substantial number are not troubled by nuclear
fears, a fact that leads some researchers to question
which children are concerned and why. Recent studies
suggest that age and socioeconomic status affect
children's level of awareness and concern. In his book
The Moral Life of Children (1986) Robert Coles reports the
results of research conducted over a period of some six

Use first name when author is very well known

years during which he interviewed and observed small
groups of children around the country, coming back to
talk to some of the children more than once and over a
period of years. Coles concludes that young children are
incapable of comprehending certain laws of physics and
chemistry, and as a consequence some have little or no
knowledge of the nature of the nuclear threat. He talked
to several children who "thought that nuclear bombs have
more 'dynamite' than other bombs" (p. 259). Others, like a
black child from Mississippi who worries what would
happen "if the Klan ever got that bomb" (p. 257),
incorporate nuclear anxieties within more absorbing
fears.

Before the age of twelve many children may have very
distorted notions about what nuclear bombs are, but once
they are old enough to comprehend the nature of nuclear
weapons, the degree of children's concern seems to be
affected by parental attitudes and social class. Poor
children are preoccupied with much more immediate fears
of hunger, parental unemployment, and violence (Coles).
Among the large number of children of lower-middle-class
families, where having enough money to maintain a certain
standard of living is a primary concern, the "end of the
world" is likely to mean always having "a bill collector
at the door" (Coles, p. 278). In more affluent families,
on the other hand, children are likely "to worry long and
hard about nuclear accidents or wars" if their parents

Effects of Nuclear Threat

7

do, and yet these are the same children who seem to be able to adapt to the nuclear world, to express their fears and to go on enjoying their privileged lives (p. 279).

Children in countries with nuclear weapons and those from non-nuclear countries seem to have comparable levels of concern. A study by Chivian and Mack (1983) comparing attitudes of U.S. and Soviet children found that although more children from this country thought that a nuclear war was likely to occur in their lifetimes, more Soviet children thought that if such a war should occur, they would not survive. Children in neutral countries that do not have nuclear weapons are anxious about the same issues. A study conducted in Sweden (Holmberg and Bergstrom, 1984) revealed that Swedish children are equally concerned, though the fears they emphasize fall halfway between those of the Soviet and U.S. children (cited in Tizard, 1984). Another study, in Finland, also found widespread anxiety about nuclear issues (cited in Tizard, 1984).

The fear that children experience is an appropriate and perhaps inevitable response to the danger posed by nuclear weapons, but it may have serious consequences for some. Beardsley and Mack (1982) noted their strongest finding to be "a general unquiet or uneasiness about the future and about the present nature of nuclear weapons and nuclear power. There is a particular uncertainty

Indicate in parentheses that a source is cited in a secondary source

Effects of Nuclear Threat

8

about nuclear war or the limiting of such a war should it occur, and the possibilities of survival" (p. 89). One of the consequences of this uncertainty about the future for some youth is a sense of futurelessness.

The fact that so many young people are generally pessimistic about whether there will be a future "might make some adolescents disillusioned and highly present-oriented rather than being willing to accept delay of gratification or to plan for the future" (Beardsley and Mack, 1983, p. 82). Goodman, Mack, Beardsley, and Snow (1983) found that some of the adolescents they interviewed say they "live for the day" and "don't hold back," behavior that they blame on their fear of a nuclear catastrophe (p. 526). Although these investigators warn that the nuclear threat is probably only one of many factors contributing to "impulsivity and immediacy in personal relationships and behavior," it does seem to make a significant contribution to that behavior (p. 526).

A number of researchers associate the lack of hope in the future with self-destructive behavior. A sense of futurelessness resulting from the nuclear threat may be the cause of drug and alcohol abuse for some young people and suicide for others. Goodman et al. (1983) had several respondents claim that the nuclear threat is responsible for excessive drug use. One sixteen-year-old made the connection explicit: "When I was doing drugs though, I was scared of nuclear [arms]" (p. 512). Carl Rogers

Use brackets around any material added to a quotation

Effects of Nuclear Threat
9

(1984), who believes that "the prospect of nuclear war" has a serious detrimental effect on the young, quotes one young alcoholic who drinks "to get wasted" because then "nothing seems to matter" (p. 11). Some psychologists attribute the alarming increase in the suicide rate among young people to a growing sense of hopelessness about the future, and Rogers (1984) insists that there can be no doubt that "the possibility of a nuclear war plays a part in that hopelessness" (p. 11). Others, however, warn of the misconceptions that could come from taking children's fear of nuclear war out of context of their other fears (Tizard). Elkind (1983), testifying before the House Select Committee on Children, Youth, and Families, argued that the recent increases in suicide, substance abuse, and crime among the young are attributable to all the stresses that they encounter, the nuclear threat being only one (Hearing, p. 54).

> Page number needed here for particular part of report

If fear of nuclear annihilation leads some young people to live for the moment, sometimes engaging in self-destructive behavior, others learn to cope by leading what Robert Lifton (1982) has called "a double life" (p. 627). Goodman et al. (1983) note that some adolescents who "fear that nuclear war is inevitable" live on two levels, fearing that there will be no future and yet planning for it. Coles (1986) tells about the teenage girl from an affluent family who answered a questionnaire in which she "quite truthfully proclaimed

Effects of Nuclear Threat
10

her horror of a nuclear war," and then that very evening attended an elegant party and had a wonderful time (p. 279). Lifton (1983) explains that living such a double life has detrimental effects, and that "children experience it with particular intensity because they lack the psychological defenses and rationalizations that adults are so skillful at constructing." He adds that it "complicates young people's already difficult task of coming to terms with death which, in turn, impairs their psychological capacity to live" (<u>Hearing</u>, p. 71).

This paragraph shifts from a presentation of the problem to the need for a solution
Children need help from responsible adults in dealing with their fears of the nuclear threat. Salguero (1983), a child psychiatrist at Yale University, argues that since all children need to feel protected by their parents from serious external threats as well as from everyday dangers, parents must recognize that many children are afraid and that their fears are affecting their psychological well-being. Salguero explains that what often happens is that in order to cope themselves, adults engage in "massive denial," and that some children who appear to deny the nuclear threat are actually "waiting for a signal" that it is all right to talk about their fears. In order to help youth "to change fear into hope," adults need to "communicate their true feelings and their own views and perceptions" (p. 95). Lifton, who has studied a form of denial that he calls "psychic numbing" (1982), explains that adolescents have

problems when they suppress fears in childhood because
the denial of fears does not last forever. The images
suppressed in childhood come back to haunt them in
adolescence.

Some children hold adults responsible for what they
consider to be an absurd situation. Interpreting the work
of Carey, who has studied the effects of bomb shelter
drills on children during the 1950s, Lifton (1982)
explains that children who were told that they could
protect themselves from a nuclear blast by diving under a
desk and covering their heads with paper knew that what
they were doing was ridiculous. Testifying before the
House Select Committee on Children, Youth, and Families,
Lifton explained that children sense that their parents
doubt their ability to see them safely into adulthood and
they "associate it with an overall inability on the part
of the adult world to guarantee the safety of the young"
(p. 68). Some researchers speculate that young people's
perception of the absurdity of "duck-and-cover drills"
may have contributed in the sixties to the breakdown of
confidence in the elders, who some young people felt were
"unreliable, perhaps even insane" (Gittelson, 1982, p.
145). Mack (1982) found that teenagers' attitudes toward
the nuclear threat include "a protest at the arrogance of
adults who have put them in this situation" (p. 593).
Salguero (1983) goes a step further, arguing that unless
parents talk to their children and take steps with them

to cope with the nuclear threat, "adolescents will view the adults' denial as numbness and folly, responsible for the world's destruction" (p. 96).

Children and adolescents need to have solutions, hope for the future, and a first step in creating that hope is for adults to work to rebuild confidence between themselves and youth. According to Escalona (1982), the way adults respond to "ultimate danger" is to children "the ultimate test of the trustworthiness of adult society" (p. 607). To be hopeful about the future, young people "need to know that there are adults struggling to see that reason prevails in human affairs--strong adults, whom they can depend upon" (Schwebel, 1982, p. 613). They need to be engaged in dialogues in which they can "see adults confronting the danger and acting responsibly" (Goodman et al., p. 529).

There is no single solution to the nuclear threat or to the problems it creates for children and adolescents, but one significant aspect of any set of solutions must be education. Although some people argue that youth should be shielded from the horrible facts of the nuclear threat (Hearings, Voth, 1983, p. 11), most people realize that it is impossible to protect even very small children from knowledge of the nuclear danger. They already know, and they want to know more. Goodman et al. found that when questioned about the issue, young people repeatedly insisted that they wanted information about nuclear

After first
citation of a
source with more
than two authors
give first
author's name
followed by et al.

weapons in order to "overcome an overwhelming sense of
frustration and helplessness" (p. 528). Among the
teenagers interviewed for Goodman's study, many said that
they want to learn more about nuclear issues. One girl
expressed a desire to "know more," though she did not
know where to go for information. Another insisted that
"the public . . . has to be educated," while still
another saw the only chance for change to be in "people
being more aware." One seventeen-year-old who had taken a
course in nuclear weapons felt that the fear of the
unknown was much greater than the known: "Before, I just
didn't understand it. It was just this huge fear, like a
black hole" (p. 521). After reviewing the literature on
children's understanding of nuclear war, Tizard (1984)
concludes that significant numbers of young people are
anxious about the nuclear threat, that their level of
understanding of the issue is low, and that they want to
be "better informed" (p. 280).

Education, then, seems to be the logical first step
in dealing with the psychological problems caused by the
nuclear threat, but to begin that process, adults must
deal with what Mack (1984) calls "resistance to knowing"
(p. 263). Educators and other responsible adults must end
their own denial of the problem and learn more about the
effects that living in the nuclear age is having on
today's youth. The mechanisms by which people draw back
from the contemplation of intense horror are often used to

avoid confronting the reality of nuclear annihilation.
Even people who have an adequate intellectual
understanding of the nuclear dilemma need to reduce what
Mack calls "the margin between intellectual and emotional
knowing" (p. 264) in order to become effective educators.

Researchers may not know very much about how to help
young people deal with their fears, but most agree with
Lifton that they can begin with "the sharing of
knowledge" (Hearing, 1983, p. 73). Goodman et al. (1983)
note that when young people are educated to the realities
of the threat, "they can overcome at least that aspect of
fear that stems from ignorance and that leaves them
powerless" (p. 528). Goldenring (1983) urges that adults
must find a forum to discuss the nuclear threat with
children "in churches, in schools, in communities, and in
families throughout the US and indeed throughout the
world" (Hearing, p. 63), while Mack (1983) notes the need
for educational programs in the schools and for
opportunities for young people to talk about the issue
(Hearing, p. 46).

Concluding
paragraph sum-
marizes main
points of paper
and notes
conclusions
drawn.

There are significant numbers of children and
adolescents in the United States and other countries who
are affected by the nuclear threat, and for some, fears
of a nuclear disaster may be causing serious psychological
problems, ranging from drug abuse to the consequences of
psychic numbing. Responsible adults--psychologists,
educators, legislators, and parents--must help troubled
youth cope with their fears first by confronting their

own fears and by demonstrating to young people that there
are concerned people struggling to prevent a catastrophe.
The next step is to work to devise means to educate young
people in a way that will help them have or gain a sense
of control over an issue that troubles so many. There is a
need for more research both on the impact of the arms
race on youth and, since there is considerable controversy
about how to provide children and adolescents with
information appropriate to their age and level of
development, on the kinds of educational experiences that
will be most helpful. Adults must not wait until there is
a consensus about the best course of action, however.
They must do the best they can with the information they
have to talk to children, to teach them, and to provide
them with an opportunity to express their fears. Children
are having nightmares now.

Effects of Nuclear Threat
16

References

Bachman, J. G. (1983). American high school seniors view the military: 1976–1982. Armed Forces and Society, 10, 86–104.

Beardsley, W., and Mack, J. E. (1982). The impact on children and adolescents of nuclear development. In Psychological Aspects of Nuclear Developments, Task Force Report #20. Washington, DC: American Psychiatric Association.

Beardsley, W. and Mack, J. E. (1983). Adolescents and the threat of nuclear war: the evolution of a perspective. Yale Journal of Biology and Medicine, 56, 79–91.

Coles, Robert. (1986). The moral life of children. Boston: Atlantic Monthly Press.

Escalona, S. K. (1965). Children and the threat of nuclear war. In M. Schwebel (Ed.), Behavioral Science and Human Survival (pp. 201–209). Palo Alto, CA: Science and Behavior Books.

Escalona, S. K. (1982). Growing up with the threat of nuclear war: some indirect effects on personality development. American Journal of Orthopsychiatry, 52, 600–607.

Gittelson, N. (1982, May). The fear that haunts children. McCalls, 77–146.

Goodman, L., Mack, J., Beardsley, W., Snow, R. (1983). The threat of nuclear war and the nuclear arms race: adolescent experience and perceptions. Political Psychology, 4 (3), 501–514.

Hearing before The House of Representative Select
    Committee on Children, Youth, and Families. (1983).
    Children's Fear of War. Washington, DC: U.S.
    Government Printing Office.
Lifton, R. J. (1982). Beyond psychic numbing: A call to
    awareness. American Journal of Orthopsychiatry, 52,
    619–629.
Mack, J. E. (1984). Resistances to knowing in the
    nuclear age. Harvard Educational Review, 54, 260–270.
Rogers, C. R. (1982). A psychologist looks at nuclear
    war: its threat, its possible prevention. Journal of
    Humanistic Psychology, 22 (4), 9–20.
Salguero, C. (1983). Children and the nuclear threat: A
    child psychiatrist's personal reflections. Yale
    Journal of Biology and Medicine, 56, 93–96.
Schwebel, M. (1965). In M. Schwebel (Ed.), Behavioral
    Science and Human Survival (pp. 210–223). Palo Alto,
    CA: Science and Behavior Books.
Schwebel, M. (1984). Effects of the nuclear war threat
    on children and teenagers: Implications for
    professionals. American Journal of Orthopsychiatry,
    52, 608–617.
Tizard, B. (1984). Problematic aspects of nuclear
    education. Harvard Educational Review, 54, 271–281.
Turco, R. P., Toon, O. B., Ackerman, T. P., Pollack, J.
    B., & Sagan, C. (1983). Nuclear winter: Global
    consequences of multiple nuclear explosions. Science,
    222, 1283–1292.

13

WRITING RESEARCH PAPERS IN THE NATURAL AND APPLIED SCIENCES

Approaches to Research in the Natural and Applied Sciences

The natural sciences are divided into three groups: physical sciences—chemistry, physics, and astronomy; the earth sciences—geology, paleontology, oceanography, and meteorology; and the life sciences—biology and medicine. Each of the individual disciplines is divided into different branches, and a student who does research in one of the sciences would focus on a very narrow aspect of one of the subdisciplines, such as a single chemical reaction.

Students who do research in the sciences might write papers based on one of the following: their own original research projects; a review of the literature in scholarly journals on a particular topic; a study of review articles; or an examination of articles in popular science journals such as *Scientific American.*

In chemistry, senior-level students might do research to develop a method for a particular chemical analysis—toxic wastes, for example—and then write a paper based on the research. Such a paper is divided into three parts. The first is a review of the history of the problem to be studied; the second is a discussion of the methods used, the results obtained, and an interpretation of the results; and the third section is a detailed description of the methods.

Undergraduate students of chemistry may also write research papers based strictly on what other people have done. In a class requiring a research paper, one student might review the literature published in scholarly journals on a topic like the absorption of light by inorganic compounds, bioluminescence (why fireflies light up), or the conversion of coal to oil. Another student might read review articles on a single topic like the synthesis of a chemical compound, while yet another might consult a

212

number of articles in popular science periodicals to write a paper on phero-mones or DNA chemistry.

Undergraduate students majoring in biology will probably write research papers that review the literature on a topic studied in conjunction with a lab project or, as in other sciences, they might review the literature and write a paper on topics that are being discussed in class. The topics that students might research in order to write a review paper range from the effects of acid rain on the growth and development of spruces, firs, and pines to how cell membranes function.

Students of physics, geology, and the remaining natural sciences might write research papers to accompany a laboratory or field project, review the literature on a topic considered in class, or explore the practical application of a natural phenomenon.

The applied sciences include the traditional fields of engineering—mechanical, civil, electrical, architectural, chemical, aeronautical—as well as the rapidly expanding fields of technology related to computer science. Students might research new synthetic building materials, explore the use of computers in diagnosing heart disease, or study and evaluate the achievement of a particularly influential architect.

Making a Reference List for Papers in the Sciences

If you are writing a scientific paper as part of an assignment for a science class, your instructor will probably give you instructions about the particular form to follow. Many students, however, write papers on scientific topics as part of a composition course taught by English departments. Such papers should use the scientific documentation style that is illustrated in this chapter.

Carol Garcia documented her paper by listing all reference sources at the end of her paper in the order cited, numbering them consecutively, and then inserting the number in parentheses within the text. When she wanted to specify page or volume number, she inserted it within the parentheses. When she repeated a reference, she used the original reference number rather than a new number. This system is widely used, simple and clear, and appropriate for most undergraduate papers in the sciences. It is one of the styles recommended by the *ACS Style Guide* (1986) published by the American Chemical Society. This style is used not only in chemistry, but in engineering and by various publications in other scientific disciplines. The list of references at the end of Carol's paper provides models for citing various materials found in books. Samples of three other commonly cited kinds of references are given on the following page.

Some scientific publications vary this system slightly by making the numbers in the text superscripts rather than enclosing them in parentheses. Others list the sources at the end of the paper in alphabetical order according to author and insert the author's name and the year of publication in parentheses within the text.

Styles of documentation vary more in the natural and applied sciences than in the humanities and social sciences. When in doubt, you should ask your instructor to specify the preferred style or should look in a professional journal in the field. At least once a year, and often in each issue, journals will publish "instructions for authors" that give the preferred style.

When scientists publish papers in professional journals, they do not place page numbers within parentheses in the text, but instead cite the full work. Instructors, however, often request that students indicate the exact page of each reference. Carol's instructor advised her to note page numbers in the text for those references cited more than once.

The form for citing an author's name varies considerably in scientific research. Journal articles typically use initials and the last name. Books often include the given name. In every case, you should cite the author's name as it appears on the title page of your source.

The following sample entries supplement the models in Carol's list of references (see p. 225):

(1) Grimmer, D. P. Solar Energy 1981, 26(1), 49.

Note: The title of the article is not given, only the title of the journal; the volume number (here, 26) is underlined; the issue number (1) follows in parentheses with no space between it and the volume; only the first page number of the article is noted.

(2) Drew, M. S.; Selvage, R. B. G. Energy 1981, 5, 407.

Note: No issue number is included since the pages of the journal are numbered consecutively throughout a volume. The names of all the authors are given and joined by a semicolon.

(3) "Retrofitting a Residence for Solar Heating and Cooling." Natl. Bur. Stand. (U.S.) Tech. Note Nov. 1975, No. 892.

Note: Do give titles for government bulletins along with all other information needed to retrieve the document.

A Sample Paper in the Natural and Applied Sciences

Carol Garcia, whose paper is reproduced in this chapter, was a student in a freshman English class. She was also taking a course in physics and was allowed to use the paper to fulfill part of her requirements for that course as well. She chose to write a paper that combines the principles of physics with architectural design.

Carol Garcia
Physics 121, Sec. 4
December 2, 1982

DESIGN FOR THE FUTURE:
PASSIVE SOLAR HOMES

    In recent years many Americans who have always
enjoyed living in comfortably heated and cooled homes find
that they can no longer afford to do so. The problem, of
course, is that the cost of energy has risen dramatically
in the last few years and that most apartments and houses
built in the United States since World War II were designed
with the idea that there would always be a supply of cheap
energy. But the most commonly used source of energy--
fossil fuel--is being rapidly used up and is becoming
increasingly expensive; and the future usefulness of
nuclear power--once thought to be an attractive
substitute for fossil fuels--is controversial (1).

    There is, however, an unlimited source of energy
available to us in the form of sunlight. The simplest,
most economical, and most effective way to use the sun's
energy is to design houses that capture and retain the
sun's heat in the winter and exclude it in the summer. To
create buildings that maximize solar heat collection in
cold months and minimize it in the summer, it is necessary
to understand how solar heat may be collected,
transferred, and stored (2, p 5).

    Solar radiation (sunlight) passes through transparent
or translucent materials--glazing--and is experienced as
light and heat. When sunlight hits a mass, it is either

First number in
parentheses
refers to first item
in bibliography

Thesis statement
or controlling
idea

Parenthetical
numbers refer to
p. 5 of the second
item in
bibliography

2

reflected or absorbed. Effective masses for absorbing heat waves are dark masonry objects or dark containers filled with water. Collecting solar heat requires a glazed wall situated for maximum solar exposure and containing a dark mass to absorb the heat waves (2, p 28).

Conduction is the process of moving heat energy through molecules of a mass. By transferring energy from one molecule to another, a mass can take on more and more heat. Solar energy can be effectively stored in an object that is a good conductor of heat, such as cement, brick, adobe, and water, all of which can be incorporated into house design (2, p 29).

Convection is the transfer of heat between a mass and a fluid substance (liquid or gas) or within a fluid causing a flow as the warmer, less dense portion rises and the colder and denser portion falls under the influence of gravity. The process of convection allows for moving heat from a storage medium into living space and for circulating the air within a living space as warm air rises, is cooled by contact with a cooler surface, and falls to be heated again by the storage medium (2, p 21).

Passive solar design refers to those features of a building that collect, store, and distribute heat from the sun by converting sunlight to heat, conducting it into a storage medium, and finally moving it about a living space through convection. One way to bring sunlight into a building is through south-facing windows, a method known as direct gain (see illus. 1). Sunlight passes through windows and is absorbed by objects or parts of the building, which convert it into heat. Effective solar buildings usually have one of these features: heavy walls

Directs readers to first illustration

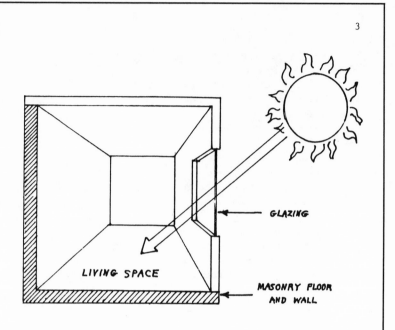

Illus. 1: Direct Gain

of brick or masonry, floors of brick or tile over concrete,
or large containers of water within the living space (3, p
330). Each of these features adds to the amount of heat
that can be stored in a building, and some solar designs
intended for houses in cold climates employ all three.

Rooms with a floor-to-ceiling thermal storage wall
placed between large south-facing glazed panels and the
living space itself have less temperature fluctuation than
those heated only through south-facing windows. Heat is

4

generated as sunlight passes through the glass and warms
the walls--usually made of masonry or water-filled
containers--where it is stored. It is then radiated back
into the living space. Since thermal storage walls built of
masonry were popularized by Felix Trombe, who incorporated
masonry walls into row houses in the South of France (2, p
45), masonry thermal storage walls are referred to as
Trombe walls (see illus. 2).

   A third method of passive solar heating is to attach
an extra glazed space to the south side of a structure

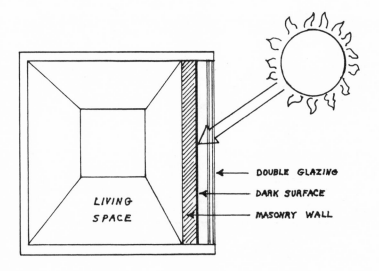

DOUBLE GLAZING

DARK SURFACE

MASONRY WALL

LIVING
SPACE

Illus. 2: Trombe Wall

5

that can be closed off from the adjacent living space,
creating a sunspace, called a greenhouse if it is used for
growing plants (4) (see illus. 3). Sunspaces must have
some thermal mass to collect or store heat, such as a dark
masonry floor, water-filled containers, or a common
masonry wall between the sunspace and adjacent living
space (4, p 195-6). There must be some arrangement of vents
or windows to allow warm air to flow into the adjacent

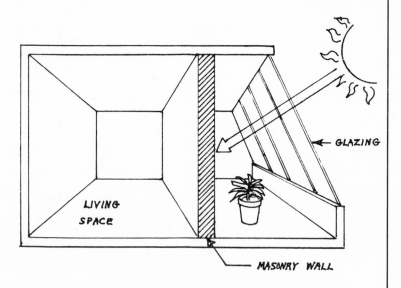

Illus. 3: Attached Greenhouse

6

living areas and to exhaust excess heat in the summer (2, p 181). Some sunspaces use electrically powered blowers to bring the heat into the interior rooms (5). Large sunspaces can provide attractive and pleasant living space, and they can be used to grow flowers and vegetables (5).

A convective loop collector--consisting of glass panels attached to an existing south wall, which is painted a dark color--is an inexpensive structure for solar heating. The wall of the house is vented at the top and bottom of the frame to bring cool air out of the house through the bottom vent and to send heated air into the adjoining rooms through the top vent, thus forming a convective loop (see illus. 4). The convective loop collector is simple, easy to install, and economical. It has no storage capacity for night heating, however, and therefore only provides heat during the day (6, v1, p 9).

Source number 6, volume 1, page 9

Designs for solar houses may use one or any combination of these features, and the amount of glazing and mass, as well as the ideal size of a sunspace, vary according to site, economic resources, climate, and taste (5). The passive solar elements of a building should be chosen along with other features, such as the shape of the house and placement and size of rooms. Solar houses are generally elongated along an east-west axis to provide large areas for glazing on the south side; and bedrooms, living rooms, and the kitchen are typically placed on the south side for maximum lighting and solar heat (2, p 90).

A successful solar design includes features for retaining heat that would otherwise be lost by conduction and radiation through walls, roofs, windows, and floors,

7

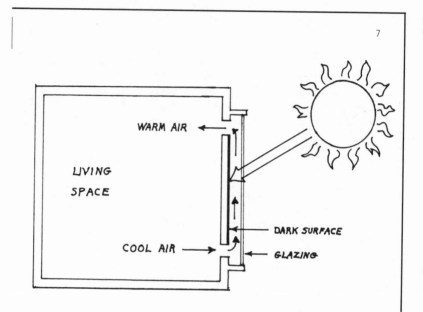

Illus. 4: Convective Loop Collector

especially at night as the outside air cools, and by
convection as it moves through cracks around windows,
doors, foundations, and even electrical outlets. Cold air
leaking in replaces the warm air. All of the air in a
typical house is replaced from one to two times per hour
(7). The use of weather stripping, caulking, storm windows,
double glazing, and seals for air leaks will reduce
convective heat loss; and insulating materials--materials
that resist heat conduction--added to exterior walls,
attics, and the airspace beneath a house will reduce heat

loss by conduction (6, v 3, p 6). The ideal amount of
insulation, like the size of glazed area and the amount of
thermal mass, will vary according to climate and site (5).
Effective reduction of heat loss in most homes requires
careful attention to many small details that in combination
can have large results. The Report of the Energy Project
at the Harvard Business School estimates that by installing
"six-inch insulation in the ceiling, adding storm windows
and doors, and sealing air leaks with caulking and weather
stripping in twenty million homes which are currently
inadequately insulated, residential consumption of energy
could be reduced by twenty-five per cent" (8). Some
experts say that the first step people should take to make
their homes more energy efficient is to add more
insulation (5).

Another common design feature for retaining heat in
solar homes is earth sheltering, sometimes called earth
berming. The rate of heat conduction through an exterior
wall depends on the difference in temperature between the
inside and the outside of the house, and since the
temperature of the earth two feet below the surface is
always warmer than the air in winter, sufficient earth
piled against the north, east, or west walls of a house
will slow the heat loss. Some solar homes even use earth
sheltering on the roof, but they must be designed to
support the additional weight. All surfaces exposed to the
earth require special waterproofing (9).

Any successful solar design must minimize cooling
requirements during hot weather. Passive design features
that can limit the heat entering a house during hot
weather are earth sheltering, shading, ventilation, and

9

reflective surfaces. Since the earth temperature below the
surface is usually significantly cooler than the air in
hot climates, the part of a house that is below the
surface will lose heat to the cooler earth (6, v 1, p 18).
Shading, which prevents the sun's rays from penetrating
the house, can be accomplished with awnings, overhangs,
deciduous trees, or vines on trellises (2, p 225). To
increase air movement, windows should be placed for cross
ventilation, rooms arranged so that doors can be opened to
allow air to flow freely, and attics and other areas that
collect heat vented to allow hot air to escape. Light-
colored roof surfaces, exterior walls, and window coverings
can also reflect the heat away from a house (2, p 262-6).

People who design, build, and live in successful
solar homes or who retrofit old ones with solar features
experience psychological, economic, and social benefits.
They know the pleasure of working with rather than against
nature, and they enjoy the feeling of well-being created
by the warmth of the sun captured in their own homes.
Their initial financial investment earns dividends in lower
utility bills, and over the lifetime of the home, the
investment will be returned many times (5).

Conclusion shows why the paper's topic is important

10

References

(1) Lovins, Amory B. "Soft Energy Paths"; Friends of the Earth: San Francisco, 1977.

(2) Mazria, Edward. "The Passive Solar Energy Book"; Rodale Press: Emmaus, PA, 1979.

(3) Farallones Institute. "The Integral Urban House: Self-Reliant Living in the City"; Sierra Club Books: San Francisco, 1979, p 330.

(4) McCullagh, James C., Ed. "The Solar Greenhouse Book"; Rodale Press: Emmaus, PA, 1978.

(5) Creech, Dennis, Director of the Georgia Solar Coalition, Atlanta, GA, personal communication, 1982.

(6) Georgia Solar Coalition. "Putting the Sun to Work: A Guide to Residential Solar Options in Georgia," 3 vols.; Georgia Office of Energy Resources: Atlanta, GA, 1981.

(7) Langdon, William K. "Movable Insulation"; Rodale: Emmaus, PA, 1980, p 9.

(8) Yergin, Daniel. In "Energy Future: Report of the Energy Project of the Harvard Business School"; Stobaugh, Robert; Yergin, Daniel, Eds.; Random House: New York, 1979, p 172.

(9) The Underground Space Center: University of Minnesota. "Earth Sheltered Homes"; Van Nostrand Reinhold: New York, 1978, p 129.

Appendix A

THE MLA ALTERNATIVE: DOCUMENTING WITH NOTES

Some instructors may request that you document your papers with both notes and a list of sources, though you may be asked to document a paper with endnotes or footnotes only. Since all the information needed to identify a source is included in a note, notes provide adequate documentation. Footnotes differ from endnotes only in their placement in the text. Footnotes are placed at the bottom of the page—the same page on which the citation is found. Endnotes are consolidated in one list and placed at the end of the paper.

Number notes consecutively throughout your paper, beginning with 1. Place the number at the end of a phrase, sentence, or paragraph, or immediately following any quoted material, even if only a single word. Raise the number slightly above the line; such numbers are called superscripts.

The form used for notes is slightly different from that of a list of sources. For example, an author's first name is given first since notes are not listed alphabetically. There are also variations in punctuation and indentation. Compare the bibliographic citation below with the note that follows.

Bibliographic citation:

```
Lash, Joseph P.  Eleanor: The Years Alone.  New York: Norton,
     1972.
```

Note citation:

```
     Joseph P. Lash, Eleanor: The Years Alone (New York: Norton,
1972) 220.
```

Documentary Notes (Endnotes and Footnotes)

The following models, using the MLA style, will help you design documentary endnotes, footnotes, and content notes. For the APA style and the scientific number system mentioned above, see chapters 12 and 13.

BOOKS

1. A book with one author:

   M. H. Abrams, *The Mirror and the Lamp* (New York: Oxford UP, 1953) 234.

2. Two or more books by the same author:

   Give the author's complete name in each note.

3. A book with two authors:

   James W. Davidson and Mark Lytle, *After the Fact* (New York: Knopf, 1982) 272.

4. A book with three authors:

   Herman Kahn, William Brown, and Leon Martel, *The Next 200 Years* (New York: William Morrow, 1976) 84.

5. A book with more than three authors:

   Bernard Bailyn et al., *The Great Republic: A History of The American People* (Lexington, MA: Heath, 1977) 959.

   Note: The abbreviation "et al." stands for "and others."

6. A book with a corporate author:

   U.S. Department of Energy, *An Assessment of Thermal Insulation Materials* (Washington, DC: GPO, 1978) 57.

   Note: GPO is an abbreviation for Government Printing Office.

7. A book with an anonymous author:

> Writers' and Artists' Yearbook, 1980 (London: Adam and
> Charles Black, 1980) 93.

8. A book with an author who uses a pseudonym (a fictitious name):

> Michael Innes [J. I. M. Stewart], Going It Alone (New
> York: Dodd, 1980) 23.

Note: The author's real name may be supplied in brackets.

9. A scholarly edition:

> Charles Dickens, Oliver Twist, ed. Kathleen Tillotson,
> The Clarendon Dickens (Oxford: Clarendon, 1966) 211.

Note: If the work of the editor is being discussed or cited, the editor's name comes first:

> Kathleen Tillotson, ed., Oliver Twist, by Charles Dickens,
> The Clarendon Dickens (Oxford: Clarendon, 1966) 211.

10. A work in a series:

> Donald H. Reiman, Shelley's "The Triumph of Life": A
> Critical Study, Illinois Studies in Lang. and Lit. 55 (Urbana:
> U of Illinois P, 1965) 34.

11. A single work published in more than one volume (with continuous pagination):

> Edgar Johnson, Sir Walter Scott: The Great Unknown, 2
> vols. (London: Hamish Hamilton, 1970) 117.

12. A book that is part of a multivolume work with a single title:

> Arnold Kettle, An Introduction to the English Novel
> (London: Hutchinson U Library, 1953) 2: 74.

13. A book that is part of a multivolume work by one author when each volume has a separate title:

> Robert Coles, Privileged Ones, vol. 5 of Children of
> Crisis (Boston: Little, 1977) 506.

14. A book that is part of a multivolume work when each volume has a separate title and author:

> J. I. M. Stewart, Eight Modern Writers, vol. 12 of Oxford History of English Literature (Oxford: Oxford UP, 1963) 519.

15. A book with different authors for each chapter and a single editor:

> Daniel Hoffman, ed., Harvard Guide to Contemporary American Writing (Cambridge, MA: Harvard UP, 1979) iv.

16. A reprint of an older edition:

> Christina Stead, The Man Who Loved Children (1940; rpt. New York: Holt, 1965) 132.

17. A paperback reprint of a hardback edition:

> Rosellen Brown, Civil Wars (1984; New York: Penguin, 1985) 185–190.

Note: The date, but not the publisher, of the first edition is given immediately after the title.

18. A revised edition:

> Richard Ellmann, James Joyce, 2nd ed. (New York: Oxford UP, 1982) 395.

19. A revised version of a work of literature:

> John Fowles, The Magus, rev. version (Boston: Little, 1977) 245.

20. A translation:

> Homer, The Iliad, trans. Richmond Lattimore (Chicago: U of Chicago P, 1951) 142.

Note: If the work of the translator is being discussed, this should be cited as follows:

> Richmond Lattimore, trans., The Iliad, by Homer (Chicago: U of Chicago P, 1953) 142.

21. Sacred writings: Citations from the Bible and other sacred writings are
    usually documented within parentheses in the text of the paper: (Gen.
    20:1–17). Sacred writings referred to in a note are neither underlined
    nor placed in quotation marks.

PARTS OF BOOKS

1. An article, essay, chapter, or other part of a book with a single author:

   > Doris Lessing, "The Temptation of Jack Orkney," in
   > Stories (New York: Knopf, 1978) 564.

2. An introduction, afterword, preface, or foreword to a book written by
   someone other than the book's author:

   > Alice Walker, Afterword, I Love Myself: A Zora Neale
   > Hurston Reader, ed. Alice Walker (Old Westbury, NY: The
   > Feminist Press, 1979) 297.

3. A previously published essay or article from a collection of writings by
   different authors:

   > M. H. Abrams, "The Correspondent Breeze," Kenyon Review
   > 19 (1957): 113–30, rpt. in English Romantic Poets, ed. M. H.
   > Abrams (New York: Oxford UP, 1960) 37–54.

4. An essay or article from a collection of works not previously published:

   > Dennis Brutus, "English and the Dynamics of South African
   > Creative Writing," English Literature: Opening Up the Canon,
   > Selected Papers from the English Institute, 1979, ed. Leslie
   > A. Fiedler and Houston Baker, Jr. (Baltimore: Johns Hopkins
   > UP, 1981) 1–14.

5. A short story, poem, or essay from an anthology:

   > George Herbert, "The Flower," Seventeenth-Century Prose
   > and Poetics, ed. Alexander M. Witherspoon and Frank J. Warnke,
   > 2nd ed. (New York: Harcourt, 1963) 857.
   > Alexander Pope, "The Rape of the Lock," The Norton
   > Anthology of World Masterpieces, ed. Maynard Mack et al., 5th
   > ed., 2 vols. (New York: Norton, 1985) 2: 305–326.

6. A novel or play from an anthology:

> Toni Morrison, <u>Sula</u>, <u>The Norton Introduction to the Short Novel</u>, ed. Jerome Beaty (New York: Norton, 1982) 581.

7. Afterword, preface, introduction, or other editorial comment on individual pieces in a collection:

> Jerome Beaty, afterword to <u>Sula</u>, <u>The Norton Introduction to the Short Novel</u>, ed. Jerome Beaty (New York: Norton, 1982) 661.

8. An unsigned article in a widely known reference work:

> "Solar Energy," <u>The New Columbia Encyclopedia</u>, 4th ed. (1975) 2556.

9. A signed article in a widely known reference work:

> Howard Suber, "Motion Picture," <u>Encyclopedia Americana</u>, 1981 ed., 19: 516.

10. An article in a specialized, less familiar reference work:

> D. H. Monro, "William Godwin," <u>The Encyclopedia of Philosophy</u>, ed. Paul Edwards, 8 vols. (New York: Macmillan, 1967) 3: 358.

PERIODICALS

1. A signed article from a daily newspaper divided into sections paginated separately:

> Milton R. Benjamin, "U.S. Is Allowing Argentina to Buy Critical A-System," <u>Washington Post</u> 19 July 1982: A1+.

2. A signed article from a daily newspaper paginated continuously:

> Joseph Lelyveld, "V. S. Pritchett, in Step with the Years, Writes On," <u>New York Times</u> 16 Dec. 1985, natl. ed.: 4.

Note: Some newspapers are published in more than one edition, and the pagination varies from one to another. Indicate the edition if it is specified on the masthead.

3. An unsigned article from a daily newspaper:

"Soviet Group Presses for Broader Arms 'Dialog,'" <u>New York Times</u> 5 Sept. 1982, Sec. 1: 16.

4. A signed article from a weekly magazine or newspaper:

Bruno Bettelheim, "Reflections: Freud and the Soul," <u>New Yorker</u> 1 March 1982: 52+.

Note: Use "+" for an article that begins in one part of a periodical and continues elsewhere.

James Lewis, "Jobless Reality Fails to Impress Thatcher's Cabinet," <u>Manchester Guardian Weekly</u> 5 Sept. 1982: 3.

5. An unsigned article from a weekly publication:

"Computers," <u>Time</u> 2 Aug. 1982: 72.

6. A serialized article:

William J. Broad, "Science Showmanship: A Deep 'Star Wars' Rift," <u>New York Times</u> 16 Dec. 1985, pt. 2 of a series begun on 15 Dec. 1985: 1+.

7. A signed editorial:

Gerard Smith, "Toward Arms Control," Editorial, <u>New York Times</u> 29 June 1982: A23.

8. An unsigned editorial:

"Tuition Subsidies Are Not Benign," editorial, <u>New York Times</u> 3 July 1982: 20.

9. An article from a monthly magazine:

William Greider, "The Education of David Stockman," <u>Atlantic</u> Dec. 1981: 27.

10. An article in a journal with pages numbered continually through each yearly volume:

> Blanche H. Gelfant, "Mingling and Sharing in American Literature: Teaching Ethnic Fiction," College English 43 (1981): 763.

Note: The numbers after the title of the journal refer to the volume number, the date, and the pages of the article cited.

11. An article in a journal that numbers pages separately for each issue:

> Clare Sprague, "Dialectic and Counter-Dialectic in the Martha Quest Novels," Journal of Commonwealth Literature 14 (1979): 39.

Note: Where there is no volume number, treat the issue number as though it were a volume number.

> Peter Biskind, "Rebel without a Cause: Nicholas Ray in the Fifties," Film Quarterly 28.5 (1974): 32.

Note: The numbers following the journal title refer to the volume (28) and issue (5).

12. A signed review with a title:

> Peter L. Berger, "A Woman of This Century," rev. of Hannah Arendt: For Love of the World, by Elizabeth Young Bruehl, New York Times Book Review 25 April 1982: 1, 20-21.

13. A signed, untitled review:

> John F. C. Harrison, rev. of The Age of Capital, 1848-1875, by E. G. Hobsbawm, Victorian Studies 20 (1977): 423.

14. An unsigned, untitled review:

> Rev. of The French Lieutenant's Woman, by John Fowles, Times Literary Supplement 12 June 1969: 629.

15. A letter to the editor:

R. W. Flint, letter, New Republic 18 Feb. 1957: 23.

16. A response to a letter or letters:

Nicholas Lemann, Reply to letters of Roger Williams and Virginia K. Williams, Atlantic Dec. 1984: 14.

17. A speech or address for a special occasion printed in a periodical:

Toni Morrison, "Address to the American Writers Congress," 9 Oct. 1981, in Nation 24 Oct. 1981: 396.

18. An article from *Dissertation Abstracts* or *Dissertation Abstracts International*:

John Bryan Webb, "Utopian Fantasy and Social Change," DA 43 (1982): 8214250 (State U of New York at Buffalo).

19. An article from a volume of abstracts:

John W. C. Johnstone, "Who Controls the News," American Journal of Sociology 87 (1982): 1174-81, abstract from America: History and Life 20.A (1983): 2120.

20. An article from a newsletter:

Douglas Cliggott, "Proposed Tax Reform Will Have Negative Effect on Capital Investment," Business Executive Expectations Third Quarter 1985: 2.

Note: Newsletters may not include volume and issue numbers, dates, or even pagination. In cases where a publication does employ the usual conventions needed for a citation, adapt what information you have to a form as close as possible to that of a conventional periodical citation, making sure that you provide enough information for readers to find the source.

OTHER WRITTEN SOURCES

1. The published proceedings of a conference:

> Conserving the Historical and Cultural Landscape, Proc.
> of the Conference of the National Trust for Historic
> Preservation, Western Region, 2-3 May, 1975, Denver, CO
> (Washington, DC: Preservation Press, 1975) 54.

2. A government publication:

> Office of the Federal Register, United States Government
> Manual, 1980-81 (Washington, DC: GPO, 1980) 37.

3. A legal reference:

> Brown v. Board of Education of Topeka, 347 US 483 (US
> Supreme Court 1954).

4. A pamphlet:

> Jules Saltman, Teenagers and Alcohol: Patterns and Dangers
> (New York: Public Affairs Comm., 1983) 3.

5. A letter from a volume of published letters:

> "To Alfred Kazin," 8 July 1961, Edmund Wilson: Letters
> on Literature and Politics, 1912-1972, ed. Elena Wilson (New
> York: Farrar, 1977) 602.

6. A letter printed in a volume of collected letters:

> Edmund Wilson, "To William Faulkner," 25 Sept. 1956, in
> Letters on Literature and Politics: 1912–1972, ed. Elena
> Wilson (New York: Farrar, 1977) 540.

7. An unpublished letter from a collection:

> Adlai E. Stevenson, Letter to Ralph McGill, 11 May 1954,
> Ralph McGill Papers, Emory University, Atlanta, GA.

8. A personal letter:

> Letter received from Grace Paley, 30 July 1981.

9. A dissertation:

> Donald Joseph Gray, "Victorian Verse Humor," diss., Ohio
> State U, 1956, 29.

10. A document from an information service:

> Paul V. Delker, Adult Education--1980 and Beyond,
> Occasional Paper No. 59 (Columbus: Ohio State University,
> 1979), 19 (ERIC ED 189 309).

11. A manuscript or typescript:

> Hart Crane, manuscript of The Bridge, Hart Crane
> Collection, Columbia University, New York.

NON-PRINT SOURCES

1. A lecture or publicly delivered paper:

> George Levine, "George Eliot's Scientific Ideal: The
> Hypothesis of Reality," The English Institute, Cambridge, MA,
> 1 Sept. 1979.

2. A radio or television program:

> The Doomsayers, prod. Brian Capener, PBS Special, 8 Sept.
> 1982.
> "Maya Angelou," narr. Bill Moyers, Creativity, PBS
> Special, Atlanta, GA, Ch. 30, 8 Jan. 1982.

Note: When you want to refer to a particular individual (producer, director, narrator, or actor), cite that person's name first:

> Bill Moyers, narr., "Maya Angelou," Creativity, PBS
> Special, Atlanta, GA, Ch. 30, 8 Jan. 1982.

3. A performance of music, dance, or drama:

La Bohème, cond. James Levine, with Teresa Stratas, Metropolitan Opera, Metropolitan Opera House, New York, 13 Jan. 1982.

Note: When you want to refer to a particular individual (conductor, director, choreographer), cite that person's name first:

James Levine, cond., La Bohème, with Teresa Stratas, Metropolitan Opera, Metropolitan Opera House, New York, 13 Jan. 1982.

4. A film:

Vietnam: An American Journey, Films Inc., 1979.
Rebel without a Cause, dir. Nicholas Ray, with James Dean, Sal Mineo, and Natalie Wood, Warner Brothers, 1955.

Note: When you want to refer to a particular individual, cite that person's name first.

Nicholas Ray, dir., Rebel without a Cause, with James Dean, Sal Mineo, and Natalie Wood, Warner Brothers, 1955.

5. A face-to-face interview:

Personal interview with Dennis Creech, Director of the Georgia Solar Coalition, Atlanta, GA, 30 Jan. 1982.

6. A telephone interview:

Telephone interview with Coretta Scott King, 1 Nov. 1982.

7. A work of art:

Paul Cézanne, A Modern Olympia, Louvre, Paris.

8. A work of art with a cited illustration:

Pierre Bonnard, The Open Window, The Phillips Collection, illus. in Master Paintings from the Phillips Collection, by Eleanor Green et al. (New York: Penghurst Books, 1981) 71.

9. A musical composition:

> George Frideric Handel, <u>Messiah</u>, ed. Watkins Shaw, Novello Handel Edition (Sevenoaks, Eng.: Novello, n.d.).

Note: Use n.d. (no date) for any undated material.

10. An audio recording:

> The Police, <u>Synchronicity</u> (A & M, SP-3735, 1983).

11. An audio recording from which a particular song is referred to or quoted.

> The Beatles, "Revolution," from <u>The Beatles/1967-1970</u> (Capital, SEBX-11843, 1973).

12. An audio recording when the work of the performer or performers is discussed:

> Marilyn Horne, <u>Orfeo ed Euridice</u>, by Christoph Willibald Gluck, cond. by Georg Solti, Orchestra and Chorus of the Royal Opera House, Covent Garden (London, OSA1285, 1970).

13. A videotape or videorecording:

> <u>The Nuclear Dilemma</u>, videorecording, BBC-TV (New York: Time Life Multimedia, 1974).

14. A computer program on tape or disk:

> Richard J. Ward, <u>The Executive Game</u>, computer program (Bowling Green State University, Hewlett-Packard, A880-2232A).

Note: Computer programs vary considerably. For this reason you will have to adapt a citation to the information you have. When possible, you should include an author, title, place of production, company or organization that produces the program, identifying number, and date.

15. Material from a computer service:

> "Salk, Jonas Edward," <u>American Men and Women of Science</u>, 15th ed. (Bowker, 1983) (DIALOG 236, item 0090936).

Note: Cite material from a computer service such as DIALOG or BRS like printed material found in books and periodicals, but add a reference to the service at the end of the citation, giving the name of the service and the numbers identifying the database and the particular item from that base.

SUBSEQUENT CITATIONS IN NOTES

If you are using documentary notes—as in the sample paper in this chapter—you should fully identify each source in the first citation, including, when appropriate, author, title, place of publication, publisher, date, and page. For each note after the first, indicate the source as briefly as possible and give the page for that reference. Follow these guidelines for references to a source after the first full citation note:

1. When only one work by an author is listed, cite the author's last name and the page number:

   ```
   Hareven 307.
   ```

2. When there is more than one work by an author, use the author's last name, a shortened title, and the page:

   ```
   Lash, Love 213.
   Lash, E&F 201.
   ```

(*E&F* is an abbreviation for *Eleanor and Franklin.*)

3. For citations without an author, use an abbreviated title and the page:

   ```
   "Reflections," 52.
   ```

A Sample Paper with Endnotes

Sara Maxfield cited her sources with both documentary notes and a bibliography, using the form for citations recommended by the Modern Language Association in the *MLA Handbook* (1984). The preferred form of the Modern Language Association is that used by Michael Gold, but the style used by Sara is an acceptable alternative.

People who write about literature often combine critical analysis with research findings, and that is what Sara Maxfield has done. Her paper might be called a documented essay since she combines what she has learned from researching the two authors and the critical response to the two novels with her own interpretation.

History, Choice, and the Individual:
Toni Morrison's Sula and
Alice Walker's Meridian
Sara Maxfield
Professor Johnston
English 121
May 9, 1983

Maxfield 1

How much choice do people have about who they are
and how they behave? How important are family, community,
and historical events in determining character and life
choices? Is it possible for people to alter significantly
their own lives and those of others? Two contemporary
novels that explore the forces determining character and
behavior are Toni Morrison's <u>Sula</u> and Alice Walker's
<u>Meridian</u>. Morrison follows the lives of people who are
tied to the past and whose behavior and feelings are the
product of their families and of a closed community;
Walker traces the lives of three young people who grow
away from their families and communities and become part
of the greater world. Morrison sees personality as
determined by personal interaction; Walker, as the product
of the interaction of private lives and public events.
Yet these two books, while conveying very different
visions of human experience, relate to each other in
striking ways.

    Both are relatively short novels made up of a series
of brief chapters, told in the third person, and using
the name of a female character for the title. Each novel
is set in the author's home state--Morrison's in Ohio and
Walker's in Georgia. Each includes a family history that
tells of grandmothers. Both tell of female friends who
become estranged because of a man; of violence, drowned
children, dismemberings, and murder; of parents renounced,
children rejected, friends betrayed. Both are second
novels written by talented black women who have since
been recognized as major writers. Morrison was featured
on the cover of <u>Newsweek</u> in March of 1981; Walker, on the
cover of <u>Ms.</u> in June of 1982. Morrison won the National

*Thesis statement
or controlling
idea*

*Expansion of
thesis*

Maxfield 2

Book Critics Circle Award for <u>Song of Solomon</u> in 1978,
and Walker won the American Book Award and the Pulitzer
Prize in 1983 for <u>The Color Purple</u>.[1]

Raised numerals (superscripts) send the reader to endnotes, here a content note giving information that is relevant but not central to the main points

Each woman has been in her own way what Morrison
calls "at the barricades," fighting for right and
justice.[2] Morrison seems to have chosen to fight the
battle through her profession, both as a writer and an
editor, working to help good writers publish their books.
Even before she published her own first novel, <u>The Bluest
Eye</u> in 1970, she was working as a teacher and an editor.[3]
Walker has chosen the challenging battles of a political
activist, and her interests have ranged from the struggle
for civil rights to protests against nuclear weapons.[4]

These superscripts refer to documentary endnotes

Both women, however, also consider that writing
novels is one way of meeting their social and moral
responsibilities. Morrison has said that "art can be both
uncompromisingly beautiful and socially responsible."[5]
Walker, who doubts if bad people can write good books,
asks: "If art doesn't make us better, then what on earth
is it for?"[6] Just as in her own life Morrison has chosen
to work for good on the personal level as a teacher and
editor, helping other authors write good books, so in her
novel <u>Sula</u> she explores the personal aspects of human
development. Walker's political activism is reflected in
<u>Meridian</u> as she examines the personal aspects of human
development in the context of political action.

The essential difference between Morrison's vision
of the highly personal development of character and
Walker's vision of the public forces that determine lives
is reflected in each author's basic plot, in her use of
history and her treatment of the issue of choice and

Maxfield 3

change. The central plot of <u>Sula</u> focuses on the friendship
of two girls, Nel Wright and Sula Peace, who grow up
together and who temporarily grow apart when Nel marries
and Sula leaves home. Throughout their girlhoods, Sula
and Nel, like most of the other characters, seem to be
guided by forces outside themselves. Their friendship is
resumed after ten years, but is irreparably broken when
Sula betrays Nel by becoming involved with her husband.
Though Morrison does not tell us exactly why, each of the
two comes to resemble her own mother: Nel is a
conventional wife and mother; Sula, a single woman who
lives as she pleases without regard to moral values or the
feelings of others.

Summary of the two novels for readers who are not familiar with them

    Walker's young characters, on the other hand, seem
to direct their own lives, and they do so in the public
sphere. Meridian begins to take charge of her life when
she joins the civil rights movement and accepts a
scholarship to college. Meridian works hard at her
studies and becomes friends with Truman Held, Lynne
Rabinowitz, and Anne-Marion Coles, three of her
contemporaries who are also involved in the movement.
Meridian and her friends change rapidly, largely because
of their politics, and as they change, so do their
relationships with each other. Truman, for example, who
is first a political activist and later a painter, is
alternately Meridian's friend, her lover, Lynne's husband,
and finally a friend to both women. Anne-Marion is first
Meridian's friend and roommate, but when Meridian refuses
to participate in violent political action, Anne-Marion
becomes, for a time, her enemy, accusing her of betraying
the cause of black people. In the end, Meridian has

become reconciled with Truman, Lynne, and Anne-Marion, but she has left behind her childhood friends and her family. She has chosen a life of political activism that requires sacrifice of personal and material comforts, a life very different from that of her mother, and one that her mother cannot understand.

The characters of Morrison and Walker relate differently to time and their place in history. In the sense that it begins historically where Sula ends, Meridian is a sequel to Sula. The events of Sula extend from 1919 to 1965, the year of the Voting Rights Act and riots in Watts; the main events of Meridian occur between 1960 and 1976, years of upheaval, hope, change, and finally serious disillusionment for many Americans.[7] Young characters in Sula either live outside of history, or they are used and discarded by it. The young in Meridian are involved in creating history, and they create their own lives in the process.

In Sula the years tick off with the chapter titles, but the characters, without a stake in the society, seem unaware of the significance of the dates: the jazz age, the depression, and the war in Europe are outside their lives. Even Shadrack and Plum, who are swept into history by World War I and then discarded when it is over, seem unaware of what has happened to them, unaware that they are members of "the lost generation."[8] The dates that mark the chapters of Sula mark not history but only the passage of time in a private world where people are essentially unconscious of the world outside.

In Meridian, though specific events are seldom mentioned, important personal events are tied to public

Maxfield 5

events: Anne-Marion notices Meridian while they watch the
funeral of John Kennedy on television; Meridian becomes
seriously disillusioned during the funeral of Martin
Luther King, and toward the end Truman is making a
sculpture for the Bicentennial, the year the novel was
published. Interpreters of Meridian note Walker's concern
with the individual in a social, historical context.
Elizabeth Janeway observes that Meridian has chosen to
bear "the conflict of our time in her soul."[9] Other
critics praise Walker's "acute sense of history," her
"historical awareness," in the person of Meridian, an
"insistence on a history without gaps."[10]

    Because the characters in Sula are cut off from
history and the society with no understanding of the past,
of the events and economic conditions of the greater
world, or of the possibility of having any impact on
society, they live without a sense of creative choice.
They are people, as critics have observed, who are
"enormously, achingly alive," who "have created a world
of their own."[11] But they are "locked in a world where
hope for the future is a foreign commodity."[12] The
choices in Sula are not positive or creative but
desperate. Sula's grandmother Eva chooses to lose her own
leg to collect the insurance she needs to feed her
children; the insane Shadrack initiates National Suicide
Day as a way of controlling his fear of sudden and
unexpected death; and Nel's mother Helene chooses to
marry Wiley Wright to escape her own mother's life in the
Sundown House in New Orleans. Even Jude and Nel, who
consciously choose to marry, do so to avoid humiliation
and hurt: he, to gain "some posture of adulthood" in a

Three sources
combined in one
sentence and
cited in a single
note

Beginning of
discussion of
Sula

Maxfield 6

community that denies him a man's work; she, "to help, to soothe," and to alleviate "his pain."[13]

Most of the time, however, the characters act not out of conscious choice, but from the seemingly unconscious urges that direct their lives. A number of events of the novel are the consequence of unwilled, spontaneous acts, such as Sula's careless drowning of a little boy (S 61) and her cutting off a piece of her own finger (S 54). Other acts that seem to derive from instinctual responses are Eva's heroic effort to save her daughter Hannah and Sula's casual encounter with Jude. Even the storming of the tunnel at the end of the novel, which Jerome Beaty has called the novel's "only 'political' event,"[14] is a childlike act of defiance, rather than a calculated act intended to change society. Throughout the novel, characters act impulsively, as if driven by unconscious forces, and they seem unaware of the possibility of effecting change.

For change to be meaningful, people must have choice, must be able to direct the course of their lives consciously and deliberately. In the beginning of part 2 of Sula, Morrison explains that the characters believe that evil forces direct their lives and that their job is to survive the onslaught of "floods, white people, tuberculosis, famine, and ignorance" (S 90). The only choice they have is to acknowledge and accept the forces of evil that direct their lives. They can try to avoid this choice, but there is nothing they can do "to alter it, to annihilate it or to prevent its happening again" (S 90). The ultimate end of evil is death, and the people of the Bottom "did not believe that death was accidental-

Passages from the novels cited with an abbreviation (see notes 13 and 15)

Single quotation marks used within a quotation

-life might be, but death was deliberate" (S 92). Toward
the end of her life, Sula herself is associated with
death-dealing evil. The people of the community are
convinced that she is a "Devil" (S 117), and as a Devil,
she cannot be destroyed, only "recognized, then dealt
with, survived, outwitted, triumphed over" (S 118). To
triumph over a person possessed by evil spirits is simply
to outlive her. Sula herself does not choose to be evil.
Rather she seems to act impulsively from internal and
poorly understood promptings. As an adult woman, she
behaves as "emotionally and irresponsibly" as she did as
a child. Nel finally realizes the truth about her friend:

> The situation was clear to her now. Sula, like
> always, was incapable of making any but the
> most trivial decisions. When it came to matters
> of grave importance, she behaved emotionally
> and irresponsibly and left it to others to
> straighten out. (S 101)

Long quotation indented 10 spaces; double-spaced before, throughout, and after quotation

In a world where the only choice people have is to
defend themselves against evil forces that they cannot
understand or destroy, where poverty is a way of life
that can be combatted but never overcome, meaningful
change and human progress are impossible. In response to
Sula's notion that "doing anything forever was hell,"
Nel counters: "Hell ain't things lasting forever. Hell is
change" (S 108). As she lies dying, Sula admits that
changing men and moving from place to place did in fact
change nothing: "Nothing was ever different. They were all
the same. All of the words and all of the smiles, every
tear and every gag just something to do" (S 147). In the
last chapter of Sula, dated "1965," Nel looks around at

Maxfield 8

a world in which "everything had changed" (S 164), but
she interprets that change as loss. She perceives even
the social and economic advantages brought about by the
civil rights movement in a negative light. She sees the
new generation as inferior to the "beautiful boys in
1921" (S 164). Sula ends where it begins with a kind of
lament, a mourning for a lost world and for the love and
human potential that never had a chance to flower. In the
end this novel is like Nel's final expression of grief
for her lost friend: "It was a fine cry--loud and long--
but it had no bottom and it had no top, just circles and
circles of sorrow" (S 174).

Beginning of
discussion of
Meridian

In Meridian Alice Walker explores the experiences of
the same young people who seem so diminished through
Nel's nostalgia-ridden vision in Sula. The main character,
significantly named Meridian, is a teenager when the
civil rights movement gets underway. She is intelligent
and conscientious, but pregnancy and early marriage
interrupt her schooling and any hope for her future. But
all this changes when she first gets involved in the
civil rights movement and then chooses to leave her baby
with her mother-in-law and to accept a scholarship to
college. As a college student in the early sixties, she
meets a number of politically active college students,
among them Lynne, Anne-Marion, and Truman. Together they
come of age at the dawn of what Alice Walker calls "the
age of choice."[15] Their story provides the context, as
one critic has observed, for what Walker "wants to say
about history and choice."[16] Repeatedly we see the
characters in the "stark, boundary-marking situations
concerning the very choices of life they must make."[17]

The characters in _Sula_ cannot imagine that they have any
choice but to survive and grapple with the forces of
evil; the characters in _Meridian_ discover that they have
various choices about how to destroy evil and create
good. But having choice and good intentions does not
insure that the best choices will be made, and certainly
all choices have consequences, some good, some bad. When
Meridian chooses to go to college, she must pay the price
of leaving her child and defying her mother. During her
college days, she learns even more about the consequences
of her choices: about how an intended act of charity can
lead to tragedy, as when her attempt to rescue a homeless
child leads to the child's death; about how a careless
remark can lead to suffering, as when she urges a child
watching a freedom march to join the demonstrators, only
to find her later crying in jail; about how acting in
accordance with her convictions can alienate friends, as
when Anne-Marion turns on her when she refuses to agree
that she could kill for the revolution.

For Meridian making choices involves a willingness
to act even though the consequences of action cannot be
fully understood. When she first walks into the local
headquarters of the civil rights movement in the spring
of 1960, she says simply, "I've come to volunteer" (M
80). Without really knowing what the movement is all
about and what she will do, she willfully offers her
services and joins with people who have become part of
something greater than themselves "at a time and place in
History that forced the trivial to fall away" (M 84). For
a while it seems that Meridian's choice will destroy her:
she suffers seizures, and her hair falls out. For a while

she has a recurring dream that "she was a character in a novel and that her existence presented an insoluble problem, one that would be solved by her death at the end" (M 117). Meridian's struggle against that perception of her own life as an "insoluble problem" leads her to search for a way of life that will justify her existence. She chooses to work at registering voters, to give other people a choice in forming their own society. Later she chooses to live her life fully. She now understands "that the respect she owed her life was to continue, against whatever obstacles, to live it, and not to give up any particle of it without a fight to the death, preferably not her own" (M 200).

Choosing to ally herself with the forces of life finally means accepting the "ambivalence" (M 219), the contradictions, and the conflict that are part of life. There are times when she feels that she will not "belong to the future," and other times when she "could bring the mightiest country to its knees" (M 201). What seems to have kept Meridian going is her confidence that change is possible. When Lynne tells her that she is making a mistake trying to change people--"You can't change them. Nothing will"--Meridian responds, "But I can change . . . I hope I will" (M 152). She hopes not that she will be able to change, but that she will choose to change.

Meridian does change. She recovers her health and at the end of the novel leaves the others behind. We assume she is still carrying the yellow pad with the words WILL YOU BE BRAVE ENOUGH TO VOTE?--brave enough to exercise both politically and personally the choices we have.

Maxfield 11

Toni Morrison, telling the story of Sula and Nel,
shows how limited people are when their vision does not
extend beyond their own personal involvements, for not to
see beyond the personal is to be determined by it. As we
read their story, we grieve for those who cannot imagine
that they have choices that may lead to a better life. As
she tells the story of Meridian and her friends, Alice
Walker suggests the range of possibilities open to people
who create their own lives in the larger society and who
want to work for a better world; and she does so with
full consciousness of the error and conflict that are part
of their effort. In the end she challenges her readers to
make choices and to make them for good.

Concluding
paragraph echoes
thesis

Maxfield 12

NOTES

[1]Morrison has also published two other novels, The
Bluest Eye and Tar Baby; Walker has published volumes of
poetry, short stories, and another novel, The Third Life
of Grange Copeland.

[2]Toni Morrison, "Address to the American Writers
Congress," 9 Oct. 1981, in Nation 24 Oct. 1981: 412.

[3]Jean Strouse, "Toni Morrison's Black Magic,"
Newsweek, 30 March 1981: 52-57.

[4]Gloria Steinem, "A Profile of Alice Walker," Ms.
June 1982: 36-94.

[5]Strouse 57.

[6]Steinem 94.

[7]For a general discussion of the historical
background to Meridian, see William Manchester, The Glory
and the Dream (Boston: Little, Brown, 1973), parts 4 and 5.

[8]For a discussion of the idea of the "lost
generation," see Robert Wohl, The Generation of 1914
(Cambridge, MA: Harvard UP, 1979), 1-4.

[9]"Women's Literature," in Harvard Guide to
Contemporary American Writing, ed. Daniel Hoffman
(Cambridge, MA: Harvard UP, 1979), 385.

[10]Margo Jefferson, "Across the Barricades," rev. of
Meridian, by Alice Walker, Newsweek 31 May 1976: 71; Mary
Helen Washington, "Her Mother's Gifts," Ms. June 1982:
38; Marcus Griel, "Limits," rev. of Meridian, by Alice
Walker, New Yorker 7 June 1976: 133-36.

[11]Sara Blackburn, rev. of Sula, by Toni Morrison,
New York Times Book Review 30 Dec. 1973: 3; Peter S.

Note
consolidates
three sources

Prescott, "Dangerous Witness," rev. of <u>Sula</u>, by Toni Morrison, <u>Newsweek</u> 7 Jan. 1974: 63.

[12]Blackburn 3.

[13]Toni Morrison, <u>Sula</u> (1973; rpt. New York: New American Library, 1982), 83. All further references to this work appear in parentheses in the text and are indicated by an <u>S</u> for <u>Sula</u> followed by the page number.

[14]Jerome Beaty, Afterword to <u>Sula</u>, in <u>The Norton Introduction to the Short Novel</u>, ed. Jerome Beaty (New York: Norton, 1982), 665.

[15]Alice Walker, <u>Meridian</u> (1976; rpt. New York: Washington Square Press, 1977), 124. All further references to this work appear in parentheses in the text and are indicated by an <u>M</u> for <u>Meridian</u> followed by the page number.

[16]Marge Piercy, rev. of <u>Meridian</u>, by Alice Walker, <u>New York Times Book Review</u> 23 May 1976: 5, 12.

[17]Michael G. Cooke, "Recent Novels: Women Bearing Violence," <u>Yale Review</u> 66 (1976): 146-60.

BIBLIOGRAPHY

Blackburn, Sara. Rev. of Sula, by Toni Morrison. New
    York Times Book Review 30 Dec. 1973: 3.
Beaty, Jerome. Afterword to Sula. In The Norton
    Introduction to the Short Novel. Ed. Jerome Beaty.
    New York: Norton, 1982. 661-66.
Cooke, Michael G. "Recent Novels: Women Bearing
    Violence." Yale Review 66 (1976): 146-60.
Griel, Marcus. "Limits." Rev. of Meridian, by Alice
    Walker. New Yorker 7 June 1976: 133-36.
Hoffman, Daniel, ed. Harvard Guide to Contemporary
    American Writing. Cambridge, MA: Harvard UP, 1979.
Jefferson, Margo. "Across the Barricades." Rev. of
    Meridian, by Alice Walker. Newsweek 31 May 1971:
    71-72.
Manchester, William. The Glory and the Dream. Boston:
    Little, Brown, 1973.
Morrison, Toni. Sula. 1973; rpt. New York: New American
    Library, 1982.
----------. "Address to the American Writers Congress."
    9 Oct. 1981. In Nation 24 Oct. 1981: 396-412.
Piercy, Marge. Rev. of Meridian, by Alice Walker. New
    York Times Book Review 23 May 1976: 5, 12.
Prescott, Peter S. "Dangerous Witness." Rev. of Sula,
    by Toni Morrison. Newsweek 7 Jan. 1976: 63.
Rev. of Sula, by Toni Morrison. Times Literary Supplement
    4 Oct. 1974: 1062.
Steinem, Gloria. "A Profile of Alice Walker." Ms. June
    1982: 38-94.

Maxfield 15

Strouse, Jean. "Toni Morrison's Black Magic."   <u>Newsweek</u>
    30 March 1981: 52-57.
Walker, Alice. <u>Meridian</u>. 1976; rpt. New York: Washington
    Square Press, 1977.
Washington, Mary Helen. "Her Mother's Gifts."   <u>Ms</u>. June
    1982: 38.
Wohl, Robert. <u>The Generation of 1914</u>. Cambridge, MA:
    Harvard UP, 1979.

Appendix B ───────────────────────────────

AN ANNOTATED LIST OF SELECTED REFERENCE WORKS

The following list of reference works represents only a small percentage of books available in the reference sections of even small libraries. By consulting this list, however, you should get a good idea about where to start researching almost any topic. If you find one reference work in a discipline, others will be shelved nearby.

It will be helpful if you understand the specialized vocabulary used to describe reference books. The word *bibliography* refers to lists of books or other material about a subject. There are very broad bibliographies that cover a whole field of studies (the humanities, for example), more limited ones that cover a discipline (psychology), and ones that list material on a very specific topic (the novels of William Faulkner). *Abstracts* are brief summaries of books, articles, research reports, dissertations, or speeches. *Indexes* are used to retrieve pieces of information from larger units—periodicals, parts of books, microform collections, or non-print materials. Some indexes include abstracts of the entries. Most *dictionaries* provide information about words, proper names, and phrases. *Encyclopedias* provide more detailed information, background, and explanations of people, places, things, events, and ideas. There is, however, often some overlap, since dictionaries may give more than definitions, and some encyclopedias include definitions of many specialized words.

Before you use a reference work, you should study the format and instructions for users. If you read the introduction or other explanation about how to use a given work, you should soon be able to use it successfully. If you have trouble, however, consult the reference librarian for assistance.

The works listed below are cited as they are usually referred to by researchers and librarians: those usually identified by the name of the author are listed with the author's name first; titles are noted first for works primarily identified by title, as in the case of encyclopedias and most other multi-volume works.

Many reference works are now produced both in book form and in computer databases (on-line), and the number of sources available on-line is increasing rapidly. If you are planning to do a computer search, you may want to ask your computer librarian whether those reference works appropriate to your topic are available on-line.

General Reference Works

BIBLIOGRAPHIES

Bibliographic Index. New York: Wilson, 1938–.
This extensive listing by subject includes bibliographies that appear in books, pamphlets, and periodical articles. It also lists bibliographies published as individual books and pamphlets.

Books in Print. New York: Bowker, 1948–.
See page 33. Available on-line.

Cumulative Book Index. New York: Wilson, 1898–.
Lists books published in English by author, subject, and title.

Farber, Evan Ira. *Classified List of Periodicals for the College Library.* 5th ed. Westwood, MA: Faxon, 1972.
This annotated list of over one thousand periodicals is intended to help librarians select periodicals for their college collection. It is useful to the student in getting a brief description of the purpose and scope of a given periodical.

Katz, Bill, and Linda Sternberger Katz. *Magazines for Libraries.* 4th ed. New York: Bowker, 1982.
Lists over sixty-five hundred periodicals. Each item is described and annotated. See page 55.

BIOGRAPHICAL SOURCES

Contemporary Authors. Detroit: Gale, 1962–.
An up-to-date source of information on living authors of fiction and non-fiction in many fields. A good place to look for material on authors who are not well known.

Current Biography. New York: Wilson, 1940–.
Attempting to cover all important living people in all fields, this is a good source of information for popular figures such as entertainers.

Dictionary of American Biography (DAB). 21 vols. New York: Scribner's, 1927, with supplements.
Covers only people not living and provides authoritative signed articles on important Americans. Also cites further sources of information.

Dictionary of American Negro Biography. Ed. Rayford W. Logan and Michael R. Winston. New York: Norton, 1982.
Spanning some three centuries, this is an invaluable source of information about more than seven hundred black Americans in all fields. Covers only those who died before 1970.

Dictionary of Canadian Biography. Toronto: U of Toronto P, 1966, with supplements.
Includes native Canadians as well as people from other countries who have contributed to Canadian life. As with DAB and DNB, no living people are included.

Dictionary of National Biography (DNB). 22 vols. London: Oxford UP, 1908–1909, with supplements.
Provides substantial biographical material for notable individuals no longer living. Covers Great Britain and colonial countries.

The McGraw-Hill Encyclopedia of World Biography. New York: McGraw-Hill, 1973.
Includes information on the living and the dead. A good place to go for biographies of women and members of minority groups less represented in more traditional sources.

Who's Who. New York: St. Martin's, 1849–.
Begun in 1849 as a list of titled British aristocracy and still primarily a British source, since 1897 these annual volumes have provided biographical information and current addresses (and for authors, a list of works) for prominent people in many fields. A reliable source for information about the living. *Who Was Who* is a compilation of biographies of people no longer living selected from *Who's Who* 1897–1970.

Who's Who in America. Chicago: Marquis, 1899–.
Up-to-date biographical information about living Americans. The standards for selection are high, as people must be well-known for significant and reputable achievements. *Who Was Who in America* is a selection from previous volumes of people now deceased. *Note:* There are many specialized biographical sources that include *Who's Who* as part of their title.

Some are published by Marquis Press of Chicago, and some are from other publishing houses. You may find one of these helpful when more general biographical sources fail. Available on-line as *Marquis Who's Who*.

Note: For indexes to biographical sources, see pp. 260–61.

DICTIONARIES

American Heritage Dictionary of the English Language. 2nd college ed. Boston: Houghton Mifflin, 1982.
A good desk dictionary that includes new words used in business, science, and technology. It also contains valuable material on the history of the English language as well as guides to punctuation, grammar, and usage.

Oxford English Dictionary (OED). 13 vols. London: Oxford UP, 1933, with supplements.
Traces the historical development of English words. Dated quotations listed in chronological order illustrate the ways each word has been used, detailing how its meaning has changed. This is a fascinating work and an invaluable resource for finding out much of what is known about the history of words.

Webster's New Collegiate Dictionary. 9th ed. Springfield, MA: Merriam, 1983.
An authoritative desk dictionary for help in understanding the English language as it is actually spoken and written today. It includes both specialized terminology and new words.

Webster's Third New International Dictionary of the English Language. Springfield, MA: Merriam, 1981.
An unabridged dictionary, this work gives brief definitions of words from both standard and spoken English. There are also quotations from contemporary sources.

ENCYCLOPEDIAS

Collier's Encyclopedia, Encyclopaedia Britannica, the *Encyclopedia Americana,* and the *New Columbia Encyclopedia* are discussed on pages 22–24.

Academic American Encyclopedia. New York: Grolier.
This comprehensive general encyclopedia, first published in 1980, has many articles that are more up-to-date than comparable ones in the older standard encyclopedias. Also available on-line.

Random House Encyclopedia. New York: Random House, 1983.
A good easy-to-use, readable reference work for a wide range of general topics. Comparable to the *New Columbia Encyclopedia.*

GEOGRAPHICAL SOURCES

Columbia Lippincott Gazetteer of the World. Ed. Leon E. Seltzer, with the cooperation of the American Geographical Society. New York: Columbia UP, 1952. Supplement 1961.
Lists places of the world alphabetically, including countries, parts of countries, cities, and towns, as well as major geographical features such as bodies of water, mountains, etc. It also gives information about industry, agriculture, size, and other details.

The Times Atlas of the World. Comprehensive (7th) ed. New York: Times Books, 1985.
Detailed maps and listings of most of the places of the world. Each item listed is coded so that you can easily find it on a map.

The Times Atlas of the World. 5 vols. London: The Times, 1955–59.
These outstanding volumes are known for the beauty and accuracy of their maps. Some of the material is, of course, out-of-date. Many of the African maps, for example, must be supplemented with more recent atlases.

The Times Index-Gazetteer of the World. London: The Times, 1965.
Lists almost three times as many communities and geographical features as *Columbia Lippincott.* It provides latitude and longitude along with map locations, but it does not include descriptions.

Webster's New Geographical Dictionary. Springfield, MA: Merriam, 1972.
Provides brief, basic information such as location, size, population, history, and economy for many places. Not as extensive as *Columbia Lippincott,* but more up-to-date.

INDEXES

Biography Index. New York: Wilson, 1946–.
You will often save time searching for biographical material by beginning with this index, as it will lead you to particular volumes or editions of reference books as well as to book-length biographies and biographical information in periodicals. It also contains a listing by profession or occupation of all the people included so that a student looking for names of important people in various fields—animal trainers, criminologists, hermits, midwives, pacifists—can easily find them.

Biography and Genealogy Master Index. Ed. Miranda C. Herbert & Barbara McNeil. Detroit: Gale, 1980–.
A consolidated index to more than 3,200,000 articles in over 350 dictionaries of biography. Material in annual volumes is accumulated every five years. Does not cover book-length biographies or biographical material in periodicals. A good place to go when you want basic information about people's lives: birth date, dates of major accomplishments, or educational background. Available on-line.

Book Review Digest. New York: Wilson, 1906–.
Cites selected reviews of works of literature and nonfiction books in all fields. The citations are alphabetized by the author of the book reviewed, and each includes a brief description of the book, quotations from selected reviews, and references to other reviews.

Book Review Index. Detroit: Gale, 1965–.
Covers more than three times as many periodicals as *Book Review Digest*, but does not provide excerpts or summaries. Publication was suspended from 1969 to 1977. Available on-line.

Essay and General Literature Index. New York: Wilson, 1900–.
Published three times a year, this index emphasizes material in the humanities and social sciences. Indexed by author, subject, and some titles, this work will lead you to individual essays and portions of books on topics that you would not be able to find in card catalogs or standard periodical indexes. For example, a general work on twentieth-century British novelists may have an important chapter on D. H. Lawrence; such a chapter would be indicated here, but not in a card catalog.

The Magazine Index. Menlo Park, CA: Information Access Corp., 1977–.
See page 26.

Monthly Catalog of United States Government Publications. Washington, D.C.: GPO, 1895–.
The most comprehensive index to government-generated materials. Indexed by author, subject, key words, title, and other categories. Before you use this index, find out—ask a librarian—if there are more specialized indexes to government publications treating your subject.

The New York Times Index. New York: The New York Times, 1913–.
See page 27. Volumes covering the years from 1851 through 1912 have been published in ten volumes as *The New York Times Index, Prior Series.*

Personal Name Index to the New York Times Index. 22 vols. Succasunna, NJ: Roxbury Data Interface, 1976–1983.
Consolidated index to name entries appearing in *The New York Times*

Index from 1851 to 1974. An excellent index for finding articles on individual people. Includes obituaries.

Readers' Guide to Periodical Literature. New York: Wilson, 1900–. See pages 25–26.

Facts on File: A Weekly World News Digest. New York: Facts on File, 30 October 1940–.
A good source for a brief overview of events and information reported in newspapers. You could start here for the basic facts about an international crisis, the highlights of sports events, or a list of the best sellers. The cumulative five-year index can be very useful for identifying the dates when long-term news events were covered. Available on-line.

Whitaker's Almanac. London: Whitaker, 1868–.
Contains valuable statistical information on government, finance, population, commerce, and general statistics of countries all over the world, with special emphasis on the British Commonwealth. A good place to go if you want information on a wide range of topics from the activities of the royal family to the winners of the London Film Festival.

The World Almanac and Book of Facts. New York: Newspaper Enterprise Assoc., 1868–.
A good source for factual material in many fields. Valuable both for current and for historical topics.

Humanities

Directory of American Scholars. 8th ed. New York: Bowker, 1982.
An excellent source for information about American scholars in the humanities who are currently active in teaching, research, and publishing. The directory is arranged in four subject volumes—History (I), English, Speech, and Drama (II), Foreign Languages, Linguistics, and Philology (III), and Philosophy, Religion, and Law (IV). Turn here to find out about the education and professional history of important figures in these fields.

Humanities Index. New York: Wilson, 1974–. (Formerly *International Index*, 1907–65; *Social Sciences and Humanities Index*, 1965–74.)
Indexes articles in periodicals by author and subject in the following fields: archaeological and classical studies, area studies, folklore, history,

language and literature, literary and political criticism, performing arts, philosophy, and religion and theology. A separate book review section is organized by author of the book reviewed.

An Index to Book Reviews in the Humanities. Detroit: Thomson, 1960–.
Organized alphabetically by the author of the book being reviewed. It cites reviews in both English- and foreign-language journals of scholarly books, serious literature, and critical considerations of popular literature.

ART

Art Index. New York: Wilson, 1930–.
An excellent index to periodicals that publish articles on archaeology, architecture, art history, fine arts, crafts, and related fields. There are subject and author entries, and there is a separate section of book reviews alphabetized by the author reviewed.

McGraw-Hill Dictionary of Art. 5 vols. London: McGraw-Hill Ltd, 1969.
An encyclopedia despite its title, this is a useful source for basic information about artistic movements, schools of art, periods, and individual artists. The articles are signed and include bibliographies.

FILM

Film Literature Index. Albany, NY: Filmdex, 1974–.
Indexes selected articles about films in some three hundred various periodicals not all chiefly concerned with film. There is also an index of reviews of books about films.

The Filmgoer's Companion. 7th ed. By Leslie Halliwell. New York: Hill and Wang, 1980.
Emphasis is on details about actors and movies rather than serious critical evaluations. Intended for the general reader rather than the student, this book is mainly useful for quickly finding the date, director, and actors of a given film or for identifying the names of films in which particular actors have played. The index is invaluable for identifying even the most obscure person associated with a film.

International Index of Film Periodicals. New York: Bowker, 1973–.
Indexes some sixty periodicals devoted exclusively to film. The best index for serious studies of films.

The New York Times Film Reviews, 1913–1968. 5 vols. New York: The New York Times and Arno Press, 1970. (Subsequent volumes update the collection.)

Reproduces film reviews in chronological order exactly as they first appeared in the *Times*, including photographs. These volumes provide critical discussion of thousands of movies, and they also serve as a fascinating history of film.

HISTORY

America: History and Life. Santa Barbara, CA: Clio Press, 1964–.
Cites articles in over two thousand periodicals. Volumes published from 1974 on include a brief abstract of each article. As with other complex indexes, you should study the format before you begin to use it, but you may find this one more cumbersome than others. Available on-line.

An Encyclopedia of World History. Ed. William L. Langer. Boston: Houghton Mifflin, 1972.
A chronological listing of world events from the time of the first historical records through 1970. The *New Illustrated Encyclopedia of World History* is the same work except for the correction of a few errors and the addition of illustrations.

Harvard Guide to American History. 2 vols. Ed. Frank Freidel. Cambridge, MA: Harvard UP, 1974.
An invaluable bibliography covering all periods of American history. The first volume also includes an introduction to the methods and materials of historical research.

Historical Abstracts. Santa Barbara, CA: Clio Press, 1955–.
Brief summaries of periodical essays on the history of the world from 1450 to the present. After 1964 *Historical Abstracts* excluded the history of the United States and Canada, which has since been treated in the companion, *America: History and Life*.

Morris, Richard et al. *Encyclopedia of American History*. New York: Harper and Row, 1982.
This valuable single-volume work is divided into three parts: a narrative of events from the founding of the colonies through the 1970s, a section treating various topics in American history, and an alphabetical listing of brief biographies of five hundred notable Americans in several different fields. The second section is useful for students who want a chronological overview of a broad subject such as American music or developments in medicine.

New Cambridge Modern History. 14 vols. Cambridge, Eng.: Cambridge UP, 1957–.
Authoritative discussion of world history from the Renaissance through the mid-twentieth century. The first twelve volumes are arranged

chronologically, with chapters—each written by a renowned authority —focusing on nations and geographical regions and subheadings treating political, religious, economic, and cultural events. Volume 13 consists of twelve essays—each written by an expert—on broad subjects such as industry, revolution, or warfare, providing a good historical overview. Volume 14 is an historical atlas.

Shepherd, William. *Historical Atlas*. New York: Barnes and Noble, 1964.
Provides maps for world history from 1450 B.C. to the early 1960s. A useful supplement to the study of many historical topics such as the territorial expansion of the Roman Empire, the countries that remained neutral during World War II, or the original members of the United Nations.

LITERATURE

Altick, Richard, and Andrew Wright. *Selective Bibliography for the Study of English and American Literature*. 6th ed. New York: Macmillan, 1979.
A highly selective, up-to-date list of the best materials available to students of English and American literature. Students doing research on almost any topic in these fields will find valuable help here. Many of the 636 items are books in related fields—philosophy, history, religion— that are important to the study of literature.

Articles on American Literature, 1900–1950. Compiled by Lewis Leary. Durham, NC: Duke UP, 1954. (Separate volumes for 1950–67 and 1968–75.)
These three volumes include an extensive—though admittedly incomplete—listing of articles on major and minor American authors.

Cambridge Bibliography of English Literature. 5 vols. Ed. F. W. Bateson. Cambridge, Eng.: Cambridge UP, 1940–57.
Covers significant literary works from the Old English through the modern periods. Arranged both by genre (poetry, drama, novel) and chronology. Cites books and articles that treat each work listed.

Kolb, Harold. *A Field Guide to the Study of American Literature*. Charlottesville: U of Virginia P, 1976.
A useful introduction to selected works on American literature. The annotations indicate the content and value of each citation. This is a good book to consult if you want to do research on some aspect of American literature or culture.

Literary History of the United States. 2 vols. Ed. Robert E. Spiller et al. New York: Macmillan, 1972 and 1974.
Volume 1 is a comprehensive history of American literature presented chronologically. Separate essays feature major writers, individual genres (poetry, fiction, drama, folklore, etc.), and various literary phenomena

and types. Also includes a selected list of books. Volume 2 is a cumulative bibliography of books and articles organized by type, period, topic, and author.

The MLA International Bibliography of Books and Articles on the Modern Languages and Literatures. (Formerly *American Bibliography,* 1921-55, *Annual Bibliography,* 1956-62.) Modern Language Association, 1963–.
Divided by national literatures and subdivided by literary periods, this index is comprehensive and thorough. Since the index has gradually expanded to include more periodicals, it is important that you study the table of contents and the format of each volume that you use. An indispensable index for topics that focus on a given author. Available on-line.

The New Cambridge Bibliography of English Literature. 5 vols. Ed. George Watson. Cambridge, Eng.: Cambridge UP, 1969–77.
An updated version of the original *Cambridge Bibliography.* Along with the original, this work provides a comprehensive overview of English literature and indicates the scope of materials available on each literary figure.

Oxford History of English Literature. 12 vols. Ed. F. P. Wilson and Bonamy Dobrée. Oxford: Oxford UP, 1945–.
A continuous history of English literature from the earliest times to the modern period, aimed at both the scholar and the general reader. Includes treatment of other fields—the arts, philosophy, science—where they relate to literature. Bibliographies accompany each volume.

Year's Work in English Studies. London: Murray, 1919/20–.
Articles and books on a selective survey of English literature. There is a brief description and usually a critical evaluation of each work cited. A good source to use to learn what kind of studies were published on authors during specific years. If you are studying an author's changing reputation, for example, you will find a record of that change here. Each volume published since 1954 contains a chapter on American literature.

MUSIC

Harvard Dictionary of Music. 2nd ed. By Willi Apel. Cambridge, MA: Harvard UP, 1969.
A storehouse of valuable information on all aspects of music, this is a classic work of music literature. Here you can learn about instruments, composers, types of music, and specific compositions, as well as definitions of musical terms. Many items are placed historically. You will find, for example, a brief history of the cello and the guitar.

Music Index. Detroit: Information Coordinators, 1949–.
Indexes periodicals that specialize in music and articles on musical topics

published in more general publications. There are citations to articles on all kinds of music, including popular, jazz, opera, dance, and many others.

The New College Encyclopedia of Music. By J. A. Westrup and F. Ll. Harrison, rev. by Conrad Wilson. New York: Norton, 1976.
This useful work contains six thousand entries on musical terms, composers, compositions, instruments, and so on. Beginning students should find the many brief bibliographies particularly helpful.

The New Grove Dictionary of Music and Musicians. 20 vols. Ed. Stanley Sadie. London: Macmillan, 1980.
An excellent source of authoritative information on all aspects of music. There are substantial signed articles on topics ranging from music in ancient times to the contemporary world. Most include bibliographies.

PHILOSOPHY AND RELIGION

A Dictionary of Comparative Religion. Ed. S. G. F. Brandon. New York: Scribners, 1970.
This one-volume work includes short informational entries and twenty-eight longer, more comprehensive articles on world religions. Good bibliographies and a helpful system of cross-references make this an excellent place to begin research, especially for quick identification of key figures and concepts.

Encyclopedia of Bioethics . 4 vols. Ed. Warren T. Reich. New York: The Free Press, 1978.
A comprehensive, detailed and easy-to-use encyclopedia that covers all aspects of a new and exciting field. Written by a large team of experts from many traditions, this work is useful both for an overview and for detailed investigation. Includes bibliographies and an index.

Encyclopedia of Philosophy. 8 vols. Ed. Paul Edwards. New York: Macmillan, 1967. (Reprinted 8 vols. in 4 vols., New York: Macmillan, 1972.)
This is the most authoritative and comprehensive reference work on philosophy available in English. Each signed article has its own bibliography. There are articles on concepts and systems in philosophy, historical essays, and over nine hundred articles on individual thinkers.

Encyclopedic Dictionary of Religion. 3 vols. Ed. Paul Kevin Meagher et al. Washington, D.C.: Corpus Publications, 1979.
This is the most up-to-date and comprehensive work of its kind available in English. Signed entries by experts in the field cover a wide range of facts, events, persons, issues, and concepts. Focuses on Western religions, but includes Eastern religions as well. Especially good on impor-

tant figures in religious thought and history. Includes a bibliography and cross references for each entry.

The Philosopher's Guide to Sources, Research Tools, Professional Life, and Related Fields. Ed. Richard T. DeGeorge. Lawrence: Regents Press of Kansas, 1980. (Replaces DeGeorge's *Guide to Philosophical Bibliography and Research.*)

This well-organized companion to philosophical research should also be helpful to students in religion, social science, the fine arts, literature, and other allied fields. In twenty-two chapters, it lists thousands of guides, handbooks, indexes, overviews, summaries, biographies, and so on. Turn here for a guide to the standard works in philosophical research.

The Philosopher's Index. Bowling Green, OH: Philosophy Documentation Center, Bowling Green State U, 1967–.

This comprehensive index to periodicals and books in philosophy and closely related fields consists of a subject index, an author index with abstracts of articles and books, and a book review index. If you are looking for a work in philosophy, it's here. Available on-line.

A Reader's Guide to the Great Religions. Ed. Charles J. Adams. New York: The Free Press, 1977.

A rich and authoritative guide to the best materials on the history and traditions of the world's major religions. Each chapter, written by an expert, provides a good introduction to a particular religion and discusses the usefulness and value of the works cited.

Religion Index I: Periodicals. Ed. G. Fay Dickerson. Chicago: American Theological Library Association, 1977–. (Formerly *Index to Religious Periodical Literature,* 1949–77.)

This major and indispensable index for religious periodicals provides a cumulative guide to over three hundred major journals. It contains a subject index with extensive cross-references and an author index with abstracts of most articles. Thus it not only locates material, but also saves time in that it allows you to judge whether an article seems appropriate for a given research topic. (*Religion Index II* covers multivolume works not generally useful to the beginning student.)

Social Sciences

GENERAL

American Men and Women of Science: Social and Behavioral Sciences. 13th ed. Ed. Jaques Cattell Press. New York: Bowker, 1978.

Excellent source for information about people currently active in the social sciences.

Encyclopaedia of the Social Sciences. 15 vols. Ed. Edwin R. A. Seligman. New York: Macmillan, 1930–35.
An invaluable work, particularly useful for learning how the social sciences were understood in the 1930s. Want to know what the established view of Freud was in the 1930s? It is here. About half the articles are biographical. Provides excellent historical information on many topics such as abortion, adoption, segregation, and unemployment.

International Encyclopedia of the Social Sciences. 8 vols. Ed. David L. Sills. New York: The Free Press, 1977.
Intended to complement rather than replace the *Encyclopaedia of the Social Sciences.* The articles, which are signed and include bibliographies, are mainly analytical and comparative, rather than historical and descriptive.

Public Affairs Information Service Bulletin [PAIS] New York: Public Affairs Information Service, 1915–.
An outstanding general index, PAIS covers all aspects of public affairs: copyright laws, interest rates, taxes, international affairs, education, social movements, political issues, and much more. Excellent for finding information and sources on current events and issues of current concern such as nuclear nonproliferation. Available on-line as PAIS INTERNATIONAL.

Social Sciences Index. New York: Wilson, 1974–. (Formerly *International Index,* 1907–65; *Social Sciences and Humanities Index,* 1965–74.)
Indexes articles and periodicals by author and subject for all the social sciences. A separate book review section is organized by author of the book reviewed.

White, Carl M. *Sources and Information in the Social Sciences.* 2nd ed. Chicago: American Library Association, 1973.
An excellent introduction to reference materials for all areas of social science, including economics, sociology, anthropology, psychology, and political science. Disciplines that overlap with these subjects—education, business administration, geography, and history—are also included. Much more than a descriptive list of sources, each chapter serves as an introduction to the discipline. Any student would do well to browse through this valuable book both to learn how information in the social sciences is organized and to discover reference tools for specific research topics.

ANTHROPOLOGY, PSYCHOLOGY, AND SOCIOLOGY

Frantz, Charles. *The Student Anthropologist's Handbook*. Cambridge, MA: Schenkman, 1972.

An interesting overview of the discipline, including a discussion of the training required to become an anthropologist, the kinds of activities professional anthropologists engage in, and an introduction to research materials and institutions.

A Guide to Library Resources in Psychology. By J. E. Brown. Dubuque, IA: Brown, 1971.

A useful introduction to the discipline of psychology and to important books in the field published before 1971. This guide, though dated, provides a wealth of information on how to use psychological literature.

Psychological Abstracts. Washington, DC: American Psychological Association, 1927–.

Covering more than those subjects strictly considered part of psychology, this work provides brief summaries (abstracts) of articles from journals and chapters from books in all the social sciences. This important index is not as easy to use as the *Social Science Index*, but it is more specialized and provides more information about each reference. To find material in the volumes from 1973 to the present, consult the *Sources of Psychological Index Terms*. As with any reference work, you should study the introductory material (instructions for the user) of the volume actually used since the format for citations may vary. Available on-line as PsycINFO.

Sociological Abstracts. New York: Sociological Abstracts, 1953–.

Like *Psychological Abstracts*, this work is useful for many disciplines within the social sciences. To use it, however, you will find it necessary to study the table of contents and the indexing system. If you find a source cited in this or other abstract volumes, you can study the abstract to decide whether you want to look for the original. The latest studies on child care, alcohol abuse, or sexism are among the thousands of sociological topics indexed here.

BUSINESS AND ECONOMICS

Business Index. Menlo Park, CA: Information Access Corp., 1979–.

Available on microform, this index is especially useful for finding very current material on business topics in general magazines, business periodicals, and newspapers (including the *Wall Street Journal*). Since the listings are cumulative, you will be able to locate material on many business topics efficiently and easily. This index is constantly updated, and older material is dropped as new listings are added.

Business Periodicals Index. New York: Wilson, 1958–.
Indexes articles in the following fields: accounting, advertising, automation, banking, communications, economics, finance and investments, insurance, labor, management, marketing, taxes, etc. An overview of articles in the significant journals. Book reviews are in a separate section.

Daniels, Lorna M. *Business Information Sources.* Berkeley: U of California P, 1985.
The best guide to sources in all aspects of business and economics. Any student interested in studying a topic related to these fields should consult this book first to learn about the available sources.

Encyclopedia of Management. 2nd ed. Ed. Carl Heyel. New York: Van Nostrand Reinhold, 1982.
A very good encyclopedic dictionary on a variety of topics such as consumer protection, data communications, motivation, and trade shows. Substantial articles on these and many other topics include references that direct the reader to important texts and articles on the subject.

McGraw-Hill Dictionary of Modern Economics: A Handbook of Terms and Organizations. 3rd ed. New York: McGraw, 1983.
A very useful dictionary; each entry includes a definition as well as at least one other source that provides more information.

Moody's Manuals. New York: Moody's Investors Service.
Moody's Manuals provide comprehensive financial information in seven annual publications, six devoted to U.S. companies, one to leading foreign companies. If you want financial information about a particular company, begin with *Moody's Complete Corporate Index,* which will lead you to the appropriate manual. Students doing substantial research on business topics should be familiar with all Moody's publications. *Moody's Corporate Profiles* is available on-line; it is useful to gain access to information in other Moody's publications.

Standard and Poor's Corporation Records. New York: Standard and Poor's Corp.
A widely used reference for information on more than 10,000 U.S. companies. Basic information on companies is revised regularly and latest developments are reported in daily updates. If you are looking for particular topics, begin with the topical index. Students doing substantial research on business topics should be familiar with all *Standard and Poor's* publications. *Standard and Poor's Corporation Records Online* provides access to current and historical business information.

Value Line Investment Survey. New York: A. Bernhard & Co.

Provides objective, authoritative information on some 1,700 companies. Excellent source for investment information.

EDUCATION

Current Index to Journals in Education (CIJE). Phoenix: Oryx Press, 1969–.

An index to almost eight hundred educational and education-related materials. The place to turn for a thorough review of the literature on a topic. Produced by the Educational Resources Information Center (ERIC), CIJE uses the same subject headings (descriptors) as *Resources in Education* described below. Available on-line through ERIC.

Education Index. New York: Wilson, 1929–.

Includes fewer periodicals than CIJE, but covers a much longer period of time. You may prefer to use this more selective index, since you will not find many of the periodicals indexed in CIJE in small or even medium-sized libraries.

The Encyclopedia of Education. 10 vols. Ed. Lee C. Deighlin. New York: Macmillan, The Free Press, 1971.

Deals primarily with American education. Describes a wide range of educational topics. If, for example, you want to get an overall picture of nursing education in the U.S., you would find here sixteen double-columned pages on the topic; a general encyclopedia such as *Collier's* offers less than two pages.

Resources in Education (RIE). [Known as ERIC] Washington, DC: GPO, 1975. Formerly *Research in Education,* 1966–74.

An index to many documents not published in journals. Contains an order form for obtaining copies of documents. These documents are stored on microform in many libraries. Copies can usually be made with a microform reader-printer. Like *CIJE,* RIE is produced by the Educational Resources Information Center; this index and the collection of documents it catalogs are often referred to by librarians and researchers as ERIC. Available on-line through ERIC.

World of Learning. London: Europa Publications, 1947–.

Gives basic information about a variety of educational institutions throughout the world, including libraries, research institutes, colleges, and universities, as well as learned societies and museums. This is a good place to find the address, telephone number, and purpose of an institution. You will also find general information on when and how an institution was founded; the number of students; and for large or prestigious schools, the names of chief officers.

POLITICAL SCIENCE AND GOVERNMENT

The Almanac of American Politics. By Michael Barone and Grant Ujifusa. Washington, DC: Barone, 1972–.
The subtitle of this delightful book tells you what you will find in it: almost anything you ever wanted to know—and then some—about "The President, the Senators, the Representatives, the Governors: Their Records and Election Results, Their States and Districts."

Brock, Clifton. *The Literature of Political Science.* New York: Bowker, 1969.
An introduction to library materials and research methods in political science. It includes descriptions of various indexes and abstracts to help you find material in periodicals. An excellent introduction to government publications and the many publications of public organizations.

Congressional Quarterly Almanac. Washington, DC: Congressional Quarterly, 1945–.
Summarizes congressional activity every year. Here you will find concise information about committee hearings, voting records, investigations, texts of presidential addresses, and lobbying efforts, as well as details of major legislation.

Congressional Quarterly's Guide to Congress. Eds. Robert A. Diamond and Patricia Ann O'Connor. Washington, DC: Congressional Quarterly, 1976.
Periodically revised, this comprehensive overview of the workings of Congress is placed in a large historical context; it explains the powers, procedures, and structures of Congress; and it discusses the relationship of Congress to the society at large.

Congressional Quarterly Weekly Report. Washington, DC: Congressional Quarterly, 1943–.
Gives a comprehensive summary of congressional activity for each week. If you are researching a specific legislative act—the Civil Rights Act of 1964, for instance—you may want to go to the *Weekly* for a summary of all the activities and debate leading to its passage.

Holler, Frederick L. *Information Sources of Political Science.* Santa Barbara, CA: Clio Press, 1981.
More up-to-date and comprehensive than *The Literature of Political Science* (see above), this work describes the important reference works in related fields such as psychology and philosophy. A pleasure to read, this guide will be very useful to students doing research on topics concerning the public aspects of social science.

The United States Government Manual. Washington, DC: GPO, 1935–.
An up-to-date source of information on all aspects of the organization of the federal government. Published every year, it includes names, addresses, and telephone numbers of public officials in all branches of government; explanations of the function of all government departments; and basic information about domestic and international organizations that are allied to the United States. Want to know the names of the Supreme Court justices, how to obtain information from the Environmental Protection Agency, or how the Department of Health and Human Services is organized? To answer these and many other questions, check the *Government Manual.*

Natural and Applied Sciences

GENERAL

American Men and Women of Science: Physical and Biological Sciences. 7 vols. 15th ed. Ed. Jaques Cattell Press. New York: Bowker, 1982.
The best source for information about living scientists who are currently active. Available on-line.

Dictionary of Scientific Biography. 16 vols. New York: Scribners, 1970–81 (Supplement, 1977; Index, 1981).
A valuable source for the history of science. The articles provide reliable information on the professional lives of thousands of scientists from classical antiquity to modern times. The twentieth-century figures have all been dead for some years, and all achieved considerable distinction.

General Science Index. New York: Wilson, 1978–.
This cumulative subject index to general science periodicals is commonly found in public libraries. It is a good source for beginning science students to use.

McGraw-Hill Encyclopedia of Science and Technology. 15 vols. 5th ed. New York: McGraw, 1982.
This high quality, up-to-date work provides excellent background reading in almost all scientific and technological topics. It is appropriate for the sophisticated student of science as well as for the beginning researcher who is investigating a scientific topic.

McGraw-Hill Yearbook of Science and Technology. New York: McGraw. Published annually.
Updates the latest edition of the *Encyclopedia.* A good source for a summary of scientific development in recent years.

Science Citation Index. Ed. Eugene Garfield. Philadelphia: Institute for Scientific Information, 1982.
An interdisciplinary index to scholarly journals in the sciences and to books since 1977. It links each publication listed with all others that cite it. Once you learn to use the *Science Citation Index*, you will find that it provides a relatively easy way to find the important information on a given topic. Available on-line as part of SCISEARCH.

ASTRONOMY

The Cambridge Encyclopaedia of Astronomy. Ed. Simon Milton. Cambridge, Eng.: Institute of Astronomy, 1977.
A well-illustrated, topically arranged survey of astronomy, this work provides an authoritative introduction to many aspects of the field.

BIOLOGY, MEDICINE, AND NURSING

Cumulative Index to Nursing and Allied Health Literature. Glendale, CA: Glendale Advertisement Medical Center 1977–. (Formerly *Cumulative Index to Nursing Literature,* 1956–1976.)
Organized by both subject and author, this comprehensive index will lead you to articles on all aspects of nursing and allied health sciences.

The Encyclopedia of the Biological Sciences. 2nd ed. Ed. Peter Gray. New York: Van Nostrand Reinhold, 1970.
This single-volume work provides accurate information on biological topics for nonexperts.

Grzimek's Animal Life Encyclopedia. 13 vols. Ed. Bernhard Grzimek. New York: Van Nostrand Reinhold, 1972–75.
This is an informative and fascinating reference work. Each volume treats its subject—fishes, birds, mammals, reptiles, and so on—with authority and style. Generous use of color plates and photographs enhances the readable text. International in scope, this is a good place to turn for an overview of the animal kingdom. Each volume has a good index and a list of suggested readings.

Index Medicus. U.S. Department of Health and Human Services. N.I.H. Publications. Washington DC: National Library of Medicine, 1960– (monthly).
This is the authoritative index to periodical literature in medicine and related fields. Biological literature is well represented. Although many of the articles cited are technical and intended for experts, you may find this index helpful if you are researching general topics in medicine or biology. Available on-line through MEDLINE.

CHEMISTRY AND PHYSICS

The Condensed Chemical Dictionary. 10th ed. New York: Van Nostrand Reinhold, 1981.

In addition to providing definitions of chemical terms, this is a useful source for concise information about commercial and trade market products and for pharmaceuticals and drugs.

The Encyclopedia of Physics. Eds. Rita G. Lerner and George L. Trigg. Reading, MA: Addison-Wesley, 1981.

This single-volume work is an authoritative source for background information and for an overview of the major principles and problems of physics. More than this, it contains speculative articles on controversial developments, written by experts engaged in current research. Extensive bibliographies and clear charts and diagrams make this a useful and usable source.

Handbook of Chemistry and Physics. 58th ed. Cleveland: Chemical Rubber Company, 1913–.

This is the most useful single-volume reference work available to the undergraduate and graduate student in chemistry and physics. It is divided into six parts with a good index and constitutes, as its subtitle indicates, "A Ready Reference Book of Chemical and Physical Data." Turn here for the facts, and go to the sources listed above for the explanations.

COMPUTER SCIENCE

Computers and Control Abstracts. Piscataway, NJ: Institute of Electric Engineers with The Institute of Electrical and Electronic Engineers, Inc., 1969—.

Part C of the three-part *Science Abstracts.* Published twice monthly, this excellent index provides sources for information on all aspects of computer science, including computer languages, equipment, software, hardware, new terminology, and latest developments in the field. Available on-line as INSPEC.

The Directory of On-line Databases. Cuadra Associates, Inc., 1980—.

Updated quarterly, this excellent directory provides accurate, concise, and useful information about databases in all fields.

ENGINEERING

Applied Science and Technology Index. Ed. Rose Manofsky. New York: Wilson, 1958–.

A multidisciplinary subject index covering a wide range of topics including several kinds of engineering, as well as the applied aspects of chemistry, geology, and physics. If you are researching general science topics, you will want to browse through this index to get an idea of the scope of its coverage.

Engineering Index. New York: Engineering Index, Inc., 1906–.
Worldwide coverage of the journal literature, publications of engineering societies and organizations, and selected government books. Available on-line as COMPENDEX.

ENVIRONMENTAL SCIENCE

Grzimek's Encyclopedia of Ecology. Ed. Bernhard Grzimek. New York: Van Nostrand Reinhold, 1976.
A comprehensive approach to the study of ecology. Beautifully illustrated and a pleasure to read, this work is a valuable source of general and detailed information on ecological topics.

McGraw-Hill Encyclopedia of Environmental Science. 2nd ed. Ed. Sybil P. Parker. New York: McGraw, 1980.
Concerned with the complex interaction between living things and environmental phenomena, this specialized encyclopedia focuses on many aspects of the earth and the ways it has been used.

INDEX